D0801388

INDIAN MAN

OLIVER LA FARGE

INDIAN MAN
A Life of Oliver La Farge

D'Arcy McNickle

INDIANA UNIVERSITY PRESS

Bloomington / London

92
2159 m

SECOND PRINTING 1971

COPYRIGHT © 1971 BY INDIANA UNIVERSITY PRESS

Published in Canada by Fitzhenry & Whiteside Limited, Don Mills, Ontario
Library of Congress catalog card number 70-135010
ISBN 253-14000-5
MANUFACTURED IN THE UNITED STATES OF AMERICA

FH

To Viola

❖ Contents ❖

❖ Acknowledgments ❖

MANY OF Oliver La Farge's kin, his associates, and close friends contributed to the preparation of this biography. Their helpfulness, and their patience through what turned out to be a long waiting period, is acknowledged as a double debt of gratitude. I am first of all indebted to Consuelo (Mrs. Oliver La Farge) for allowing me full freedom in working my way through a mountainous mass of private papers—even putting at my disposal the personal letters between herself and her husband, including those of their courting days. To this were added many long discussions in Mrs. La Farge's Santa Fe home.

W. E. R. La Farge, second son of Oliver's brother Christopher, made available a great quantity of letters between Oliver and Christopher and other members of the family, especially letters between Oliver and his mother. Included in the collection is the "Saunderstown Diary," in which Mrs. Grant La Farge, Oliver's mother, reported the great and small affairs of rural Rhode Island over a thirty-year period. W. E. R. La Farge's hospitality included a delightful autumn day at River Farm near the site of the Saunderstown home where Oliver spent his childhood.

Others of the family who patiently answered questions and volunteered information were Oliver's surviving brother, Francis, his sister, Mrs. Margaret Osborn, his cousin, Mrs. M. L. Knox, and his nephew, Grant La Farge.

Alden Stevens, who succeeded Oliver as president of the Association on American Indian Affairs, allowed full access to the files of the association. Mr. Stevens' long friendship with La Farge provided insights as well as information. Richard Schifter, counsel for the association, was equally cooperative in opening the files of the association's legal work and copying relevant documents.

Of the many friends who shared their personal experiences, Bartlett H. Hayes, Jr., and Douglas S. Byers, both in Andover, Massachusetts, were members of the Peabody Museum field party which Oliver led to the Navajo country in 1924. Both had vivid recollections of that expedition, which provided the landscape and the imaginative awakening for the writing of *Laughing Boy*. Their perceptive discussion of La Farge's career was most helpful.

Others who were associated with La Farge, from early to recent times, and who contributed generously of remembrance and impression, were Corliss Lamont, a Harvard classmate; Moris Burge, at one time a field representative and later executive director of the association; John Collier, Commissioner of Indian Affairs in the Roosevelt administration, and his Assistant Commissioner, William Zimmerman, Jr., who became a staff member of the association; Miguel Pijoan, Oliver's personal physician; Marie Rodell, his literary agent; William Maxwell, his editor at *The New Yorker;* Winfield Townley Scott, who edited a selection of Oliver's newspaper columns; Mrs. Corinne Locker, Oliver's secretary for many years; Edward H. Dozier, professor of anthropology at the University of Arizona, and his brothers, Pete and Tom, members of Santa Clara Pueblo.

Here, also, acknowledgment must be made of other assistance which materially advanced the work in progress. The University of Saskatchewan Regina Campus granted a year's leave of absence from a seriously shorthanded staff. The Association on American Indian Affairs made funds available for an extended eastern trip at the start of the project. A grant from the Louis M. Rabinowitz Foundation of New York helped to finance the final period of writing. To all of these, my heartfelt thanks.

❖ Bibliographical Source Notes ❖

THROUGH THE KINDNESS of Mrs. Oliver La Farge, before the papers were acquired by the University of Texas at Austin, I had full access to Oliver La Farge's private papers, including correspondence, ethnographic field notes, war journals, publishers' contracts, and a variety of published and unpublished writings. The material is not cited specifically in the bibliography since, at the time I worked with it, it had not been catalogued and was not yet accessible.

In addition to the above, a considerable volume of correspondence between Oliver and members of his family has not been collected but is privately owned by his brother Francis W. La Farge, by his nephews Christopher Grant and W. E. R. La Farge, and by Mrs. La Farge. The letters cited in this biography are to be found in one or another of these private collections. Again, specific references are not mentioned in the text, since the letters are not indexed or otherwise identified. The letters that passed between the three brothers, Christopher, Oliver, and Francis, are vividly descriptive of a closely integrated family and its social integuments.

The La Farge Family Collection of letters and documents, in the custody of the New York Historical Society, was not available to the public.

A major source of information for La Farge's long career in Indian causes, of course, are the files of the Association on American Indian Affairs in New York City. In addition to correspondence, the materials include historical sketches, reports, speeches, and internal office memoranda, all bearing La Farge's imprint, and usually his signature. Of special importance is *The American Indian* series, containing articles by La Farge and other writers dealing with aspects of Indian life and the political consequences of being Indian.

La Farge's literary career has been the subject of several graduate studies and critical articles appearing in university publications. A representative selection of these, though possibly not a complete list, are the following:

Allen, Charles, "The Fiction of Oliver La Farge." *University of Arizona Quarterly I.* Winter 1945.

Brokaw, Zoanne Sherlock, "Oliver La Farge: His Fictional Navajo." M.A. thesis, University of Arizona, 1965.

Friedman, Philip, "Oliver La Farge: the Scientist as Literary Artist." M.A. thesis, University of New Mexico, 1959.

Gillis, Everett, "Oliver La Farge." Austin, Texas, 1967.

McHenry, Carol S., "Tradition: Ballast in Transition, a Literary Biography of Oliver La Farge." M.A. thesis, University of New Mexico, 1966.

Among general works consulted, the following are listed because they illuminate some area of La Farge's career, or direct reference is made to them in the text.

Amsden, Charles A., "Prehistoric Southwesterners, from Basketmaker to Pueblos." Los Angeles, 1949.

Ashburn, Frank D., "Peabody of Groton." New York, 1944.

Austin, Mary, "Earth Horizon." Boston, 1932.

Baltzell, E. Digby, "Philadelphia Gentlemen." Glencoe, Ill., 1958.

Brett, Dorothy, "Lawrence and Brett." New York, 1933.

Bunzel, Ruth, "Chichicastenango: A Guatemalan Village." American Ethnological Society, New York, 1952.

Bynner, Witter, and Oliver La Farge, "Alice Corbin, An Appreciation." *New Mexico Quarterly,* Spring 1949.

Coolidge, Dane, "Lorenzo the Magnificent." New York, 1925.

Cortissoz, Royal, "John La Farge," in *Dictionary of American Biography,* Vol. 10, pp. 530–535. New York, 1933.

Gillman, Frances, and Louisa Wade Wetherill, "Traders to the Navajos." University of New Mexico Press, 1953.

Guernsey, S. J., and A. V. Kidder, "Basketmaker Caves of

Northeastern Arizona." *Papers of the Peabody Museum of American Archaeology and Ethnology,* vol. 8, no. 2. Cambridge, 1921.

James, Henry, "Notes of a Son and Brother" in *Autobiography.* New York, 1956.

Kazin, Alfred, "Starting out in the Thirties." Boston, 1965.

Kidder, A. V. "An Introduction to the Study of Southwestern Archaeology." New Haven, 1924.

Kidder, A. V., and S. J. Guernsey, "Peabody Museum Arizona Exploration, 1920." *Proceedings of the National Academy of Sciences,* vol. 7, pp. 69–71, 1921.

La Farge, Reverend John, *The Manner is Ordinary.* New York, 1954.

Link, Margaret Schevill, "The Pollen Path." Stanford University Press, 1956.

Lujan, Mabel Dodge, "Lorenzo in Taos." New York, 1932.

McGregor, John C. "Southwestern Archaeology." University of Illinois Press, 1965.

MacLeish, Archibald, "There was Something About the Twenties," *Saturday Review,* Dec. 31, 1966.

Nevins, Allan, "The Emergence of Modern America." New York, 1927.

Thompson, J. Eric, "Maya Hieroglyphics: Introduction." *Publication 589, Carnegie Institution of Washington,* 1950.

White, G. Edward, "The Eastern Establishment and the Western Experience." Yale University Press, 1968.

Wilmsen, Edwin N., "An Outline of Early Man Studies in the United States." *American Antiquity,* vol. 31, no. 2, pt. 1. 1965.

Wister, Owen, "Roosevelt, the Story of a Friendship." New York, 1930.

INDIAN MAN

Beginnings

OLIVER LA FARGE'S long association with Indian people and Indian causes had a quality of inevitability, born of his beginnings and his proper self. What was at first an enchantment became an encompassing environment, and when he tried to break away, as an individual and as a writer intent on avoiding the loss of identity in a stereotype, he found that the invisible had become form and substance.

He went to the Indian country following a whim, romantic and escapist—as he recognized—and found that he had escaped into reality.

The years between his first wide-eyed encounter with Navajo Indians in Arizona and his last visit to an Indian community were filled with promise and denial, with high success and thwarted accomplishment, and through these incongruities, or because of them, his environment grew steadily greater. His final effort was a journey from Santa Fe to Taos Pueblo, in New Mexico, in which he was supported by a tank of oxygen, a seriously sick man. He had promised to help his Pueblo friends prepare an appeal for the recovery of the lands containing and safeguarding their sacred Blue Lake. He returned home and collapsed soon after.

Indians entered Oliver La Farge's consciousness in childhood. His father, Christopher Grant La Farge (1862–1938), one of the original architects for the Cathedral of St. John the Divine in New York, knew a variety of Indians. He had personal friends among several southwestern tribes. He had camped and hunted with Canadian Indians and was expert with canoe and gun. He taught each of his three sons, of whom Oliver was second born, the skills of moving in the forest and on water. Oliver reported that his father, at seventy and twice Oliver's age, drew a stronger canoe paddle than his own.

Grant La Farge belonged in that small group of Easterners, men like Owen Wister, Frederic Remington, and Theodore Roosevelt, who were discovering that the United States had a considerable extension westward. Mostly the sons of wellborn though not always wealthy families, these men went west, somewhat like British colonials in search of big game, but they stayed long enough and were perceptive enough to learn from Indians and cowboys the harshness and majesty of the land.

The west shore of Narragansett Bay in Rhode Island, where Oliver spent his summers from earliest childhood, had its share of the incidents of colonial settlement among the Indians of New England. The region owes its name to the Narragansett tribe, which occupied most of Rhode Island west of the Bay when Roger Williams in 1636 begged leave to establish a plantation among them. Canonicut Island, which lies in the Bay, just opposite Saunderstown where the La Farges had their summer homes, was named for a Narragansett chief who aided the English in the Pequot War of 1637. Modern Kingston, not far from Saunderstown, was the site of the Great Swamp Fight of December 1675, when King Philip, the Wampanoag leader, lost his bid for mastery of the young colony. He and some Narragansetts who joined his cause were destroyed together. A surviving remnant of the tribe, at least in name, lingers on in southern Rhode Island.

Groton, Massachusetts, which contains the school where Oliver spent an anguished adolescence, is built on the site of an Indian settlement; and Groton was destroyed in an Indian raid in 1676—all of which is commemorated on a plaque in the village.

Apart from such casual childhood encounters with the Indian past, Oliver La Farge was probably made most conscious of Indianness by his personal appearance and by his mother's familiar name for him. Everyone else in the family called him "Ink" or

"Inky." His mother called him "Indian Man," and until her death he signed his letters "Thine Indian Man." She used the name because of his notable Indian features—straight black hair, pronounced facial bones, and a skin which tanned readily to a deep brown. He had the lithe frame of a forest runner and his toes turned slightly inward, which in classical Indian romance is the natural gait of the red man.

There is a family tradition, not entirely substantiated, of an Indian ancestor up the line, presumably in the Hazard branch of the Perry family. Oliver's great-great-grandfather was the naval hero of the war of 1812, Commodore Oliver Hazard Perry, hence his full name, Oliver Hazard Perry La Farge. An uncle bore the same full name, and post offices and mailmen never discovered how to distinguish between them. The name-bearers were constantly forwarding mail intended for the other. There was a second naval hero in that family, Commodore Matthew Calbraith Perry, brother of Oliver, who persuaded the Japanese to open their ports to Western trade (1854). It was a versatile, talented family of strong individuals, whether or not an Indian lurked in the shadowy background.

The first to bring the name to North America was Jean-Frédéric de la Farge—anglicized to John La Farge to conform to New World democratic practice. He was born in 1786 at Juriac, near Angoulême, in the province of Charente-Inférieure, of a family of small landowners, Bonapartist partisans. While serving with the French navy in the West Indies, Jean-Frédéric went ashore with a landing party during the Haitian uprising in 1803 and was taken prisoner. After three years he escaped, first to Cuba, then he moved on to New Orleans, and eventually to Philadelphia. Still later he carried on an import business as La Farge and Russell in New York and invested in real estate. He held land in Louisiana and northern New York, some of which he obtained in settlement of debts owed him by European clients. The town of La Fargeville in Jefferson County, New York, marks his residence in that area. It is told within the family that Jean-Frédéric and his French wife,

Louisa Binsse, daughter of a painter of miniatures, because they were foreigners and Catholic, were not liked in the neighborhood.

It was Jean-Frédéric's son John, the painter, muralist, and worker in stained glass, who fully launched the family in the American stream. In marrying Margaret Mason Perry, a Newport beauty, he allied himself with ancestral lines descending from Benjamin Franklin; Thomas Sergeant, a prominent Pennsylvania jurist; and the seafaring Perrys. Of the nine children born of this marriage, one was a practicing architect (Oliver's father), three others were painters, one of whom painted professionally, and the youngest, John, a Jesuit priest, was a writer, editor, and worker in the field of race relations.

The spread of family talent provided the occasion for an unusual exhibition offered by a New York gallery in 1931. In this showing of "Paintings by John La Farge and his descendants," ten children and grandchildren and one non-La Farge wife were represented.

Grant La Farge married Florence Bayard Lockwood, daughter of Benoni and Florence (Bayard) Lockwood and niece of Thomas J. Bayard, United States Senator from Delaware and Secretary of State in President Cleveland's first cabinet. Her ancestry also included New England sea captains. Oliver's elder brother, Christopher, trained as an architect but left that field to pursue a writing career.

Oliver considered himself a Rhode Islander, though he was born in New York City, December 19, 1901, in "a very small house with a mansard roof" on East 19th Street, between Fourth Avenue and Irving Place. Later the family lived for many years at 124 East 22nd Street. The family owned no property in the city but returned regularly for the winter season. For a child, the city meant school and the constraints of city streets and parks and block-solid residences. But Rhode Island in the summer, with water and shore and woodland, an abundance of birds and animal life, and freedom to roam, was a child's dream.

The area around Saunderstown had once been occupied by

small family farms running down to the water's edge and fishing supplemented the land's produce. As subsistence farming yielded to the growing industrialization of the northeast, families moved away and the farms were either abandoned or sold to summer people, who bought for "a view," not to farm. The lands went back to native growth and stone boundary walls disappeared under a mat of vegetation. So wild and thorny was this overgrowth, as Oliver's mother described it on one occasion, that "When a bird drops into a very thick tangle of bramble, bull-briar, wild rose and grape, no dog, let alone a human, can get to it." She was explaining why it was that her husband and a companion on the opening day of the hunting season shot fourteen quail but came home with only ten.

Such wilderness was perfect for summering children. The La Farges and their relatives had been buying bits and pieces of abandoned farmland until they owned a strip two miles long and half a mile deep along the west shore of the bay. This area, and of course all the woodlot berry patches, creeks, marshes, and tidal runs for miles around, as well as the open water, was theirs to explore.

Oliver was one of a group of eleven children who were together for most of his growing years: three sets of cousins, Whartons, Lockwoods, and La Farges. They were adventuresome, imaginative, and carefree. Oliver's mother, as he explains in his autobiographical *Raw Material,* wanted her children to grow up without fear and tried never to show her uneasiness or plain fright over their escapades. They sailed, swam, rode horses—in effect, occupied the countryside.

It was a home in which the children were encouraged to participate in high-minded discussions. Everyone was expected to share in the conversation at table within certain rules. The talk had to be general, or specifically about what one was reading or doing. It was not a time for airing grievances. When grownups were visiting, children were allowed, and expected, to present themselves and to speak individually to guests before withdrawing.

Reading was an admired pursuit in that era and it was especially valued in the La Farge colony. Adults read out loud to each other and to the children. The children read to themselves or to each other.

Oliver was especially bookish, devouring whole encyclopedias. Once when his mother had the neighborhood ladies in to tea—her teas and readings were regular Thursday afternoon affairs—Oliver, then age ten, entered the room to pay his respects and announced to his mother that there were more bastards in Sweden than in any other country. The ladies gasped, blushed, or frowned, but Mrs. La Farge remained calm. She asked the boy how he knew about the state of affairs in Sweden. It seemed that he had been reading about baseball in the encyclopedia and kept right on reading until he came upon that interesting article.

By such following his nose in his reading he acquired an early knowledge of biology and was able to explain to a younger female cousin, when they came upon a cow heavy with calf, the essential details of mammalian reproduction. About the birth process itself he was heard to say, "And I can tell you it is a very painful experience."

The habit of daydreaming, of romanticizing his surroundings, which caused him such distress when he looked back as an adult upon his childhood, was nourished by these beginnings. For years, even after they had grown beyond childish play, he and a favorite cousin carried on a game in which they inhabited a kind of idyllic legendary kingdom, he as the Crown Prince, she as the Archduchess. When they first invented the game, he was very thorough in creating the setting: he devised a coat of arms, with appropriate Latin motto, a history, and even a language—a kind of mutilated French.

Taken in any measure, his mother was an extraordinary person, and because she always remained her own person, with definite views and tastes which she expressed but never imposed, her influence upon Oliver remained constant. Their letters to each other never wavered in their expressions of respect, trust, and love.

One of the cousins of that play group, writing to Oliver after his mother's death in 1944, remembered her: "She was one of the warmest and most kind and generous people I have ever known. And one of the most brilliant. As a child I sat at her feet and when I grew older she became my friend. In a way she was Saunderstown for me. I always went to call on her the very evening I arrived. Walking through the familiar woods and cutting down behind the pumphouse and being greeted with shouts of delight and then embarking upon long discussions about the British empire."

Her style of life and thought is encapsulated in a letter written to Oliver in her seventieth year (1934). She was in Saunderstown, as always in summer, a house full of people. She sat at her desk to write:

> You can't imagine how often I have started to write to you these last few weeks, but one thing and another has had to be done, or I think it has to be, and so I tumble into bed. August, as you know, is the hectic month here and just as I think I have a clear day to myself there comes a knock on the door and in come some people either to spend an hour or to stay the night. I care more for hospitality than for almost anything else and I also have the habit, but as one grows older and also has less help in the house it leaves one with less and less strength and you push aside all sorts of things that you adore doing really quite as much. In the world that one "remolds nearer to the heart's desire," I should have older people spared poverty rather than the young. I felt this when I was a young woman so it is not only a selfish idea. Extreme poverty is good for no one, but moderate poverty does make for character and in the contest of life opens many doors to understanding and enjoyment if taken in the right way. When your father and I started housekeeping I rather enjoyed proving that the things of the mind and spirit did not depend on physical support. All this is an explanation of my silence. Not that you need it, but as I noticed in Henry James' letters that began with this sort of an explanation, when you finished reading it you had a lot of information about what he had been doing and thinking.

The contrast between mother and father is strikingly revealed in their letters, in style and content. The mother's style was cursive, to say the least, and the cryptic handwriting grew progressively more obscure, while the father wrote a bold clear script, but the content was excessively brief.

Christopher expresses this in a long letter to Oliver written in July 1932 from England. He had just dissolved his architectural partnership with his father, and before leaving New York he had sorted out his childhood memorabilia, reading and throwing out old correspondence and souvenirs. "What correspondents we were, you and I," he told Oliver. And then he made a discovery: "Curiously enough, I was horribly disappointed in almost all of Daddy's letters—except their appearance, which was uniformly beautiful. They were always plans: 'I'll meet you at Queen's River on such and such a day and such a train,' and inevitably, in each: 'Sorry to be so brief, but no time to write now.' It became embarrassing, because the continuity of letters reread en masse is hideously revealing. Over and over again, 'I have no time to write more,' 'I am rushed.' And these to a boy at school!"

His mother's references to poverty and to less household help had a special pertinence when she wrote in 1934 describing her household. The family was never wealthy, but the style of living assumed a basis of at least moderate wealth. It was a large household of fluctuating numbers as relatives and friends moved in and out. There had always been servants—a cook, an Irish maid; nurses and governesses, as needed; a groom to teach riding and horse handling; two houses to maintain; boats and boathouses, and always horses and hunting dogs.

Grant La Farge was a man of high achievement and still higher promise, whose career had been truncated by a series of events and decisions.

His original architectural firm, Heins and La Farge, of which George L. Heins, a classmate at Massachusetts Institute of Technology, was the senior partner, had been awarded the contract to design and build the Cathedral of St. John the Divine on Morningside Heights in New York. This was in 1891, after a three-year competition among the nation's leading architects.

The winning design called for a vast edifice in which Romanesque and Byzantine traditions were to be blended in a symbolic union of East and West. For the next twenty years La Farge devoted himself to the realization of a project that would extend beyond his lifetime. By 1911 the great choir had been completed and also the crossing, from which a massive central tower was to rise. At that point, the founding bishop having died, the Cathedral trustees decided to abandon the Romanesque style and change to Gothic.

Heins, his classmate and partner, had died in 1907, and this left the trustees at liberty to invoke a clause in the contract permitting them to transfer it to another architect. The trustees then approached Ralph Adams Cram, a leading Gothic stylist, and he promptly accepted. This caused some unhappiness among architects, some of whom appealed to Cram, on the basis of professional ethics, to withdraw. One of the partners in his own firm of Cram, Goodhue, and Ferguson, withdrew from the partnership soon afterward.

Grant La Farge accepted the decision of the trustees and never challenged the propriety of Cram's action. Indeed, he refused to discuss the matter, then or at any time later. He continued his career, largely specializing in church architecture; the achievements were distinguished, but they were bread-and-butter, not a consuming passion.

He knew Indians, visited them in their homes as a young man, painted portraits of tribal leaders, wrote knowingly about Indian religious ceremony—and it must have occurred to him that his behavior in the St. John's affair was in the Indian tradition of keeping his troubles to himself. In learning about Indians as he grew up, Oliver learned first from his father.

The depression years brought construction in the United States virtually to a halt, and the architectural profession suffered in consequence. When Christopher withdrew in 1932 to devote himself to a writing career, Grant La Farge was seventy years of age, too old to hustle for new business, but he managed after a fashion as a consultant to schools of architecture and as a lecturer. These earnings were sporadic, however, and he used the money largely to supply his tastes of long habit. He was a lonely man in those last years, an alien within his own domain. The mention of "less help in the house" was probably the only occasion when Mrs. La Farge alluded to the problem she faced as manager of a household that lacked a driving force.

In that summer of 1934 his mother wrote Oliver: "Your father is extremely well and already there are a number of lectures arranged for the coming winter and also some connections with different foundations which may prove both profitable and interesting. He never was cerebrating better and is full of ideas. He takes all sorts of people out sailing and they get younger and younger."

Her letters were full of the commonplaces of country living. All the countryside and its people were within her sight and her hearing, and she recorded all—the marriages, deaths and funerals, the newborn, and the multitudinous land sales, often with complete sales data going back over several generations. When she visited the county old people's home, she brought bright aprons for the women and smoking and chewing tobacco for the men. She made the countryside her own.

During the Prohibition years, Narragansett bay was alive with rumrunners and the surrounding shore had its incidents of hijacking and bizarre happenings, all of which she watched with a certain satisfaction. As in the fall of 1931: "At 11 P.M. there was a tremendous explosion at the Big Dock and we all rushed to [our dock]. Flames mounting high and a continuous fusillade of artillery. Fire engines from Wickford, streams of water, shouting, hubbub, wind offshore. Then a rumrunner *The Black Duck* appeared and towed the burning Coast Guard boat out into the Bay, where it made a very beautiful conflagration, accompanied all the time by the explosion of Uncle Sam's ammunition."

She was not a prohibitionist—sherry before dinner was a way of life. Occasionally she scoured the back roads looking for potable wine to put on her table.

Reading books and writing and talking about them afterward were deeply ingrained habits. Throughout her adult life, until she suffered a general decline in her late seventies, she had the neighborhood ladies in for the Thursday afternoon reading. Her letters to Oliver invariably contained a paragraph or two on something she was reading or some comment on style and content in a writer's work.

On one occasion: "I am reading Dubois' book and I wish that someone had been near to steady his English. He writes well and at times with eloquence, but it has not been properly proofread or something like that."

Again: "If you can lay your hands on it do read the new book by Bertrand Russell, 'Freedom versus Organization.' It is thrilling in places, clever, witty, honest, and sometimes flippant and quite unfair. But immensely of this time and day."

Her ear for word usage—a trait passed on to her children, especially Oliver and Christopher—remained alert even into old age. She was a talker rather than a writer, as she explained in one of her letters, but her diction was usually crisp (if unpunctuated) and precise. When she caught herself describing someone as "an awful nuisance," she noted: "Do you know I remember the time when the use of the word 'awful' as an adjective for 'very' which it is now was a much disputed novelty and one just did not use it in polite society and then one suddenly did it here and in England too. *Punch* in the seventies was very funny about it."

And she could compose vivid word pictures, as when she wrote of a Saunderstown spring:

> It is such an exciting time in the garden and everything gets ahead of one and there is something to do every minute. I am living in a white world, not snow but so many white blossoms that the whole tone of the sea is changed in contrast. Magnolias, apples, pears, white lilacs, and pyrus japonica and purple lilacs as a combination. The black buds of the black ash against the full moon were like a witch's picture. As lovely and as eerie as the scene in *Macbeth*.

It was a changing world which soon would dissolve and be refashioned in new forms. The older families watched with dismay as "developers" bought solid properties and split them up into cottage sites and parts of the familiar landscape soon filled with rows of cracker boxes.

The La Farge home at Saunderstown was not a pretentious house, the furniture was worn, the rugs threadbare in spots, the surrounding lawns and planted areas were weed-grown at times, but it was comfortable, a place of great talk and great laughter— and sharp practices on the croquet lawn. A year after Mrs. La Farge's death in 1944, the house was destroyed by fire that caught in the night when no one was around.

The children who grew up in the earlier time held it in their minds as they had experienced it. The same cousin who wrote Oliver about visiting his mother described how she felt when she came back later, before the house burned: "It is so darned lovely and just the way it used to be. . . . The whole landscape touches my heart as no place in the world. How did Horace put it? I never could quote and haven't the energy to look it up—this corner of the earth, above all others, laughs for me—*hic angula terrae.* I suppose all expatriates have some corner of the earth which does that for them. Something about the cedars and the brown barren places where we used to canter the ponies. . . . I can see them and smell them now, as I write, with such awful homesickness."

Out of such experiences, concern, and loving response Oliver La Farge fashioned his own world. He stayed close to these beginnings even as he moved away from them. The habit of sharing himself deeply and unreservedly with the members of his primary group, especially with his mother but extending to both brothers, constantly renewed these attachments. Until her failing faculties, particularly memory, effectively immobilized her, he sent his writings in draft form to his mother and she passed them to other members of the family, whoever happened to be at hand. She would reply with words of encouragement but also with critical suggestions, assuring him, however: "I never read your character or personal actions into your work. It has never occurred to me to do so since you began to write at Groton."

As he moved more closely and more prominently into the world of Indians and the politics of Indian affairs, he continued to share his experiences with members of his family. It was not that he expected critical guidance in the specific problems with which he dealt, but it served his need for continuity.

In the summer of 1936 Indian Commissioner John Collier asked Oliver to spend some time with the Hopi Indians in Arizona and to assist in drafting a written constitution. The task required knowledge of Hopi social structure, first of all, and also great tactfulness in bringing together the several autonomous Hopi villages and attempting to reconcile Hopi traditionalism with modern political practices. The *Running Narrative* which he prepared, a kind of journal of his meetings and conversations with village leaders and others, was sent to the family at Saunderstown. His mother sat up all night to read it and return it air mail. And she wrote with a certain clear discernment: "One thing that strikes me is that all the groups are different from each other. . . . I suppose it is really the fact that with all human nature, when one gets into really close contact with it one ceases to generalize. . . . Common characteristics, yes, but modified in each instance."

And as always, she tried to put it into perspective for him: "If you can do the thing you are trying to do, it will lay the right foundation for right things for all these people for many years to come. And not only in the acceptance of the law but in their approach to their responsibilities as they see them and as they are in nature."

It would have amazed the Hopi leaders to have learned that an elderly gentlewoman in distant Rhode Island was concerned that they should come to a proper understanding of their responsibilities—but that was no more unlikely than that Oliver La Farge should himself have come from Rhode Island by way of Groton and Harvard and the Century Club in New York to sit in their Kivas and urge them to remake their ancient institutions.

In part that journey arose from these beginnings, from his father's feeling for the Indian and from his mother's image of a moral world. As she wrote him: "I am much interested in your job and have a feeling that you are doing something that hardly anyone else can do for these people. In the present state of confusion and upset in the world, the people who are doing something constructive and useful for other people or groups of people are keeping the world sane and sound and will be our salvation, if we are to be saved at all."

By themselves, such influences should have carried him to wherever it was he intended to go, as similar influences had borne others of his class and generation to high places. But the insights and especially the modes of proceeding of one generation do not function in the succeeding generation, and each age discovers for itself what will serve its purposes. In that summer of 1936, Oliver La Farge was thirty-five years of age—he had already won the Pulitzer Prize for fiction—but he had yet to discover his proper self.

❖ II ❖

Learning How

As an adult writing about his childhood and the experiences that shaped his growing up, Oliver La Farge seldom mentions New York, and yet the greater part of each year continuing into adolescence was spent in the city. He never became city-bound, though he labored and played in the city at different times, and his livelihood throughout his life was city-derived. It was a place of beginnings and of returnings, never a resting place. But he was an urbanite.

St. Bernard's, where his formal education began, was a no-nonsense grammar school founded in 1904 by two Englishmen, Francis Hebard Tabor and John Card Jenkins. According to the testimony of their students, these schoolmasters had a gift for inspiring young boys to work at hard tasks and to respect their taskmasters. Boys as young as ten and twelve were dosed heavily with Milton and Shakespeare and the Latin classics.

A roster of the school's former students includes a fair sampling of individuals who became leaders in banking, business, law, and academic life. The school drew its students from that segment of the upper class which had roots in the traditions of the city and the nation. The sons who were enrolled at St. Bernard's were not always from wealthy families and certainly not from newly rich families, but from long-established households, mostly of Anglo-Saxon derivation, and of course Protestant, though it was not a church school.

The La Farge brothers, Christopher first, then Oliver, then Francis, went through St. Bernard's in age-spaced succession. The

17

school was first located on Fifth Avenue at midtown, then it moved to the East Sixties, and later to East 98th Street. In those first years—he was there during the years 1909–1914—Oliver recalled the physical arrangements, equipment, and space were cramped and improvised, adapted from private residences. When the school operated out of a brownstone house in the East Sixties, the students walked around the block at recess, for lack of recreational facilities. To play soccer, they traveled to a public playground in the Bronx, and since the school lacked kitchen and dining space—these rooms having been converted into classrooms —the students brought lunches from home. The sons of the well-to-do had elegant lunches prepared by a professional chef, while the poorer boys carried the crude but substantial creations of the family cook. The boys noticed such distinctions.

In spite of its shortcomings, the school influenced its students in important ways. Oliver remarked once that the teachers at St. Bernard's "were not afraid to expose children's minds to college-level concepts." Language was not taught simply by rote memory, but as living form, with beginnings and continuities. The fact that English derived in part from Latin, and on that account bore a certain relationship to French and to other Romance languages, might not have stirred a response in other boys, but Oliver was quickened by that kind of insight. He became aware of process, of growth and change through time, and this encouraged a habit that would grow, a curiosity about why things were so and how they became so.

The habit of curiosity was encouraged at home. The La Farge children, with whatever cousins happened to be visiting, lived in a constant uproar of debate, with someone jumping up from a meal to quote from a reference book and demolish an opponent. No subject was out of bounds because of its complexity, no one too young to participate. It was enough to drive any adult into quick retreat, all except Mrs. La Farge, who attentively presided and was a court of final appeal when the facts went against a wavering argument.

Those were the first school years. A visitor to St. Bernard's took note of young Oliver reading obliviously in a corner while hubbub swirled around him at noon recess. He played Jessica in the school production of *The Merchant of Venice,* and before an appreciative audience stood on one foot while he scratched the back of his leg with the toe of his other foot.

Groton, his next encounter with formal education, was an unmitigated disaster, as La Farge wrote about it thirty years later. He was troubled there by something deeper than the first rude shock which schoolboys are likely to experience when they leave the security of home. It was more than homesickness, the usual symptom of that early crisis.

In *Raw Material* he wrote a blistering attack on Groton, on the forces compelling unquestioning conformity to the preparatory school establishment. The "Groton Boy" was a paragon of sterling but bland virtues, a seeker after impeccable mediocrity, the avowed enemy of thoughtful and creative imagination. In some of his aspects, as when pursuing his self-appointed task of enforcing the rules of the herd, the "Groton Boy" could be cruel and tasteless. It was this clash, coming unexpectedly, from which Oliver recoiled and which he afterward condemned.

In his story "By the Boys Themselves," collected in the volume *A Pause in the Desert,* he described with less rancor how the parts of the system reinforced each other: "The Head did his best to keep his finger on the workings of the traditions among the boys, which, quite as much as the formal disciplines of constituted authority, controlled St. Peter's school. He depended upon his Prefect's meetings, and particularly upon consultations with the Major Prefect. . . . Experience had taught him that his contact [with the boys] would always be incomplete, for even the most responsive of Sixth Formers were still dominated by an ingrained tradition of secrecy, an almost mechanical defense against adults."

All of Oliver's boyhood until then had been lived in an open environment, with freedom to investigate, to inquire, to stretch his capacities. Groton seemed to deny this; it seemed to insist upon his becoming something he did not want to be. He might not know what that was, or what he wanted for himself, but instinctively he rebelled. His resistance, of course, drew contempt from his peers; they assailed him for being different. And that is what he wrote about in *Raw Material.*

Physical appearance will set a boy apart from his mates—a physical anomaly such as extra large ears, bulging eyes, brick red hair. Oliver was not a physical standout. He was not unusually tall for his age, though his thinness suggested height. Like all growing boys, he was an assemblage of loose parts, mostly elbows, knees, and feet. He had a thin, bony face, black hair, and flashing dark eyes.

Part of the problem—perhaps a major difficulty—was that in confronting boys who were bigger and stronger, more adept in the classroom or on the athletic field, he became aware for the first time of a sense of inadequacy. He began to expect defeat in whatever he attempted. Even when he triumphed in individual encounters or in competitive sports, he was certain failure would come on the next try. It was a new and troubling experience. Only after many years was he able to look back at Groton and understand what had happened. In 1942, for example, when he was writing those chapters on Groton which were included in *Raw Material,* he told his brother Christopher: "The Groton [material] is pretty hostile, but I've tried to make it clear that it isn't intended to be an essay on or a description of Groton so much as a description of one individual's evolution within Groton."

On other occasions he referred to those years in more favorable perspective. He was at the school all through the First World War years and shared with his schoolmates a patriotic fervor which sometimes led to ridiculous situations, as when he found himself drillmaster for a platoon of Girl Scouts and Brownies. The awkward incident is retold with aplomb in the *Texas Quarterly* (posthumously, in 1964).

Writing in the *Atlantic Monthly* in February 1954, in an article entitled "We Need Private Schools," he explained: "When I wrote what I did about Groton—none of which I would change—I left a world of favorable things unsaid because I took them for granted and assumed that everybody else would. . . . It is only recently that it has become apparent to me that a great many schools, including a number of private schools, fail to provide that most fundamental thing of all, an education." In that article he took exception to Harvard president James Conant's proposal that private schools should be closed, that the American scheme of life required that all should be educated in public schools.

Oliver's problem at Groton was not lack of awareness of who he was. He was well aware of that and troubled by it. The La Farges and their relatives for generations had been doers and creators—artists, architects, writers, career statesmen. The question for Oliver, then and later, was, could he belong in that company? His competitors were not the taunting, bullying schoolboys who trampled on his privacy, but the elitists who made up his ancestry. Writing from Harvard on his twenty-first birthday, he explained to his mother: "People expect me to be artistic and literary, and I can't draw, I can't paint, and nobody but me thinks I can write."

It was overdrawn, perhaps, but he had before him always the example of Christopher, his elder brother, who could do all these things. In the very year (1914) that Oliver entered Groton, Christopher, still in school at that time, was complimented on his writing by no less a person than Theodore Roosevelt, a close friend of the family. No jealousy was involved, but Oliver carried an abiding doubt which success would never entirely demolish.

The one positive satisfaction that emerged from the Groton years was his discovery of anthropology. If he could not make it as a creative artist, in the La Farge tradition, then perhaps life as a scientist would allow him to live with himself. The two possibilities were not poles apart, but they had a polarizing effect on La Farge's career.

The appeal of anthropology was akin to the fascination he had discovered in language as a developing process. Anthropology had to do with beginnings, with growth, and with first causes. It all began during his second year at Groton with a reading of

Henry Fairfield Osborne's *Men of the Old Stone Age,* to which he had been directed by Theodore Roosevelt's detailed review of the book. His mother sent him the review, partly no doubt because both Osborne and Roosevelt were family friends. The Osborne volume led him to further reading and to more disciplined study habits.

He finished at Groton, if not in a blaze of glory, certainly not the discomfited boy he had been at times. Growing out of the stage of being all arms and legs and feet, he found that he had athletic ability and surprised himself by starring at high-jumping, rowing, and football.

The summer after leaving Groton, in anticipation of Harvard, he and Christopher traveled for six weeks in Europe—England, the Low Countries, France—the traditional educational tour. It was the first time that Oliver had moved outside of the family circle and his class consciousness was painfully visible. The ship going over was full of "dull Americans" and "boorish Germans"; only the Dutch were "pleasant and intelligent and not fat." He noted that the stewards tended to be patronizing, even "pretty flip," toward other passengers, especially "those Americans high class enough to wish to be ladies, and who tip," but toward his brother and himself they were always respectful, "entirely different." He and his brother expected to be served and were sparing in their tips.

Wherever they went in England, they had letters from their mother, who had herself before her marriage lived in England and was obviously well remembered. "All your friends are coming through like a million dollars," Oliver wrote. Invitations for luncheon, for dinner, for an overnight stay carried them into the Lake Country, to the important cathedral towns, to Stratford, to London. Lord Haldane wrote from London to Mrs. La Farge: "Your son [Christopher] dined here last night, and afterwards remained for a talk alone. . . . I was greatly interested in him. In keenness of mind he reminds me of his mother, and I can see how closely you have watched over his literary development. With such young men your country is secure—ethically as well as intellectually."

Their encounter at Stratford-on-Avon with the novelist, Marie Corelli, to whom they had a letter of introduction from a friend of their mother's, was a shock. "She insulted us outrageously, and America, and talked like a fool. First it was herself and Mr. Asquith. Then came the remark that America had produced but one great man in art and literature—Emerson. She swept Lincoln aside as oratory—and 'what is oratory?' So, has that fat and very middle-class little woman ever written anything good?" He had never heard of her, but reported, "She simply thinks she's the second great pen of Stratford."

They saw castles and cathedrals, the industrial Midlands, and the sights of London. For Christopher it seems to have been a fairly serious sketching tour, but Oliver only occasionally mentions his own efforts with pad and pencil. His brother's talent was so much better trained that Oliver felt diffident about working at his side. He exclaimed once: "When I draw a picture that's pretty fair, people say 'Goodness, Inky, I think that's very nice,' in the tone of pleased surprise you use when a child says a new word. If Kipper drew it, they'd think he was joking." It was said without rancor, an indication of how close the brothers were. The respect each felt for the other was deep and lasting. Oliver wrote about this to one of Christopher's sons many years later.

The European tour was not, on the surface at least, a liberalizing experience. It seemed only to confirm and reinforce a vein of arrogance which never entirely mellowed, and often came to the surface at inopportune times. After he had toured Belgium, he wrote to his father: "I went to Belgium almost in fear, for I had heard an awful lot of bad things about the Belgians. . . . Well, I want to say that it's a mighty fine country. The people are Europeans, and can't help it, but they are clean and the shops are honest."

The anglophile also emerged, as when he stood in Notre Dame Cathedral in Paris and gazed up at one of the great rose windows and afterward wrote to his father: "By gum, up at the top was the old cabbage, the cabbage and waffle iron—you know what I mean, the rose and portcullis of the Tudors—all around. I blinked, then

I made out the old English cats and fleur-de-lys, and I felt as if I was at home—I mean in England, for England isn't abroad, you know."

That fall he registered at Harvard with the class of 1924. He still was unsure of himself and of what he wished to do. His summer of observing tourists and studying cathedrals had not added to his self-understanding.

Because of this lack of assurance, he acknowledged later, he sought a very active life at Harvard, although a close friend, Douglas S. Byers, was not aware that lack of confidence was the motivation. He remarked that if La Farge had plunged into activities in order to build up his self-esteem, it was well disguised behind a façade of genuine enjoyment and comradeship.

At any rate, Oliver tried out for football that first autumn and almost at once suffered a shoulder separation. After carrying his arm in a sling for some weeks, he went out for high-jumping, a sport at which he had done well at Groton. His attachment to home was still close and he wrote detailed descriptions, including pen and ink sketches, of his jumping technique. His mother responded with appropriate encouragement. The freshman track team was defeated in an early spring meet by Worcester Academy, however, and he abandoned the notion of becoming a track star.

Rowing turned out to be the sport at which he could hold his own, as he had previously discovered at Groton. Some Eastern schools, Harvard among them, had just established a special division within the sport, limited to 150-pound crews, for men not quite big enough for the varsity boats. They rowed with the same equipment and under the same rules, and they were often capable of holding their own against a good varsity crew over a short course. Oliver wrote his mother in the spring: "I have been shifted to five [oar], which is, with six, the driving position deluxe." He won a place with the first 150-pound varsity crew at Harvard. His description of rowing, "The Eight Oared Shell," written in 1942 and included in *Raw Material,* moved one correspondent to extravagant praise: "The best piece on rowing that's ever been written."

When he was not immediately taken into one of Harvard's social clubs at the beginning of his sophomore year, he grew uneasy. "There is something wrong with your son, somewhere, and I wish I could spot it," he wrote home. What troubled him especially was that various cousins and sons of old family friends held strategic offices in some of these clubs, and yet he received no bids. "The clubs," he wrote, "[won't] make or break my young life," but his worry was genuine. He was finally taken into two clubs, including the one to which he most aspired, but not until his junior year.

The desire to be a writer was still an unformed longing born of chronic daydreaming, and he had yet to discover whether he had talent to match desire. This was where success must come, or the promise of success. Wherever else he might fail, here he could not. Actually, he had fewer self-doubts about finding himself as a writer than he usually experienced in meeting challenges. He well knew that writing was not solely a matter of talent, though that had to be part of the equipment; it was something to be learned. One had to work at it. One had to be critical of one's own efforts.

These things he knew—he could hardly have avoided learning them in that family. Christopher, four years his senior, had a sharp ear for the factitious. If an older brother's presence was not enough to stimulate self-criticism, there was a father who despised dilettantism. Grant La Farge, who wrote a vigorous prose, insisted that art be taken seriously or left alone. It was idle to talk about such matters unless one were willing to submit to the rigors of learning how.

Standing farther back but casting a strong shadow across the careers of all later La Farges was the giant of the family, John La Farge, landscapist, muralist, painter of exquisite flower studies, a genius with stained glass. With his close friend, Henry Adams, he traveled in Asia and was one of the first Western painters to capture something of the color and texture of native life in the South Pacific. His *An Artist's Letters from Japan* and his essays on painting reveal a vigorous intellect, a man deeply committed to life.

Henry James, who knew John La Farge in Newport in the 1860's wrote of him, in his amazing serpentine prose: "It was as a man of the world that, for all his youth, La Farge rose or, still better, bowed, before us, his inclinations of obeisance, his considerations of address being such as we had never seen and now almost publicly celebrated. . . . He was really an artistic, an esthetic nature of wondrous homogeneity."

John La Farge came to painting only after a period of self-doubt, according to his own statement. With freedom to choose a career in art (one of his grandfathers in France was a painter), he hesitated. He thought he wanted to read law, and even after his father, Jean-Frédéric, sent him to Europe for travel and art study, he returned to New York still inclined toward a law practice. "No one struggled more against his destiny than I," he told his biographer, Royal Cortissoz. He did not "acquiesce" in being a painter, "though I learned the methods and studied the problems of my art." He needed to know that what he could do would be worth doing, something that "would be living, would be impossible to duplicate." Some striking early successes on canvas lessened the doubt, but his final commitment to art was a process involving the whole man.

This was the tradition out of which Grant La Farge counseled his sons. Do it well, or leave it alone. Whether he could do it well was what Oliver had to discover.

His letters from Harvard contained mostly references to high-jumping and rowing and social arrangements during holiday breaks, but when his writing efforts are mentioned it is apparent that he was moving cautiously in a troubled area. In the spring term of his freshman year he was awarded honorable mention in a short story competition sponsored by the *Harvard Advocate,* and he reports: "There was a winner and two mentions, mine came first. The others were both juniors." A small triumph, but obviously cherished. Later, *Scribner's Magazine* accepted and published a brief essay ("The Human Boy and the Microscope," November 1922), and in announcing this at home he commented: "They sent me two copies. It strikes me they're a pretty decent bunch."

He found encouragement at Harvard. The *Advocate* published his stories and poems and in his junior year he was elected its president. He also made the editorial staff of the *Lampoon*. He served on the student council, which placed him at the center of student activities. The final nod of approval was his election as class poet in his senior year, about which he wrote Christopher: "The class elections have now come off and I am class poet, getting 171 votes and the three men who were up against me totaling 178 between them."

Among other accomplishments, he cultivated a robust sense of fun during these undergraduate years. In his senior year a Harvard man, class of '90, protested the singing of *Johnnie Harvard,* a drinking song, and to the embarrassment of all Harvard drinking men offered a cash prize for the best opprobrious term for those who defied Prohibition and persisted in their now illegal practice. Out of this public competition emerged the uncouth epithet, "scofflaw." La Farge then offered in the *Advocate* a cash prize for the best counter irritant, and to everybody's surprise newspapers across the country joined in the campaign. Entries came from as far away as California and Bermuda. The *Advocate* gave the award to "Spigot-bigot," with "Camelouse" a close second and "Puritank" closing in.

Also in that last year at Harvard, while participating in a pageant staged in Newport to commemorate events in Rhode Island history, including a skit showing Commodore Matthew Calbraith Perry being received at the Japanese Imperial Court, Oliver went on to a house party where he did such a vigorous clog dance that he tore the cartilage in his left knee and was immobilized just as the rowing season was warming up. He was left with a trick knee for the rest of his life.

He graduated *cum laude* in 1924 and, what was of more significance for his future career, he was awarded the Hemenway Fellowship for graduate study in anthropology. This, too, was a culmination—a recognition of quiet accomplishment in a sphere of interest about which he rarely wrote in his family letters. While experiencing doubt and some small success in his writing efforts, he had been acquiring unexpected competence elsewhere.

❖ III ❖

Journey of Discovery

From about the 1880's the Southwest had been Harvard's backyard, where her anthropology students went to dig, to measure skulls, to study kinship systems—to perform all the obscure rites that anthropologists practice. When La Farge entered Harvard the anthropology faculty included men who had served their apprenticeship in the Southwest and went on to influence the development of the science in the United States—among these, A. M. Tozzer, A. V. Kidder, S. J. Guernesy, and E. A. Hooton. Inevitably, La Farge, too, went to the Southwest.

He had not anticipated such a turn because, until he got to Harvard, he had not associated anthropology with the Western Hemisphere. His reading of *Men of the Old Stone Age* and similar works had filled his fancy with such exploits as discovering cave paintings in the Dordogne and digging up Neanderthal skulls at La Chapelle-aux-Saints. Archaeology in America in the early 1920's was still the domain of antiquarians looking for museum specimens; only a handful of obscure scientists worked at it seriously.

Oliver's father arranged for him to meet Professor Tozzer during his first weeks at Harvard, and in making the arrangement Grant La Farge pursued vicariously his own interest in Indians. His familiarity with the Southwest was more than casual, as Oliver discovered when he was in the Hopi country in 1924 and talked with Indians who knew Grant La Farge. On one occasion he wrote Oliver: "You may remember I once wrote a paper on the Pueblo churches. Bridges [at Scribner's] refused it, because he had a paper about to be published, written by a woman, covering the same subject. Well, it was some sentimental flapdoodle about Isleta, written by a silly tourist abysmally ignorant of all that means the Southwest."

During the same period the elder La Farge was commissioned by Elsie Clews Parsons to illustrate *American Indian Life,* a remarkable volume in that day, which she edited and published in 1922. The contributors included Kroeber, Lowie, Wissler, Radin —all the top names, each writing about a tribe with which he had worked. La Farge's illustrations, romantic in tone, were carefully accurate in detail and reveal how more than casually he had responded to Indian life. He had perhaps discovered something of himself in the unassuming but prideful people and in their adaptation to the natural world. He warmed to the idea of a son learning to value the same wide horizons as he had, especially since his first son, Christopher, had chosen architecture, and thereby the urban experience.

Oliver soon went to take tea with Professor Tozzer, and in time he met other members of the anthropology faculty informally. Before the end of the spring semester he had signed on for his first archaeological expedition. What happened to him then paralleled what had happened earlier to Alfred Kidder, who went to southern Utah on his first field trip in 1907 fully committed to a career in medicine, and returned a "confirmed archaeologist," as he later remarked. Oliver came back from his first experience, while not a dedicated archaeologist, conscious that a new and wholly unexpected dimension had been added to his view of the future. Standing squarely in the center of that view were the Navajo Indians.

If the invitation to join the 1921 field party was intended as a challenge to his professional interest in anthropology and to test his stamina at the end of a shovel, as he surmised, he obviously satisfied his challengers. He was included in the field party of the following year, again as a laborer and mapmaker, and in 1924 he went out as chief of party, with a crew of workers under his direction. During the summer when he did not go to the Southwest, he did some exploratory archaeology near Saunderstown, about which his mother reported: "Drove over to the River Farm and buried in the north graveyard the bones of the Indian Oliver dug up for the Peabody Museum. . . . It's rather nice to have a grave of one's own."

The expeditions in which La Farge participated were more than training exercises for a select group of students. They centered on the so-called Four Corners area—where the four states of Colorado, New Mexico, Arizona, and Utah meet—and they were aimed at gathering information about what was at the time one of the most perplexing questions in American prehistory.

Beginning in 1914, Peabody Museum of Harvard had sponsored expeditions to northeastern Arizona to determine whether the Southwest had been occupied by man before the cliff-dwelling people who built the monumental structures at Mesa Verde and other sites in the vicinity of the San Juan River. The Wetherill brothers, who had discovered many of these sites in the 1880's and gave them wide publicity, had made the claim that an earlier people had lived in the same area, and in some instances the so-called Cliff Dwellers had actually erected their houses on top of older structures. Richard Wetherill, the most active in the area, had named the earlier settlers Basket People or Basket Makers, because of the prevalence of finely wrought basketry, matting, and woven sandals among their remains. No reliable methods for dating prehistoric remains had yet been developed and the assignment of comparative antiquities was left largely to speculation, within certain gross age factors derived from geological events. The Wetherills were not scientifically trained and their guesses were generally not acceptable to the professional students, who defended the right to blunder scientifically.

The question of fixing comparative dates for the Southwestern materials was part of a larger controversy which had rocked the academic world since the end of the nineteenth century, erupting at times into bitter factional divisions and some ungentlemanly name-calling. The discoveries of early man in Europe beginning after mid-century had led to enthusiastic digging in America, in the hope of finding New World counterparts. Some of the excavated materials were reported to be from 10,000 to 100,000 years old. About 1890 a reaction set in, largely as a result of a countering movement led by scientists of the Smithsonian Institution, who flatly refused to recognize an antiquity greater than a few thousand years for New World settlement, and they wrote scholarly articles demolishing all other claims. In the absence of reliable dating methods, no effective rebuttal was available.

The Harvard Southwest expeditions were directed at least in part to solving this problem. Year after year, interrupted briefly by the First World War, field parties explored and excavated and published reports. The findings demonstrated beyond doubt that the Basketmaker people did, in fact, precede the Cliff Dwellers, who in turn were recognized as the immediate ancestors of the modern Pueblo tribes of the Rio Grande Valley, western New Mexico, and the Hopi villages of Arizona. Of more significance to archaeology, the field work resulted in improved techniques in excavation and artifact retrieval. This made possible the identification and separation of stratigraphic horizons and thus contributed to comparative dating of occupation sites. Exact dating came later, with the development of tree ring counts and, still later, radiocarbon analysis. When A. V. Kidder convened the First Pecos Conference in 1927, it was possible to identify eight distinctive time periods, based in large part on the materials gathered by the Harvard University field parties. The classification system established by the Pecos Conference is still followed, with modifications, in detailing the prehistory of the Southwest. In other words, the base lines of modern American archaeology were being laid out during those early years of Southwestern digs.

The experience was invaluable training in tool-handling, ground-mapping, detailed observation, and descriptive reporting. But the experience was also useful in convincing La Farge that exploring the caves of France or even digging in the Southwest was not what he wanted to do. He would not be an archaeologist—but the living, singing, free-moving Navajo Indians were suddenly a new force in his life. To live among them and to become knowledgeable about their ways of life seemed to answer his need for a focal point around which to organize his energies.

The 1924 field party completed its activities in early August, and then, with equipment, specimens, and maps and notes packed up and shipped off to Cambridge, La Farge and two companions, Bartlett H. Hayes, Jr., and Douglas S. Byers, set out on a cross-country horseback trip through the Navajo country—the footloose adventure that Oliver had yearned for since his first trip to Arizona.

They outfitted at Lukachukai, near the northeastern corner of Arizona, where Oliver became acquainted with Father Berard Haile, the linguist and collector of Navajo mythology. For three saddle horses complete with saddles, and a pack horse with appropriate gear, they paid $215. Their destination was the Grand Canyon, one hundred seventy-five miles to the west, with stops at the Hopi villages.

It was unfenced, open country, and the people were friendly—somewhat amazed by the sight of the three strange white men riding along Indian style, but never unmannerly. When asked, they never hesitated to give directions about where to find water and grass for the horses. When the travelers camped near a Navajo hogan, they were invariably invited to share the evening meal with the family. The young men reciprocated by asking the family to come to breakfast the next morning. This always proved to be a winning formula—a breakfast of rice boiled with dried Hopi peaches, eaten with evaporated milk and brown sugar, and topped off with coffee and soda bread flavored with cinnamon. They had discovered that sharing a meal with an Indian was a sure way to win his respect and good will. The rice-and-Hopi-peaches combination was especially effective. On one occasion Oliver made dinner for a family by boiling a thick beef sirloin (which a Navajo had given him earlier) with a handful of rice, a handful of dried peaches, and some onions—"a daring mixture," he wrote, "but a great success. They certainly loved the onions, and we cooked up some more."

They also discovered that by riding cross-country and living off the land, instead of traveling by motor along established roads in the manner of white people, they invited friendly talk. When they reached Oraibi, one of the Hopi villages, and replied to an inquiring Navajo that they had come horseback from Lukachukai, there was a smile and exclamation "That's far!" A Navajo might not have thought such a feat worth mentioning, but it was extraordinary for a white man to perform it and to seem to have enjoyed himself. It also helped a great deal that, by then, Oliver had learned some basic Navajo and could talk to the people in their own tongue. His ear for linguistic nuances was a valuable asset.

An ailing horse forced Byers to quit the party when they reached the Hopi villages, and La Farge and Hayes, by then thoroughly native, continued by themselves.

Openhanded hospitality was not limited to the Indians they encountered. At Oraibi La Farge and Hayes found themselves short of cash, which could not be replenished until they reached Tuba City, two days' ride to the west. It was suggested that they explain their predicament to the trader, Lorenzo Hubbell, since they needed to purchase supplies.

Hubbell was already a legend in the Southwest, respected and trusted by Hopis and Navajos alike, the genial host to every passing stranger, and a shrewd trader. *Lorenzo the Magnificent,* the title of Dane Coolidge's biography, aptly describes the regard in which Hubbell was held throughout the area and beyond.

One visitor of that period, Margaret Schevill Link (*The Pollen Path*) wrote: "I had heard of his exquisite courtesy and politeness of heart. But I was not prepared for the warm charm and generosity with which he treated truck drivers, mail carriers, artists, the Governor of Arizona, and me."

La Farge wrote of his encounter: "I had heard of him for years. So I pictured myself a tall, dark old-timer (he is half Mexican and the Indians call him Nakai Tso—big Mexican). Well, he is fat and wheezy and jovial, he showed us over his quarters, he clapped our backs, he did us right in every way, stuffed fifteen dollars down our throats, lost three hours sleep getting us a guide, jested and laughed and gave us the run of the house. . . . We were reaping a harvest on our horse travel, youth, and coming just enough ahead of time [of the Hopi Snake Dance] to be excluded from the label 'tourist.' "

No one, however, exceeded in hospitality the Tewa Indian from the village of Hano on First Mesa. During the week La Farge and Hayes spent watching various events associated with the Snake Dance and moving back and forth between the villages on Second and Third Mesa, they found themselves more or less adopted by the Indian, Nelson Oyaping, who was a member of the Hopi tribal police force. He introduced them to members of his family and to fellow police officers, always as "my friends." They invited him to their camp, where they fed him their boiled rice-and-peaches specialty. He thought it was excellent, and helped himself to four servings. On one occasion he and Oliver raced their horses, to the delight of Indian spectators. The Tewa won, "by half a length," according to La Farge's report, and that pleased the Indians even more.

On the final evening, as they were eating together in camp, the Tewa asked La Farge if he wanted the "little blue roan" that had won the race on the previous afternoon.

"Yes," said La Farge. "It is a good horse, but I have no money." He considered it a friendly gesture and expected his answer would close the matter.

But no. "I don't want money. You're my friend. You take the horse."

La Farge gulped that down and explained that they would sell their outfit to strangers at the end of the trip and it would be too bad to have the little blue roan leave the Hopi country. "Tie that and paint it blue!" Oliver wrote to his mother. It was a favorite expression of his just then.

The friendliness they encountered on every hand could scarcely have been inspired by the appearance of the two young men. When they called on Mrs. Laura Armer, the painter and writer, just then residing at Oraibi, and found her manner rather diffident, they turned and looked at each other, and could not quite believe what they saw. Oliver wrote afterward:

> Bart, who was six-feet one, boasted his lovely golden beard and longish golden hair, both utterly unkempt. His white shirt was gray, his trousers—old dark ones from home—white in places with dust and adobe. He wore sneakers patched with sticking plaster. His hat, once a snappy gray Eastern felt, was green where it showed through dirt and dust. . . . I had a week's beard and a month's pitiful mustache. My glasses were mended with tape. I wore a blue shirt that was actually stiff, and blue trousers that had all of Bart's accumulation plus flour and baking grease. I wore moccasins and a belt set with silver buttons a la Indian. I looked like a low grade Norman smuggler turned *courier du bois*.

So on they went, up over Black Mesa, and two nights out from Oraibi they were befriended by a camp of Navajos and taken along to the first night of a three-day sing, from which they returned at dawn; then on again, mounting higher into the rough plateau country, and "suddenly, at sunset, we came out on the north side of Black Mesa, where it drops straight down for fourteen-hundred feet. Such a view as you never saw in the world. Beyond the Canyon, beyond anything! All the grim North country, and the distant mountains that hold up the sky, all in a red sunset! Then down a narrow zigzag trail, into lavender shadows."

Riding across Black Mesa, a journey that occupied most of two weeks, was an extraordinary experience for both men, as Bart Hayes reminisced about it many years later. They were alone and, as far as they knew, they were the only white men in the area. They talked, and rode, and sang Navajo songs in loud if not very tuneful voices, but in a land of tolerant space the artless sounds provoked no echoes.

In Kayenta, Bart Hayes was a sensation because of his long blond hair and beard. A missionary had been busy in the area distributing chromos of a blond Christ, along with suitable biblical texts, and the Navajo countrymen came to gaze and to marvel. And there La Farge and Hayes met the Wetherills, legendary traders in that north country, from whom they heard incredible tales. One such told of a time when Louisa Wetherill looked out from the trading post to observe Navajos streaming past, driving their sheep and other livestock, their wagons loaded with household goods. When she went out to inquire the reason, she was told that they were moving to high ground to escape the coming flood. A missionary, having acquired some smattering of the Navajo language, had told about Noah and the flood, but he gave his startled audience to understand that the flood was imminent, not a tale of the past. It had upset the countryside.

Oliver La Farge, listening, felt ashamed for those of his own kind who traded upon the fears and uncertainties of a simple people. In the Navajo world he encountered his own world in a different light and found it repugnant. That summer, and that journey, brought many strivings into focus.

When he returned to Harvard in the fall to begin his tenure as Hemenway fellow and to pursue graduate study, he had a clear objective. That was to establish himself as a student of the Navajos and their linguistic kinsmen, the Apaches. As he wrote his brother, Christopher, a little later: "One must lay down for oneself certain conditions essential to life, and stick to them. I am beginning to find mine, and I am feathering my arrows and dancing the Ghost Dance. . . .

" 'I am thinking about the Enemy Gods, I walk among their weapons. . . .' "

He had been reading Washington Matthews' translations of Navajo ceremonial chants, and he explained:

> I wonder if there is any literature that does not repay one somewhat. When I first went below the surface of Indian myths and songs, I expected little from it, and now I find that I use it as much as Horace or Virgil to apply to daily life. . . . One of our obstacles in taking up such literature is that our own poetic feelings are conventionalized around certain subjects, and one has to lift one's mind over symbols and similes that to us are incongruous. . . . The underside of a Magpie's wings are white, hence the Navajo:

"Magpie, Magpie, in the white of his wings are the footsteps of morning."

"It dawns!"

Oliver interrupted his graduate study at mid-year, however, and he did not complete his Master's thesis, "Derivation of Apache and Navajo Culture," until 1929.

❖ IV ❖

Acquiring Skill

THE INTERRUPTION in mid-career of his graduate program carried La Farge to far places, to at least one embarrassing setback, and then to instant success. He was a young man in a hurry and he lost little time along the way.

It began with Frans Blom, another young man in a hurry, who had come to Harvard to train as an archaeologist during Oliver's last undergraduate year. Up to that time, Blom had had a varied career characterized in the beginning by a succession of escapades that resulted in his being shipped away from his well-to-do home in Denmark. His training had been in art and he was an accomplished linguist in at least four languages. Upon arriving in the New World he began to work for an oil company in southern Mexico. That was in 1919, when he was twenty-six years old. In pursuing exploratory field work for Compañia Petrolera El Aguila in the highlands of Chiapas, he was soon searching out old Mayan ruins and making drawings of monuments. These came to the attention of Sylvanus Griswold Morley of the Carnegie Institution, then working in Guatemala, and Morley encouraged him to continue. Blom presently deserted petroleum exploration in favor of archaeology and worked under Manuel Gamio at Palenque, one of the earliest known of the great Maya centers, in the state of Chiapas. Later he joined the Carnegie Institution project of excavating and restoring the large center at Uaxactun in Guatemala. Having progressed to that point in the practice of archaeology, Blom decided that he needed a theoretical grounding, hence his appearance at Harvard and enrollment in Professor Tozzer's class in Mayan archaeology and hieroglyphics.

Blom had a second reason for going to Harvard, which was to recruit a junior staff member for the Carnegie field program. Blom had approached Oliver just before the 1924 expedition left Cambridge, and he wrote his mother: "Frans Blom has offered me a job in Central America with the Carnegie Institution in 1925 and I have accepted it immediately, as he wanted to know in a hurry. I have asked for $200 a month, probably I shan't get it, but still."

After further correspondence Oliver wrote in July from his camp on the Chinle Wash near the Utah border: "I have a letter from Blom, offering me $100 a month and expenses. He says it may develop into a life job, so I shall take it. That's the usual pay for beginners, Tozzer writes me."

Then the plan seemed to run into difficulty. Back at Harvard for the fall term, Oliver wrote: "Guatemala is cancelled and just now I don't know quite where I'm at. However, the signs and omens are that this may be going to produce something even better and, all else besides, Blom is one who habitually lands on his feet, and he appears very much to want me with him in his work. I've been doing some drawings for Tozzer and they impressed him very much."

The "something better," it turned out, was the creation of the Department of Middle-American Research at Tulane University, with which Blom had become associated. If the department came into existence, as planned, Oliver might get a permanent staff appointment as well as the chance for field investigations in the Maya country.

Oliver was not anxious. He had been well received at Peabody Museum in giving an oral account of the summer's field work; he had found comfortable lodgings which he shared with his brother, Francis, and Doug Byers, and he prepared to continue his work as Hemenway fellow.

Very suddenly the Tulane plans materialized and he was asked to join the first field expedition. He left Cambridge in early March, 1925, and in Mexico City joined Blom, who had gone by boat from New Orleans with all the field equipment. The planning had proceeded even while the financing of the expedition had hung in mid-air, and as soon as that was settled, Blom had his gear ready to go. He had spent enough time in the tropical jungles and highlands to know exactly what was needed, while his early training in the Danish Navy had taught him orderliness and management. What had attracted him to La Farge, apart from the academic background, was Oliver's practical experience with horses and with camp routine. They made a good working team.

Between the middle of March and the end of July, traveling by narrow-gauge railways, oil tankers, fruit boats, horse- and mule-back—and sometimes on foot, dragging their reluctant mounts up mountainsides—they covered more than 1,200 miles. Although the year was 1925, they visited ruins which had not been observed or reported since John Lloyd Stephens traveled through the Maya country in the 1840's. They also found ancient monuments from which various shapes and sizes of the carved stones had been taken, out of ignorance of their history, and used as building blocks, even as street-paving.

Blom was at heart an explorer, in the tradition of the Viking men who pushed into unknown seas and their descendants who reached the Poles of the earth. Years later Douglas Byers wrote of him in an obituary notice, "He was meticulous in his attention to every detail. Notes were always made with indelible ink with a carbon that was mailed home from the first town with a post office. His pack outfit was the acme of efficiency, allowing room for only a few supplies, for his parties lived off the land. . . . As leader, he demanded the liver of every chicken, young or old." He and La Farge made a vigorous pair, always pushing on, whatever the weather or traveling conditions, in order not to fall behind schedule. And they had the eyes and sensibilities of young men as they rode through the countryside. At one village they reported, "The women dress in gaudy colored striped skirts held up by firmly woven white belts. Shoulders and breasts are naked, and as they are well-built they certainly gave a pleasant impression."

Elsewhere he wrote, "Evening in the jungle is beautiful, dawn is magnificent. . . . Little by little the light sifted down, and as it reached the bottom of the forest the sun threw a glimmer of gold on the treetops."

Their reporting was not confined to dull statistics and measurements but had something of the flavor of an old motion picture travelog. "We jumped into our saddles and while our Indian guides led the pack animals towards the forest wall, we bade farewell to our American friends who had treated us so royally, and hurried after our outfit."

While the expedition was purely exploratory and was not equipped for site excavation—the permit issued by the Mexican government specified no digging or removal of artifacts—it was intended as something more than a long horseback ride. In concluding the report which they prepared, *Tribes and Temples,* published in 1927, the joint authors declared, "It is our hope that our report may help to awaken the interest of the public in the history of an ancient American people, as few modern Americans realize the stupendous role the ancient American cultures play in our daily life."

To be plain about it, the authors remark: "Vast sums are spent by American institutions in distant fields, while only a few of them conduct explorations on American soil."

The expedition was especially valuable to La Farge's development as a social scientist, as a writer, and as a student of contemporary Indian life. In the division of labor between the two men, Blom was responsible for archaeological observations and reporting, while La Farge concentrated on ethnology, which meant gathering vocabulary lists and making linguistic comparisons, also observing customs, beliefs, modes of living and material possessions of the groups they visited. From his previous association with Indians in the Southwest, he had accepted the notion then current that the Indian people and their way of life were destined to assimilate to the white world and to disappear. But in southern Mexico and Guatemala, he saw tribes large and small that had experienced profound change yet remained staunchly Indian. Their agricultural practices and the foods they ate were those of their ancestors of four hundred years earlier. Their housing remained the same, even certain articles of dress were pre-European. They had, of course, been deprived of political and social autonomy, and nominally they were all devout Christians, but in their daily lives and in their relationships with each other, they functioned as Indian communities as if the Europeans had never come among them.

La Farge described some of these groups: "The Indians of Bachajon and the Indians of Ocosingo and the neighboring valleys, living as they do, cut-off from the outside world, strong in numbers and of a rather independent disposition, gave us the first evidences of how little the Indians of the Chiapas Highlands have changed since the days before Columbus.

"The Bachajon live on the threshold of the pine country. Their farms may be found tucked away in the thick jungleland of mahogany and palms, through which their little hidden trails lead to houses tucked away out of sight of alien travelers. Their capital, Bachajon Village, is among the pines. There, periodically, the Spaniards used to round them up, that they might more easily be policed, and for the benefit of the church established there. After every concentration, the Indians drifted away again like blown smoke."

Toward the end of that journey, as they paused at Comitan in Chiapas, they were told that across the border in neighboring Guatemala a certain ceremony still survived, a ceremony associated with the ancient Maya calendar. Scholars had assumed that all such ceremonies had long since disappeared, along with knowledge of the calendar and the Maya system of reckoning time. The information came to Blom and La Farge casually, in the course of a conversation with a citizen of the town, but it fired the imaginations of both. Knowledge of the calendar and its permutations, even at the height of Mayan civilization, had been restricted to the priesthood and commoners were kept in ignorance of its operation. The casual information, if correct, must mean that a priesthood, or at least knowledgeable practitioners, still functioned after more than 400 years of Christian domination. It might also mean—and at this possibility both men felt a sharp rise in pulse rate—it might mean that astronomical observations were still being recorded in the Mayan system of writing. It could even mean that men still lived who understood how to read the old hieroglyphic inscriptions. The possibility was fantastic, since scientists had puzzled over the inscriptions at least since Stephens' time and had progressed only to the point of being able to decipher dates and to follow the intricacies of the Mayan vigesimal arithmetic.

The expedition had come to an end, however, and it was time to pack up the equipment and return to the States. Further investigation of the rumor would have to wait.

La Farge returned to Harvard that fall and resumed his Hemenway Fellowship. He completed a draft of his Navajo-Apache thesis and then turned to his field notebooks to prepare the linguistic and material culture sections for *Tribes and Temples,* the report of the first Tulane University expedition to Middle America.

Meanwhile, Frans Blom was getting the necessary approval and early in 1926 Oliver joined the Department of Middle American Research, as assistant in ethnology. The two and a half years in New Orleans which followed constituted his first permanent break from home. At age twenty-four he was on his own.

While he now seemed committed to a career in science and to academic research, he did not seek out the academic community. He chose rather to live in the Old French Quarter and developed friends among a group of writers and artists, most of whom were young, talented, and unknown—William Faulkner was among them. His own writing was relegated to a part-time activity, but one story from this period, "North Is Black," a Navajo tale, was published in *The Dial.* The story was subsequently included in the Edward J. O'Brien collection, *Best American Short Stories for 1927.*

His encounters with the Navajo world—riding to ceremonials at night, watching the red rocks waver in firelight, sharing a hogan meal—lived vividly in his consciousness, underlining its curious contrasts with his daily life in New Orleans, urging him to express the strange but deep sentiments the Navajos had aroused in him. These stirrings were encouraged by his reading for his Master's thesis, which involved a searching analysis of Navajo culture and its derivation from many sources. He felt that he knew Navajo life, not just as a tourist traveling through the country, pausing to observe a chance ceremony, but in historical depth and with some insight into Navajo values and goals. The question was, and here he hesitated—could he write about it? Could any white man write about a Navajo and bring him to life? The articles and stories he had written up to then, some of which had appeared in the Harvard *Advocate,* dealt only with surfaces, what a tourist might see.

In a letter to Christopher he gave the first intimation that he had embarked on the story that was to emerge as *Laughing Boy.* "I've started on a novel," he wrote from New Orleans. "It is a most painful process, for here, in this weather, a long day at the office really exhausts one. I've been dabbing at it since last November, and have now written eighty-five sheets, or about 20,000 words. I have about twice as much to go, and the comforting realization that everything I have done will have to be rewritten." That was in July 1927, after he had returned from his second, Tulane University's third, expedition to Middle America.

La Farge led the 1927 two-man expedition, with Douglas Byers as assistant. Byers, who had been a member of the 1924 Peabody Museum field party, was about to become a banker when La Farge enticed him away to the Guatemala highlands, and the banking world lost a promising young candidate. Byers, like Alfred Kidder before him, stayed in archaeology. Eventually he became director of the Robert S. Peabody Foundation for Archaeology, Phillips Academy, Andover.

They arrived in Guatemala in February, picking up where the 1925 expedition had ended by going directly to the Indian village, Jacaltenango, where the ancient ceremony honoring the Year Bearer was still celebrated, as Blom and La Farge had been told.

By the nature of its quest, it was quite a different kind of expedition. Some archaeological probes were managed along the way, but the primary interest was in the living society, and a special sector of it.

> We were engaged on a fairly delicate diplomatic mission. Certain Indians, we did not know which ones, possessed important secret information. We had a general idea of what it was about, but how much they knew, in just what form, we could not tell. We had three months in which to ingratiate ourselves and extract the information, meanwhile making a complete survey of the general culture.

Earlier students of Middle America had concerned themselves almost exclusively with the ancient Mayans and their achievements as mathematicians, astronomers, and builders of monumental temples, and only a few studies, including Tozzer's work with the Lacandones, focused on the contemporary people and their living conditions. La Farge and Byers explained their presence in the village by asking endless questions about the language, farming methods, house building, craftwork—all the normal activities about which the people were willing to talk. But as they asked these questions they also looked for informants who knew and were willing to discuss the belief systems which were so carefully shielded from inquiring strangers. They encountered many blank walls, evasions, even fear. On one occasion an informant who told more than he had intended simply disappeared for a while. The man's wife explained: "He has been in prison twice because people accused him of witchcraft, my husband. That is not true; he has not made witchcraft. Now he is afraid, that man, my husband. He thinks the venerable Presidente has sent you from Guatemala to take him to prison. When he left the little house now, the tears were streaming down his face." Four hundred years of temple looting, of pulling down monuments, of sacred book burning, of coerced conversions had marked the people deeply.

When they finally won the people's confidence information came from many sources, and a segment of the history of the Indian race came to light. It was a history which La Farge would encounter in many settings. The details would vary greatly from tribe to tribe across North America, but a common theme ran through each experience.

There at Jacaltenango, the old knowledge was gone, even from among those who followed the ways of their ancestral priests. The hieroglyphic writing was meaningless. The names of the gods had been lost or replaced or they were mingled in the Christian hierarchy of saints. But the calendar still lived, as tradition and as a guide to life. The calendar related them to the past.

The elaborate ceremonial worship which in the Classic period had tied the Mayan people to time, to time as a divinity, had been eroded to not much more than set formulas used in forecasting good and bad fortune, in determining dates when events should take place, and even in such mundane matters as finding lost articles. Notwithstanding the erosions, an Indian past endured in the present.

In introducing his report of the expedition, La Farge observed that the Jacalteco Indians "present a picture of a thoroughly primitive people whose background is highly civilized, subjected strongly to the influence of a foreign culture, and out of these factors evolving a tight pattern peculiarly their own. . . . There is about them an unconscious clinging to the remnants of something that once was glamorous." While the Spanish conquerors had attempted to Christianize the entire Indian population and to obliterate the heathen past, they had failed. Conversion to Christianity took place, but the past also remained. He wrote,

> At first, there was conscious opposition to Christianity on the part of adherents to the old gods, as one might well expect, considering that, for the upper classes, their temporal power and the sway of the native gods must stand or fall together. This stopped in time, to be replaced by a process of adapting the two religions to suit each other. The tolerance of the Indian, and the facility with which he accepts beliefs from other creeds, are well known in all parts of the New World; he has what might be called a genius for adding new religions or parts of religions to his own.

La Farge's linguistic skill was considerably sharpened by his experiences with the Jacalteco Indians. Because good interpreters were not available, or the information to be transmitted could not be trusted to a layman, he and the principal ceremonial official found themselves struggling together to achieve understanding, La Farge stretching his knowledge of the local Maya dialect, and the Indian limping along in Spanish, of which he had first professed complete ignorance. To achieve such a degree of willing cooperation was an accomplishment in itself.

Oliver's facility for making friends which served him so well in the Navajo country also opened doors in Guatemala, even among Indians who remembered being exploited by men of La Farge's race. It gained him access equally to the homes of Ladinos, the people of mixed origin who hold themselves aloof from the Indians, though they live among them and make use of their labor and skills. La Farge mentions an occasion when he and Byers, while traveling to some ruins, stopped at a ranch house by prior arrangement for food and shelter. The Ladino ranch manager apologized, since he had not known when the two would arrive and consequently had "nothing in the house" to feed them.

La Farge reports: "Barring that we lived like kings during our two days' stay, that he himself put off a business trip so as to help and guide us, refusing pay, and that his wife, without being asked, went through our packs and washed all our dirty clothes, nothing was done for us!"

This, of course, is part of the field method which the successful ethnographer learns to practice: to win confidence where there is distrust and hostility, to obtain information forbidden to the outsider, and to do these things without betrayal, maintaining friendships that have been won. It is a theme that La Farge repeatedly builds upon in the anthropological stories collected in *The Door in the Wall*.

"Ethnology," his character muses in the title story, "is a slow process of gaining acceptance. And if you don't gain acceptance? You just go on being friendly with everyone, even the ones you would like to haul off and kick in the butt."

In "The Little Stone Man," in the same collection, where the setting is a Rio Grande Pueblo in New Mexico, he describes what can happen when secret knowledge is betrayed, even inadvertently.

By the time the expedition returned to New Orleans in the early summer of 1927, La Farge was becoming an accomplished Mayan scholar. Not only had he read exhaustively in the literature, but his field experiences had provided the firsthand contact with surviving customs which gave perspective and occasional verification to the older studies. He had acquired a certain mastery of the Mayan calendar as a secular instrument and as it functioned in its religious usages. The testing of this knowledge came five years later, when he made a third trip to Guatemala. He found himself in a situation where he had to demonstrate his ability as a diviner in order to win the confidence of the people and to disarm the suspicion which might have had tragic consequences.

As a practicing scientist, he had developed keen powers of observation and a meticulous concern for accuracy. Byers remarked, in writing about the 1927 expedition: "My ear was insensitive to the slight differences which his ear could spot, but I knew he was checking each word to be sure he had recorded it correctly. While I was working on Jacalteco material culture, Oliver would sit (with an informant) going over words and phrases. He and I, together, worked out the more difficult details of roof structures and of looms—I drew and he checked. Then we went back and checked details again to be sure."

Out of such tedium are monographs born. Back in New Orleans, with bundles of field notes and sketches, he settled down to the duties of a staff member and the immediate task of preparing a report. This, however, did not appear until 1931, with the title *The Year Bearer's People*. In the interval Oliver's career was pulled apart and put together again.

❖ V ❖

Laughing Boy

Iɴ ᴡʀɪᴛɪɴɢ *Laughing Boy* many beginnings came into focus for Oliver La Farge, although his view of Indians, center of the focus, was still skewed by the social climate then prevailing in America. He had yet to go beyond the limitations of current attitudes and assumptions—limitations which, in time, he helped to demolish.

His first association with Indians in the United States occurred in a period when cultural and biological extinction seemed imminent and inevitable. Mortality rates ran high; whole communities suffered from trachoma, an eye infection which resulted in blindness; tuberculous infections crippled when they did not kill outright; hunger was the common lot. The Indian future was further strictured by a callous and often hostile public policy, based on a presumption of racial extinction. In reacting to such universal and unrelieved negativism, the Indian people seemed to invite final disaster by clinging to meaningless symbols of the past.

La Farge responded with surprise and delight to the rich pageantry of Navajo society and the free running of Navajo lives—but when he reflected on it, he could see only doom. The tribe could not withstand for long the pressures from the outside or the inner corruption wrought by liquor, the falling away of the young people, and white man's schooling. In a letter to his mother, written during the 1924 Harvard expedition, Oliver remarked that the Navajos at Lukachukai (on the east side of the reservation) "are rich and untrustworthy, owing to too much schooling." At the same place he admired the unschooled seventy-three-year-old head man, "a fine fellow, served as a scout under General Scott. I wish there were more like that."

All that was strong and purposeful and still beautiful in Indian life must pass away, and Oliver thought of himself as one of the few fortunate ones who could understand and appreciate what he saw and record it.

He pursued this theme in writing about *Laughing Boy* for a book club:

> It is not just their picturesqueness which is going, not just their really good crafts, but their character, their manhood, is going. . . . The Southwest is still full of unspoiled Indians, gay, proud, irritating, difficult, priceless. . . . If you will take a very small pack outfit and only one guide, if you will go where there are no conveniences for tourists, if you will keep quiet and watch and be polite, you will find them. They will make fun of you. They will try to steal from you, and when you catch them they will expect you to laugh with them. They will make you perfectly furious. Then you will make friends with them. And all your life you will remember them, even if you never come back, as something different, exciting, fine, that has made you richer and that has put it up to you to be a little more of a man, or a woman, than you ever were before.

So certain was he of this impending extinction that when he observed Indians in the State of Chiapas, Mexico, who had survived, as Indians, through four hundred years of subjugation, he could only account for it by their isolation from the outside world, their strength in numbers, and their "rather independent disposition." It was not mere rumor but a matter of documented accounts that these Indians were capable of hacking intruding strangers to pieces with their murderous machetes. The outsider learned to move cautiously in their territory. They were a new experience for him, an exception. But even if they survived another century or two, the exceptional circumstances would only prove the rule. Eventually, that outside world would reach even them.

Oliver did not write *Laughing Boy* in a single sustained effort, although it gives the effect of having been composed in one emotional thrust. He started, evidently, in November 1926, some months after taking up his duties at the Department of Middle American Research at Tulane. The 1927 expedition to Guatemala interrupted his writing for at least six months, and after that report-writing and administrative duties in the department kept him occupied. For a time he was acting director of the department, while Frans Blom was leading an expedition in Guatemala.

His progress with the novel was so slow—and perhaps also his confidence in its eventual outcome so uncertain—that he turned to other writing and submitted to *Harper's Magazine* late in 1927 a six thousand-word article derived from his Guatemalan experience. In rejecting the article, Frederick L. Allen wrote perceptively: "I want to make clear that we find your material most unusual and interesting, and that the article shows a great advance in literary skill on your part. You are becoming a writer of the sort whose stuff is pounced on . . . by hard-boiled editors." The letter carried a grain more encouragement than the usual rejection slip, but still it was a rejection.

That was not the only disappointment. During a five-month period in 1928, by his own reckoning, he wrote stories and articles which totalled up to 120,000 words—and out of this effort he sold one twelve hundred-word story to *The Dial,* a literary magazine of limited circulation.

His father wrote him during that period, "I read your little yarn and then laid it aside. After a few days read it again. It seems to me good and, on the whole, well written. . . . The other day I sat next to Bridges [of *Scribner's*] and talked to him a little about you and about the story. . . . And he asked me to let him read it so I gave it to him. I have not yet heard from him. I shall not be surprised if he refuses it. In any case don't get too discouraged but keep on plugging away and one of these days you will find the receipt."

Oliver's keenest disappointment came late in the year. He was at Harvard in September 1928, carrying out a research assignment for Tulane, when word came to him that he had lost his job. He explained to a colleague later: "I got into a row with the son and daughter of one of the Trustees at a masked dance in April 1926. The eventual fruit of this was that, when my name came up for promotion to Associate [from an assistantship], the Trustees rose up and demanded that I be fired, and I was, incontinenter." It was a curious procedure. Nothing had been said to him as he prepared to leave for the East. When his salary check did not reach him after October first, he wrote a letter of inquiry. He was then told, by mail, that he had been dismissed as of September first, before he left New Orleans.

It was a serious moment. He had not proved himself as a writer, and every indication up to then left the question in doubt. The promise was there, as it had been since the days at Groton. Encouragement, and rejection slips might be all that would ever come of it. Bad as that was, now he was baldly sent packing from the first job he had ever held, his chances at a scientific career perhaps seriously damaged.

Oliver had been betrayed by a trait of character that occasionally surfaced—the capacity for explosive rage. His brothers knew how to light the fuse, and how to get out of the way when, croquet mallet in hand, he took out to demolish a teasing opponent. An associate years later remarked that Oliver was not one to suffer fools. The brother and sister of the unidentified trustee were not the first and would not be the last to be seared by a La Farge's wrath. In his bearing were traces of hauteur, what some thought of as snobbishness, others as arrogance.

He stayed on at Harvard, jobless, and completed the requirements for his Master's degree, which was awarded *in absentia* at mid-year's in 1929. Before then, undaunted by the treatment he had received, he had returned to New Orleans to turn in the results of his Harvard assignment and pack his possessions.

The experience of poverty with the prospects of defeat now became quite real, and he wrote about them later in *Raw Material*. A friend of the New Orleans period, Vera Morel, upon reading that volume in 1945, recalled an incident which reveals his desperation. She wrote,

> In recounting your earlier attempts to market your stories, there is one incident of which you are unaware, and for historical reasons, I have decided, after this long while, to tell about it. . . . You came to me at the [New Orleans] *Item* with a manuscript, proposing to sell it to the feature section and suggesting that I offer it, for you, to the editor [Don Higgins]. It was good writing—darn good—but the editor said no, not enough local interest, in fact, who cared about the Central American Indians. . . . But if it didn't cost anything, will you print? I urged. He assented. The story was published and you received the fabulous sum of fifteen dollars, or was it twelve dollars? Never knowing that I was the purchaser.

At that point, a break went in his favor. Ferris Greenslet, a friend of his father's and one of Houghton Mifflin's editors, had seen the story "North Is Black" in *The Dial,* liked it, and asked Oliver if he were planning a novel based on his Navajo experiences. It was the kind of routine inquiry that book publishers send out to promising young authors but that only occasionally results in a published book.

The publishers liked the outline he submitted and the chapters Oliver had written up to that point and encouraged him to complete the book. They did not, however, commit themselves to publication. But encouragement was all he needed as he settled down in New Orleans once more, his few possessions still unpacked.

He had carried the idea of the novel in his mind for several years, but the material had never quite come alive. The problem was, somehow, to bring all that he knew about the Navajo people into a rational universe, to project them in their proper human form unencumbered by their habits of behavior and custom which made them picturesque but savage in the eyes of outsiders. He explained in an interview some years later: "That was the problem, but its application to the novel form proved a puzzle." Then, as he recalled, "It was while crossing Euterpe Street in New Orleans that suddenly the general scheme of *Laughing Boy* took form."

Oliver's encounters with Indians and extensive reading brought him a measure of assurance to quell the sense of inadequacy that had dogged him through the years at Groton. He found the perimeters of a domain he could make his own. Moving in upon it he saw where he had been and drew a bearing on what lay beyond.

He was dealing with fresh experiences, and his control of them placed him a stride beyond his invidious peers, whose horizons were bound by the commonplace and the conventional. The story is loaded with episodes, some deliberately introduced, that illustrate singularities of Navajo belief and custom: Mother-in-law avoidance, the rule against marriage within the clan, the etiquette about using personal names, the four-day waiting period after marriage, the fish taboo, the eastward-facing door, the return of the gods after first frost. He leaned on the ethnographer's notebook as a pillar for inner security.

The artistry consisted in blending this essentially esoteric information in a narrative carried along by imagery drawn from the usages of polite society of the Eastern seaboard. The blending was done so skillfully that the socialite sitting in her townhouse and the urban literary critic could read the narrative and have a sense of participation. He brought outlandish subject matter into the realm of acceptable experience. We see Laughing Boy, a non-lettered, non-English speaking primitive (as some reviewers called him) Navajo, watching his wife as she holds up her end in a gathering of his relatives, all of them potentially hostile. La Farge writes: "Out of the corner of his eye . . . he watched Slim Girl with relish as she said and did exactly the right things, giving an excellent impersonation of just any attractive woman."

Whether or not a young Navajo bridegroom ever felt like that, the passage aptly describes the apprehensions of a young man in American society who brings his bride home for family inspection.

Laughing Boy had been living apart from his own people, at the edge of the alien white world, and as he returned for a visit he wondered how it would be after his experiences apart from them. Would the house seem dirty? Would his own people smell badly? But no, "He found that his home was delightfully as he had imagined it. . . . That which had been intimate and dear was so still."

Later in the story, Laughing Boy has dark suspicions about his wife. He is not yet aware of the double life she is living, but he senses that something evil stands between them. His brooding is described in the imagery of a familiar Arabian Nights fable: "Like an ancient magician who, by saying the forbidden names, evoked Genii whom he could not then drive back, Laughing Boy had given form to thoughts which were not to be forgotten."

Still later, when Laughing Boy has learned the truth about his wife and wounds her with an arrow, they are reconciled at last and find a deeper love. "He was very happy, it was like a second honeymoon." La Farge has completed the illusion. The white reader has lived a Navajo life without straying too far from his own experiences—no matter that the honeymoon is not a Navajo social custom.

In the final writing, more than the artist proclaiming himself emerges from the text. The writer is a young man possessing a fund of knowledge and a moral view and he has a deep concern to make these known. The protestation in his original Introductory Note, that the story was meant "neither to instruct nor to prove a point, but to amuse," is a bit of rhetoric carried over from Professor Copeland's classes at Harvard. The pages of *Laughing Boy* are, in effect, a sustained indictment of the society that produced the writer and would, unless tempered, destroy the Navajo world. He called himself an escapist later, perhaps because he could not think of himself as a propagandist or a reformer, but if escape was his purpose, he shot over his shoulder with telling effect as he ran.

A number of reviewers commented on how skillfully La Farge had caught the simple, direct language of the Indian characters; one reviewer went so far as to say that the author had managed to think like an Indian. La Farge himself mentions in *Raw Material* that his style had been influenced by prolonged study, including translation, of certain Indian tales. This could well be, but the text of *Laughing Boy* is clearly that of an outsider looking in from a defined social position upon an alien world and seeing many admirable characteristics. Thus, when Laughing Boy expresses thanks to an elder kinsman for the use of a horse, the author intrudes to remark: "Navajos almost never say thank you, save in return for very great favors; ordinary gifts and kindnesses are offered and accepted in silence. They regard our custom as obsequious."

Events moved quickly, once the barrier was broken. The manuscript was accepted by Houghton Mifflin in May 1929, and La Farge was happy to quit New Orleans and return East. Losing his job under conditions which were at best discourteous had left him disenchanted with the city, although he maintained good relations with colleagues at Tulane.

For a while it appeared that the novel would be selected by the Book-of-the-Month Club, which would have assured a heavy immediate sale. When that misfired, in July, his younger brother, Francis, wrote: "I was terribly sorry to hear that you had missed the Book-of-the-Month. Being recommended isn't so bad—it's damn good—but it's tough when you were shooting higher." The family was keeping watch. Then the Literary Guild selected it and the book appeared in November. Almost immediately arrangements were made for publication in England, where Frank Swinnerton and Storm Jamison in critical reviews referred to the emergence of "another important" American writer.

Reviews were uniformly friendly and encouraging, and there were a great number of them. Contrary to the opinion then current among publishers, that the public did not want to read about Indians, the reception of *Laughing Boy* clearly indicated that a story that was fresh and compelling would easily find readers.

A studio photograph of Oliver shows a long, amiable face, in which the bony structure has been washed out by the studio lighting and a pencil-line mustache is barely discernible. Only the eyes speak out with sparkle and awareness. In one publicity picture he is seated on a Navajo rug surrounded by a wealth of Indian crafts and dressed for a pack trip in Stetson hat, flannel shirt, riding breeches and boots. And the face is still amiable.

No review was more cherished, perhaps, than the note he received from Professor Tozzer, his first instructor in anthropology, who wrote: "I think you have done a very wonderful and a very beautiful piece of work. . . . It reflects great credit on you personally, on Harvard, and on anthropology. We are proud of having had a part, however small, in creating your background."

When *Laughing Boy* was awarded the Pulitzer Prize in May 1930, the *New York Times* story on page one gave it the featured headline, while Marc Connelly's play, *The Green Pastures,* which subsequently had one of the longest runs in the history of Broadway, was mentioned in a subhead. Pulitzer awards rarely win universal public approval, and in this instance at least one New York critic protested that the prize should have gone to Ernest Hemingway's *A Farewell To Arms,* also published in the fall of 1929. With Owen Wister and Mary Austin among the judges, it could have been predicted that a story with a western setting, dealing with Indians, would have a prior rating as best representing the American scene. Mary Austin announced that *Laughing Boy* was "the nearest approach to a genuine primitive love story" she had ever read.

Again the family stood by. His mother wrote just after the announcement: "Everyone I meet or see squeezes my hand and says 'You must be a proud woman.' I reply 'I have been proud for years.'"

Christopher wrote, "How perfectly swell about the Pulitzer Prize! I and the whole damn family are so excited about it that we can hardly spit—which is a great deprivation."

Years later, after his brother's death in 1956, Oliver wrote to Christopher's eldest son:

> From the time we were at Groton, he was the coming writer, I was the beginner whom he helped and criticized. He won both most and best story prizes; I rated quantity only. . . . My freshman year, when he was still at Harvard, he was the kindly big brother toward my writing. All along the line, both he and I assumed that he would get there first and most.

I didn't tell anyone I was writing *Laughing Boy*. I also had no hopes for it. Then it came out and started hitting all the jackpots, and I had wiped my big brother's eye. This really hurt, especially as my success was so damned spectacular. This, incidentally, we never talked about and never needed to; we both understood all the way through. He wrestled with the damn thing and got it in hand, and then proceeded to take the position that I was the experienced writer and he the beginner.

❖ VI ❖

Involvement

INDETERMINACY HOVERED over the next few years. If La Farge expected literary success to remove doubt about how he should design his life, he quickly discovered that having one's name in the newspapers is a sure way to complicate life.

Unexpectedly his commitment to writing seemed less firm and exclusive. His early striving and anguish were no longer necessary, now that he had demonstrated that he could write for commercial publication; editors were knocking on his door, as Frederick Allen had predicted. Opportunity was his, as it had been for his grandfather, and while Oliver did not perhaps "struggle against his destiny," he shared to some degree John La Farge's need to know that he could do something unique and that, as a writer, the whole man would be committed and involved. He hesitated, much as his grandfather had hesitated after his initial successes on canvas.

While negotiations in connection with the publication of *Laughing Boy* were going forward during the summer of 1929, and after the Pulitzer award, he corresponded with linguists and archaeologists at the University of Pennsylvania, at Columbia University, and at the Carnegie Institution. He had hoped for an appointment to Columbia after Tulane dismissed him, but lack of funds postponed their decision. The University of Pennsylvania offered him a Research Associateship, which he held during 1929–31. During these years he edited and annotated manuscripts in the Berendt Collection dealing with Mayan ethnology and linguistics.

An exchange of correspondence with J. Alden Mason at Pennsylvania, in August 1930, reveals La Farge's trend of thinking at that point. Mason wrote: "I presume that you are so busy with drama and motion picture producers that you have little time to devote to scientific work. I saw a note in the paper that David Belasco is going to produce your book as a play."

Oliver replied: "As far as the drama and motion picture rights and so on and so forth, they do not involve any time at all. It is my hope, or rather my intention, that financial success in this line will mean greater freedom and ease in following up the research which interests me."

In the same letter Mason had written: "It may please you to know that Boas recommended you very highly for ethnological research. We are sending a man to Matto Grosso and when I wrote to Boas asking whom he would recommend, he said you."

The reference pleased La Farge, since he had never studied under Franz Boas, who was then the reigning Satrap in American anthropology. His reply conveyed a mild ironical twist: "I am much pleased to hear that Boas recommended me. I value his opinion, of course, and particularly as, knowing his psychology, I should have expected that a successful novel would sink me forever in his regard."

Under the auspices of Columbia University he did eventually conduct an expedition, when he returned to Guatemala in 1932 to continue field studies of Mayan linguistic and religious practices.

Following the 1927 expedition, he began serious attempts to establish the sequence of language development among the various Mayan-speaking groups. He wanted to reconstruct a chronology for Mayan civilization by tracing the language growth and diffusion and correlating these with Mayan calendar dates. Eventually he collected this material in two professional papers: "Post-Columbian Dates and the Mayan Correlation Problem" (*Maya Research,* vol. 1, no. 2, New York, 1934) and "Maya Ethnology: The Sequence of Cultures" (in *The Maya and Their Neighbors,* George C. Vaillant, ed., New York, 1940). These papers have remained landmarks in the development of Mayan studies. They marked out the beginning of a line of investigation which, had La Farge continued in that field, might have resulted in basic discoveries in the prehistory of nuclear America. At least Dr. Linton Satterthwaite, Director of the University of Pennsylvania museum, wrote to Oliver of such a possibility in August 1958, when museum researchers were excavating the great temple ruins at Tikal in northern Guatemala. Satterthwaite commented: "In my bones I have a feeling that some new inscriptional material at Tikal may permit a breakthrough on the correlation problem. If it does, a fundamental element is your post-Columbian dates, a lighthouse on a stormy coast. I don't doubt it was a good thing for the world in general when you went in for literature, but Mesoamerican archaeology-ethnology was a great loser."

Among other developments that followed on the success of his novel, La Farge found himself for the first time seriously in love. He had been a wary party-goer all through college and after, squiring many eligible girls but passing quickly from one to another. Down from Harvard during holiday breaks, tea dances, dinner dances, and theater parties occupied all his available hours. Only Christmas day did he spend at the family hearth, recuperating for the week leading to New Year's Eve. While at Harvard he wrote his mother, evidently in response to some maternal solicitude: "Don't worry about me and the ladies. I've never stopped anything yet for them. When you see me skipping my meals, you can begin to be troubled."

His wariness was so much a part of his life-style that when he was on his own living in New Orleans and encouraged by at least one passing affair, he still avoided any lasting entanglements. The girls of New Orleans made him aware of his New England restraint, without changing anything. The fact that he was often the odd man at New Orleans parties and that other young people paired up with or without benefit of ceremony made him aware of and discomfited by his single state. After his return to the East he lost little time in proposing marriage to a New York debutante, Miss Wanden Esther Matthews, and their engagement was formally announced just after the middle of May 1929. Then his fiancée was whisked off to Italy by her parents, who had a villa at Portofino.

La Farge described Miss Matthews to a friend as "a most entrancing girl, and a rising young Orientalist, student particularly of Persian and the Iranian languages." Her ancestry was not as distinguished as the La Farge line, but it included prominent business and social leaders, among them a Secretary of State in President Taft's cabinet.

With his fiancée in Europe, La Farge spent the summer at Saunderstown corresponding with scientific colleagues, reading proof on his novel, and finding the world amiable.

Miss Matthews returned from Italy in the early fall and the wedding took place at the end of September at the bride's home on East Fifty-seventh Street. The news account reported that "The bride cut the cake with a Japanese sword which had belonged to the bridegroom's grandfather, the artist John La Farge." Best man was Oliver's younger brother, Francis, and for ushers he was surrounded by male relatives and close friends—his older brother, Christopher; William Osborne, a brother-in-law; Whittemore Littell, his Harvard roommate; John Bird, who had grown up with Oliver at Saunderstown; and his two trailmates, Bartlett H. Hayes, Jr., and Douglas S. Byers. The tribal ceremony took place in full detail.

The winter was a round of social devoirs—"well-served dinners of eight, apartment houses with doormen, Irish whiskey and imported wines"—on which he looked back later with distaste. He loved to go "on-the-town" in white tie and tails, then and later, but the further he departed from his birthright class, the more he questioned his involvement in it. Not, however, that winter, newly married. In March he had to postpone a visit to Cambridge, because "we are very much tied up with the rehearsals for an amateur show."

The winter and spring were not wholly absorbed by social amenities. In February 1930, without prior discussion or forewarning, the Eastern Association on Indian Affairs elected him to its Board of Directors. While the method of securing his cooperation was informal and might have been rebuffed, the appointment actually provided the opportunity which perhaps unconsciously he had been seeking, a means of making practical use of the knowledge about the Indian people he had gained through research and personal contact. The writing of *Laughing Boy* had discharged some of this accumulated impulse, but he needed to act. He had great confidence in his own understanding, and he was equally convinced that the people officially involved as government men or missionary workers in Indian affairs were by and large a poor lot whose ministrations were hastening the doom of the Indians. In any case he probably would have accepted a place on the Board of Directors because of its eminent respectability. The members all had a common interest in Indians, otherwise they came from widely different backgrounds and all had long, successful careers. Among them were such publicly known men as Frederick Webb Hodge, of the Smithsonian Institution, editor of the *Handbook of American Indians North of Mexico;* George Bird Grinnell, authority on the Blackfeet, Cheyenne, and Pawnee Indians; Fred Dellenbaugh, one of the early explorers of the Colorado river; Herbert J. Spinden and Alfred V. Kidder, famous for their work in Mayan prehistory, and Percy Jackson, a prominent lawyer who often defended Indian cases.

The first president of the Association from its founding in November 1922 was Professor Ellwood Hendrick, a distinguished chemist and curator of the Chandler Museum of Chemistry at Columbia University. He was succeeded in the presidency in 1926 by Professor Spinden.

What La Farge did not realize until later was that the Eastern Association was anxious to co-opt him, not just because he was a rising young man in the literary world and came from a distinguished family besides, but to keep him from joining forces with a rival organization, the Indian Defense Association, then headed by John Collier, who later became Commissioner of Indian Affairs.

In the tradition of Harvard young men to speak lightly of their interests and to minify their accomplishments, Oliver wrote in the decennial report of the class of 1924 that he had taken up Indian affairs "as a pet charity," but his actions after joining the Eastern Association indicate that he took his position seriously from the beginning. He was not satisfied simply to allow his name to be used on a letterhead. He went almost at once to Washington, where he introduced himself to Charles J. Rhoads, a Philadelphia Quaker who served as Commissioner under President Hoover, and offered his services as a lay citizen. Rhoads evidently was pleased to accept the offer. The La Farge family, through interrelated kin, was as well known in Philadelphia as in Boston and New York, and young men of his background could provide useful support.

Indian Affairs administration had not been decentralized to regional offices, as it was later, and sixty-odd reservation superintendencies from Alaska to Florida and an additional number of independent schools and hospitals reported directly to the commissioner in Washington. He was expected to act with knowledge and wisdom on matters occurring thousands of miles away, and under the law then prevailing his authority and responsibility could not be delegated to lesser officials in closer contact with a field situation.

To acquaint La Farge with the vast complexity of his role, without seeming to call into question his young visitor's practical understanding of the situations about which he talked, Rhoads took the unusual step of inviting him to share his desk, to review every bit of paper that came up for signature, to listen in on every conversation with staff members. It was a chastening experience, but La Farge did not back away. He came back for more, and in the end Rhoads learned to respect both his sincerity and his capacity to absorb information. The upshot of these visits was that when La Farge went west in the spring, as he had been planning all through the winter, he had a tacit understanding with the commissioner that he would report on any conditions which he thought should come to official attention. It was the beginning of Oliver's involvement in Indian affairs which grew in complexity and immediacy through the years, and still claimed him at the end.

That spring he took his Eastern bride on a pack trip and wrote home enthusiastically about their riding horses, their three pack mules, and their Indian guide, Tom Dozier. They outfitted in Santa Fe and set off for the Jicarilla Apache Reservation in northern New Mexico. It was the first of many such trips on which Tom Dozier, or his brother Pete, served as guide and horse wrangler, and through these brothers La Farge began a long association with Santa Clara Pueblo, of which the brothers were members.

One of the elders of this Pueblo, Vidal Gutierrez (Uncle Vidal, in Oliver's letters), was attracted to Oliver and informally adopted him into his family. A man past seventy when Oliver first met him —"wearing a stiff-brimmed Stetson with a downy eagle plume in the hatband, his braids black and long and neatly wrapped, a handsome, aquiline, alert man, sitting easily in the saddle on a tall-white horse"—he lived until the end of 1961, when he was over one hundred years old. He spoke a Pueblo-type Spanish, slightly archaic, which Oliver with his good ear for linguistic shadings caught onto quickly. The old man would say that La Farge was "the only white man" who knew how to talk Spanish. Santa Clara Pueblo, highly generalized, seems to be the setting for the short story, "Little Stone Man," in the collection *The Door in the Wall.*

In these early personal contacts with Indians, La Farge assumed the role of patron as a matter of course, an assumption which individual Indians did not always respond to as expected. Pete Dozier, for one, was critical of La Farge's camping manners. Dozier was expected to do the cooking and general wrangling of horses and equipment, but when the rough work was done and the food was on the fire, La Farge took charge. Dozier did not mind this, except that La Farge did not have a Western hand when spicing food. Anything in addition to salt and pepper was excessive. Dozier was especially incensed when he brought freshly caught trout from the stream on which they had camped for the night, and watched La Farge put the trout to boil for a New England chowder.

La Farge went to the Jicarilla Reservation that spring to investigate living conditions, thus initiating another long association with an Indian community. But at Jicarilla he finally began to educate himself in Indian affairs and to get glimmerings of what Indian life was really like. He retained forever after a special fondness for the Apache people, who taught him so well. Some of his more savagely critical attacks on white men's attitudes toward Indians are based on his Apache experiences.

In those first visits he saw a small tribe facing ultimate disaster. Once a vigorous people, a segment of the marauding Athabascan bands that had come down out of the North and had overrun much of the Southwest, the Jicarillas had been shunted off onto a reservation in the mountainous northwestern corner of New Mexico and largely forgotten. They had been kept on rations for a number of years, and when the government discontinued the practice in 1907 without providing farm equipment, livestock, or training for wage work, the tribal members could only sit and starve. Between 1889 when they went on the reservation and 1920, their numbers had dwindled from 1100 to fewer than 600. Among school age children, the mortality rate reached a peak of 70 percent in 1904. The incidence of infectious tuberculosis within this age group ran to 100 percent as late as 1930.

A small sanatorium cared for eighty-five tubercular children in that year. The kitchen was on the lower floor, the bed-ridden children above, and three times a day the food trays were carried upstairs and dirty dishes carried down, for lack of a dumb waiter. There was no sterilizer in the kitchen. Kerosene lamps were used in the wooden building because the inadequate electric plant operated only during the daylight hours, yet there were no fire escapes. Across the street, the overcrowded twenty-four bed hospital had no operating room, and surgical dressings were sterilized in the oven of a kitchen stove!

These were among the items that La Farge wrote about to Mr. Rhoads and reported on to his own Association.

Along with this grim first experience, La Farge also discovered what he had been surprised to discover first among the Indians of Chiapas, Mexico—the Jicarillas still lived as a people apart, their identity intact, seemingly unaware or unconcerned that the future was closed to them. He had reasoned that the Bachajon Indians survived the onslaughts of the invading world because of their isolation and their fierce independence. But here were the Jicarillas, overwhelmed by the outside world and fast dying out—yet they unwaveringly held onto their identity.

Perhaps the clearest expression of this was communicated through the Jicarilla Fiesta, a social affair held in the early fall, when the people camped together and visitors from nearby tribes —Navajos, Utes, Taos Pueblo—came to share what was left of the past. It was mostly local, never a large gathering. La Farge returned year after year, until he had an intimate knowledge of the songs and the singers themselves.

He described one such gathering in a letter to his mother in 1932:

> The Fiesta was beautiful, although there were relatively few people this year, still we counted over seventy fires, with a full moon over the lake, and singing. . . . When I finally turned in, with my ear to the ground, the big drum sounded terrific, and I slept to the rhythm. After everyone else quit, about 2:30, eight Navajos started singing. Their songs, so unlike the others, slowly woke me, so I got up and rebuilt the fire—it was bitter cold, just at the freezing point. . . . Most of the encampment was asleep, but there was still the moon, and a few fires. . . . There were just enough of them to make the proper amount of noise and to handle the part singing, but few enough so that the words were clear. I do not know any way to describe the beauty of a really good Navajo leader's voice. It is soprano, but masculine in quality, and on the highest notes reaches a sound that exactly coincides with a coyote's yelp, and yet is musical and very beautiful. At the conclusion of the song, the group pauses, and this one voice rises straight up, high into the air—and then describes an arc, at the completion of which the others come in again, so there is this solo bridge between repetitions. . . . The Taos and Kiowas carry over with a lovely sort of overture, mostly *a* sounds, but the voice is a fine tenor pitched in a manner we cannot copy, it spreads out horizontally.

D. H. Lawrence witnessed the Jicarilla Fiesta at a slightly earlier time, and his impressions, as reported in Mabel Dodge Lujan's "Lorenzo in Taos," are curious, almost ludicrous, as an attempt to convey the meaning of what he witnessed. The imagery is vivid—movement in and out of firelight, erupting sparks, thin-tailed dogs, "steeple black hats," the thudding drum—but Lawrence brought to the spectacle only the emotional and intellectual furnishings of his European background, and to him the performance was a farce, a comic opera, which the actors presumably did not know how to play. For him, it was an absurdity.

For Oliver La Farge it was something more than song rising in the night air. What he heard quite clearly was the voice of a people, patterned and melodious, telling of generations of free men growing out of the earth and returning to it. The voice was complete in itself, it spoke of a whole race of man. Death would come to the race, but until it did the sound would rise up, not as a lamentation, certainly not as a plea for help, rather as a steady assertion of the existence of the race.

The sound as he first heard it on Black Mesa and again in Mexico and in Guatemala lived with La Farge. Whatever name these people had for themselves, this was what it meant. The white man called it Indian, but that was only a white man's way. La Farge reached for the meaning. He once wrote: "When I look in my own memory for the essences of what I've so loved in Indian camps, the summation of it, I find a tricky rhythm tapped out on a drum, a clear voice singing, and the sound of laughter."

When he was close to this strange power of utterance and could feel himself stretching to encompass it, he was deeply satisfied, as if he had arrived at a sought-for destination. It was only when he was away from it, in a moment of introspection, that the effort seemed unreal. His breeding caught up with him then and reminded him of lessons learned and obligations natural to his learning. Reason cautioned that he had no business trying to escape from what he was born to be. His dilemma was real, a constant companion. He could not be Indian; he did not want to be submerged in the power class of his generation.

After the Jicarilla visit toward the end of June, La Farge took his bride westward, to the Hopi villages and up on Black Mesa. It was a journey in which he seemed bent on recapturing for a second person the magic of the feelings which had gone into the writing of *Laughing Boy*—as if that were possible, even for a new bride. They went all the way to the Grand Canyon, where they rented mules and rode down to the bottom.

By then he was already planning his second novel, and when they returned to New York late in the summer he discovered that he had to settle down to work in earnest. Much of his first earnings from *Laughing Boy* had gone into Wall Street and had vanished.

❖ VII ❖

Citizen Action

WHEN LA FARGE joined the Eastern Association on Indian Affairs early in 1930, the government's dealings with the Indian people had undergone some reforms, but great battles lay ahead. His experiences up to then, his training in research methods, his practice in objective reporting—even the curiosity he had displayed since early school days—served him well in this new endeavor. He absorbed Indian history quickly, especially the history of government-Indian relations, and he grew familiar with the intricacies of the bureaucracy, much of which seemed totally irrational until he discovered the perverse logic which had brought it about.

What he also learned, as he wrote in *The Changing Indian,* was that until the end of the 1920's "All Indian policy was predicated upon the concept of a dying culture and a dying race." The concept had come from a long tradition of historical and fictional writing. Administrative practice was crude but explicit, as Commissioner of Indian Affairs Francis A. Walker, writing in his annual report for 1872, briefly described it: "There is no question of national dignity, be it remembered, involved in the treatment of savages by a civilized power. With wild men, as with wild beasts, the question whether in a given situation one shall fight, coax, or run, is a question merely of what is easiest and safest."

The nation of Walker's time was still raw, the frontier had not yet been brought under control, and Indians, along with grizzly bears, coyotes, rattlesnakes, and mountain lions, were part of the wild fauna, their fierceness magnified by the frontiersmen's boastful self-pride, which had to be removed to make way for "decent folks." That impression was a long time dying. Just before Walker's pronouncement, the Congress, by a rider attached to an appropriation bill on which there was no debate, declared that Indian tribes would no longer be regarded as members of separate nations with which agreements could be negotiated by treaty; their affairs would be managed by legislative fiat. And that marked the beginning of the final assault on the Indians' heritage of physical resources and traditions.

La Farge reviewed these developments in *As Long as the Grass Shall Grow* (1940); by the time it was published he was in the thick of battle. He wrote: "All were united in the philosophy of de-Indianization . . . and all joined in the next great attack upon the fundamentals of Indian life: land, unity, religion." He explained the process by which land held in common passed out of tribal ownership without benefit of Indian consent:

> If ownership in common were broken up, if each Indian owned a plot of his own, and freedom from wandering, visiting, hunting, were ended, the backbone of their resistance would be broken. The pride and responsibility of individual property would soon make them competitive, thrifty, individualistic.
>
> So, with no opposition at all from those who wished to get as much as possible of the remaining reservations for their own use, the famous Allotment Act was passed in 1887.
>
> Each member of the tribe then received an allotment of land, the sizes varying. . . . Since all history had shown that the Indians were bound to become extinct, and they were in fact dying off fairly rapidly, there was no need to make any allowance for a larger population in the future. Therefore, when the allotment [of a reservation] was finished, all remaining land was declared "surplus" and thrown open to white settlement.

In 1887, when the Allotment Act was adopted in Congress, the Indian tribes possessed 139 million acres, an area slightly larger than the State of California. By 1930 this area had been reduced, through "surplussing" and other legal conveniences, to 47 million acres. By an understandable process, most of that remainder was located in the mountainous and desert regions of the West and Southwest. The choice valley lands and the sweeping grasslands of the Plains had passed out of Indian ownership within the first years.

Commenting further on that history, La Farge wrote: "I take the year 1923 as the nadir of the Indians. In that year of our prosperity, every abuse that I have described was in full force, the bulk of the land was gone, there was no reason for any of us who went among the Indians to hope that there would be a change.

"In that year 1923 the friends of the Indians felt that, having accomplished so much to end the old ways, the time had come for the next great step . . . , [to suppress] the practice of Indian religions."

This was not a generalized observation. La Farge was referring here to specific official actions by which, for example, Commissioner Burke, urged on by missionary spokesmen, in 1923 addressed a memorandum "To all Indians" respecting their religious ceremonies, reading: "I could issue an order against these useless and harmful performances, but I would much rather have you give them up of your own free will, and therefore, I ask you now in this letter to do so. If at the end of one year the reports which I receive . . . show that you reject this plea, then some other course will have to be taken."

The "other course" mentioned by the commissioner, as it turned out, was an attempt at legal coercion. In 1925 the entire governing body of Taos Pueblo was placed under arrest and carried off to Santa Fe, seventy miles away, to stand trial for an offense vaguely defined as "religious." A temperate federal judge, fortunately, threw the case out of court.

The commissioner also urged his field superintendents to consider ways and means of putting into effect recommendations concerned missionaries had offered. Among these recommendations were (1) that Indian dances be limited to one each month in the daylight hours of one day in the mid-week and at one center in each district, except in the months of March, April, June, July, and August (these being the months of planting and harvesting) when there were to be more or none; (2) that no individuals under fifty years of age take part, as dancers or spectators; and (3) that the field employees educate public opinion against Indian dances.

La Farge explained, "These were the only friends the Indians had, these people who could not see the beauty of a Tewa Eagle Dance, were deaf to the clear music of a Kiowa singer, unable to imagine good in the wild majesty of the Navajo Fire Ceremony." In leveling these criticisms at the Indian affairs administrators, missionaries, and others who counted themselves friends of the Indian people, La Farge was speaking from his own experience in Indian camps and from the stories of his Indian friends. It was a personal, not an academic or aesthetic, involvement.

The year 1923, which he took to mark the low point in Indian survival, was also the year in which the process began to reverse itself—a reversal as imperceptible at first as a tidal change, but, like tidewater, capable of mounting energy, as events proved. The critical incident was an attempt to divest the Pueblo Indians of New Mexico of extensive land holdings. In La Farge's summary: "The eighteen Pueblo tribes are peaceful farmers, living in well built towns of great antiquity. Their existence in that arid country depends upon the strips of fertile land which they occupied long ago, and the water to irrigate them. Their lands were granted to them by the King of Spain; the Spaniards and later Mexicans respected the boundaries. In the treaty of Guadalupe-Hidalgo at the end of the Mexican War, the United States bound itself in turn to the same respect."

In time, however, white men moved in on Pueblo lands, built homes, diverted water to their private use, and the federal government, the guardian and protector, failed to defend the Indian owners. Some 3,000 families, or about 12,000 individuals, were trespassing and legally subject to eviction. A court case decided in 1913 posed the threat of government action and the trespassers sought legislative remedy. They found a willing ally in Senator Holm O. Bursum, of New Mexico, who in 1922 introduced a bill in Congress to create legal rights where none existed and to throw upon the Indians the burden of proving that their ownership was valid. This was a reversal of the usual legal procedure, in which an adverse claimant has the burden of proving his case.

At this point, a small group of citizens with no previous involvement in Indian questions, many of them writers, artists, and scientists living in the Southwest, took up the Pueblo cause. La Farge himself first heard about the Bursum Bill as a Harvard undergraduate, probably during a field trip to the Southwest. He urged his mother to solicit support in behalf of the Indians, and in December 1922 he learned from her that "Mr. [Gifford] Pinchot is on the job."

It was Oliver's initial encounter with the politics of Indian affairs. Writing in 1940 about that period, La Farge observed: "It seemed at first a small thing with a large name, the New Mexico Association on Indian Affairs, a local group to fight a local Bill, but it was competent and it found support throughout the country."

The General Federation of Women's Clubs formed a committee on Indian welfare and Mrs. Stella M. Atwood of Riverside, California, chairman of the committee, engaged John Collier to press the attack. That also marked Collier's entrance into the arena of Indian affairs politics. Previously he had served with the People's Institute in New York City and had directed programs of adult education and community organization for the State of California.

At about the same time, two additional organizations were formed for the specific purpose of defeating the Bursum Bill, the Indian Defense Association, which John Collier directed until he became Commissioner in 1933, and the Eastern Association on Indian Affairs.

In November 1922, encouraged by these organizations, the eighteen Pueblos of the Rio Grande Valley came together at Santo Domingo, a large and conservative river village, and formed an All Pueblo Council. It was the first time they had taken concerted action since 1680, when they united to drive the Spanish settlers out of New Mexico. With funds supplied by their new friends, the

Indians sent a delegation across the country to Washington and created a sensation in the capital with their native dress, their songs and dances, and their sober pleading for public support.

La Farge wrote:

> These forces working together not only defeated the Bursum Bill but won instead laws [in 1924] which cleared many of the encroachers off the Indian land and compensated the tribes for land which could not be recovered.
>
> This whole development and the warm response of Congress were startling to the Indian Bureau and the forces that surrounded it; deeply disturbing was the prospect of a continuation of this new kind of public opinion.

And he added: "There was a hope, that was all. Few people believed that the hunger and sickness of the school children could be ended or their religious liberty respected, few really thought that the steady dwindling of the land could be stopped or the death rate materially lightened. In all the efforts there was still an element of a death-bed watch, of a struggle merely to create a few exceptions."

Two other notable events marked the years before 1930. The new public opinion mentioned by La Farge led Coolidge's Secretary of the Interior, Hubert Work, to request the Brookings Institution to undertake a thorough investigation of the Indian situation. The resulting study by Lewis Meriam and associates, *The Problem of Indian Administration,* published in 1928, was the first attempt ever made to evaluate what had happened to the Indian people under the government's trusteeship. The recommendations for action which emerged from this study reversed or at least modified many of the stultifying practices of the past.

The other positive action was the appointment by President Hoover in 1929 of Charles J. Rhoads and J. Henry Scattergood as Commissioner and Assistant Commissioner of Indian Affairs. These men, a banker and a college president, both Quakers, were probably the first ever to be appointed without regard to party affiliation or political pay-off. The offices were not under the Civil

Service and had always been regarded as suitable recognition for minor political hackwork.

Upon these new men fell the responsibility of initiating the reforms recommended by the Meriam report, and in spite of the deepening depression and a Congress that grew increasingly hostile to the Hoover administration, they made impressive beginnings in the fields of health, education, and employment standards.

Having achieved an important first victory, the private organizations formed to oppose the Bursum legislation now incorporated and prepared continuing programs in the Indian field. The Indian Defense Association, under Collier's leadership, pulled away from its colleagues in the Pueblo lands battle and very quickly established itself as the most aggressive of the Indian-interest groups. It concentrated on legislation, bringing pressure on the congressional committees, but it also conducted investigations of government operations all across the country. Because of these investigations and his relentless pursuit of them, Collier quickly became a most objectionable individual among officials of the Indian Bureau.

The Eastern Association, with its board membership of conservative and influential citizens, favored a policy of cooperation with the government. Dr. Herbert Spinden in his 1928 report observed: "The past year's activities have been productive of much good without recourse to noise. While it is exciting to have a fight it is perhaps more satisfactory in the long run to get things done. The Indian children suffering from disease and undernourishment would much rather be helped than fought over." The words were direct jabs at John Collier, who had been chiding the Eastern Association, and others, for their complacency. The exchanges grew sharper in succeeding years.

As a scientist, Spinden appreciated the value of careful, objective fact-gathering as a basis for action. He wrote: "Our work began with the land-grabbing Bursum Bill, then it passed to the trachoma situation and to other problems of health and economy confronting the surviving first families of America. The pressing business in each case was to obtain and spread knowledge of the situation, accurate knowledge, to persons who could help." La Farge, working from this tradition, later wrote of establishing an applied science of Indian affairs; he thought his association had a responsibility to help develop such a science.

The Eastern Association and the New Mexico Association maintained a close working relationship all through those early years. On one occasion Dr. Spinden referred to the New Mexico group as a garrison "deep in Indian country" on which the Eastern Association relied for information. The practical effect of this close cooperation was to concentrate program activities in the Southwest.

As a consequence of the Indian Bureau's "death-bed watch" policies over the years, services to Indians had dwindled almost out of existence. In no area was the Bureau's inadequacy more apparent than in medical care and control of disease. This notoriously bad situation was cited by a health authority in the *Journal of the American Medical Association* in 1920, who charged: "There is, broadly speaking, no Indian Health Service, and very little is done to prevent the occurrence of disease. . . . The situation is so serious that the very existence of certain tribes is at stake. Other tribes suffer a decrease or stationary condition of population because of a death rate which would be inconceivable under modern conditions if it were not sustained by the official records."

In 1923 the New Mexico State Board of Public Welfare conducted a limited survey of health conditions among the Pueblo Indians, and found them "as bad as we all had imagined they were." The New Mexico Association then proposed that a public health nurse be stationed in one of the Pueblos for the purpose of demonstrating to the government that mortality rates could be reduced and sanitary conditions improved by working directly with the people. They hoped that such a demonstration might induce the government to take over and expand the program.

The Eastern Association cooperated by raising funds for the program, and within the next few years enough money was found to maintain four such nurses, including one in an eastern Navajo community. Part of the money was raised through benefit performances of *The Pirates of Penzance* and Walter Hampden's *Othello,* a practice that spared the patrons' emotions while it provided medical care of a limited sort for a handful of Indian communities.

The work was described by one of the field nurses as "pure bedside, or rather floorside [in the absence of beds] nursing, to gain the Indians' confidence. . . . It is thus that the first principles of hygiene are demonstrated. After that come lessons in the care of children, then suggestions as to cleanliness and diet. When confidence is fully established, there follows a definite attack on community problems."

By 1930, when La Farge joined the Eastern Association, Dr. Spinden was able to report of the nurses placed in the field: "Their records and methods of work proved of great value to the Indian Bureau, and when, recently, the increased appropriations made by Congress permitted it, the Bureau assumed responsibility for two of the Association's projects and took over the work." A year later Spinden noted with satisfaction: "There is no longer any necessity for further demonstration work with public health nurses in the Pueblos. The Government is committed to a policy of public health nursing and is expanding its program along these lines as fast as funds will permit and personnel can be found."

Having achieved its first objective, the association looked for another demonstration area and was soon holding benefit performances to sponsor a program to encourage Indian crafts workers. The de-Indianization attitude of earlier years had discouraged the production of native arts and there had been a steady decline in the quality as well as quantity of hand crafted articles. In this, as in other areas of Indian life, the practice had been to denigrate if not actively suppress celebration of the Indian past. The old arts would die with the older people, it was assumed, and therefore they should not be taught in the schools or exhibited in public places.

Some members of the Indian associations were quite aware of what, in the 1920's, was still government policy and they made individual efforts to encourage Indian artists by purchasing articles for their private collections and for museum displays. Navajo weaving had been particularly affected by the policy of suppression as well as by prevailing commercial practices. Once a vigorous creative expression of a tribal people, as many museum collections attested, the craftsmanship had grown shoddy. Yet despite poor quality it was estimated that the revenue derived from Navajo rug production in 1930 amounted to as much as $1 million annually. The traders who marketed the rugs got most of the money, since it was common practice to purchase rugs by the pound, without regard to quality of design or texture, and what the trader paid was usually not above the market price of the raw wool. This offered scant inducement for a weaver to improve her product.

The Eastern Association reported in 1931 that "During the past year we have been turning our attention more and more to the revival and development of the native arts and crafts among the Indians of New Mexico and Arizona." Within a year the association had developed a definite program and was working on two fronts. Because of the lack of teaching specimens from the older weaving, the first task was to make hand-colored photographs of specimen rugs from museum and private collections. The association distributed these among cooperating traders and, eventually, in schools which under Rhoads' administration actually began to teach arts and crafts. The Rhoads administration so drastically changed official attitudes toward Indian art that paintings of Indian life—even ceremonial designs—appeared on the walls of schools and hospitals, bringing the familiar into what had previously been a hostile environment.

The other approach the Eastern and New Mexico Associations pursued was public exhibition. One of the first of these was the International Exposition at Seville, Spain, in 1929. The collection of Indian art in the United States Building drew admiring attention and received a Grand Prize. In that same season works of Pueblo and Kiowa artists were shown at the Brooklyn Museum, Buffalo Museum of Science, and the Museum of Modern Art in New York City.

These and kindred activities of the Indian associations carried beyond the narrow world of Indian affairs and appealed to a widening segment of public interest. When the Exposition of Indian Tribal Arts opened at the Grand Central Art Gallery in New York in December 1931, it attracted large and enthusiastic audiences all through the month, and afterward it was taken to several cities across the country. La Farge and John Sloan, the painter, collaborated in writing an *Introduction to American Indian Art* which served not only as a catalog to the show but as a reminder that "we white Americans have been painfully slow to realize the Indians' value to us, although his work has won recognition abroad." Some thirty tribes were represented in the exposition and, in addition to contemporary products, it contained specimen artifacts from the prehistoric Southwest and the Hopewellian culture of the Ohio River valley. This interest carried over into the Roosevelt administration and resulted in the creation by Act of Congress in 1935 of the United States Indian Arts and Crafts Board, which was given the responsibility of fostering Indian art, encouraging quality production, and seeking market outlets.

As a Pulitzer Prize author and a student of the Navajo people, La Farge was sought after in many quarters, and so in September 1931 he found himself serving as a judge for Navajo rugs at the Gallup, New Mexico, Inter-Tribal Ceremonial, which was then becoming an important annual Indian show. His fellow judges were the Governor of New Mexico—a knowledgeable collector— and the buyer for the Fred Harvey Company, whose occupation presupposed expert knowledge. Oliver wrote his mother, "The judging was difficult, exhausting, everything was most inconveniently arranged, and I learned a great deal."

What particularly pleased him was that many of the reservation traders seemed to have read *Laughing Boy,* and they liked it. This was surprising since the attitude toward traders reflected by the Navajo characters in the book was anything but flattering. "Everyone did me favors, everyone went out of his way to be nice to me." The traders even sold him items at "reservation" prices instead of "tourist" prices, which meant a discount of about 30 percent. "I bought a lot," he wrote.

After leaving Gallup Oliver and his bride made a pack trip from the Jicarilla reservation in northern New Mexico, down the west side of the Jemez mountains, to Santa Fe, a ride of about 150 miles. This was the trip, in reverse, he had made in the spring, with Pete Dozier serving as guide and wrangler. "Our trip was splendid in every way," he reported, "save for almost daily rain. Pete Dozier turned out to be about as fine as Tom, and we got as fond of him. With the addition that he is much more Indian, has taken part in the dances and all that."

These horseback trips were ventures into a new life, carrying him away from what he had been brought up to be, into something different and as yet only dimly grasped. He was never a passive receptacle for experience, never an acquiescent onlooker. He lived with an unrest that stirred him into action. When among people, he was the story-teller, the leading conversationalist. This trait once moved a friend to remark, with perhaps qualified admiration, "In any situation, Oliver was always the Archbishop."

The Indian world, the whole Southwest, challenged this disposition toward active participation. He had to be *of* and *in* any milieu, to master its style and content. This he had worked at with growing-up vigor all through his Narragansett boyhood, as he explored the open and the hidden bounds of the waters, the shore, and the woodlands. The story "Thick on the Bay," in *A Pause in the Desert,* and the chapter "Salt Water," in *Raw Material,* are drawn directly from these early experiences of pushing out against boundaries. He had learned to sail, to fish and hunt, and to ride and care for a horse. And now, in the West, he went about seriously making himself over into an acceptable Westerner.

The process of assimilation to which he subjected himself he described in a long letter to Christopher:

This June I forced myself to make a five days' trip alone, not camping, but traveling from one acquaintance's place to another —Allen Clark's house, Santa Clara Pueblo, Santa Clara Ranger Station, Señor Suazo's house in a hamlet called Barranco, the Ghost Ranch (a high-fanny dude ranch), Abel Sanchez "Hotel" at Tierra Amarilla, Ed Sargent's cattle ranch, Jicarilla Apache

Agency—an almost complete cross-section of this part of New Mexico. This involved finding my way in new country, and taking care of my horses.

Up until that trip, he explained, he had always traveled with a guide, someone who helped with camp chores and made the decisions about routes to follow. Now he felt released from such dependence.

So in September I started out with a pack, camping part of the time. It worked fine until I took sick in the middle of one night, and then I was very, very lonely, and in the end I had to give up the trip after a week of it and several days' travel on a diet of tomato juice and bicarbonate of soda. But even that added to my confidence. I traveled a good seventy miles and made two camps while being really quite ill. During part of the time I guided some Indians who were going the same way and experienced no great difficulty, only great relief when I reached the Apaches and put my bed under a wagon and went to sleep at midday. So I concluded that, all in all, I am free of the country, to travel where and as I please. I now really consider that I am out of the "dude" class, of which I was never sure before, barring that I can't rope worth a damn.

Apparently he expected his new bride to share his enthusiasm for pushing out the walls of experience. In an earlier letter to his mother he remarked, "Wanden is developing into a crack pistol shot, consistently better than me. I'm only medium, and she is really good. With a rifle I have a slight edge on her, and we are both a little better than most westerners."

⟐ VIII ⟐

The Deepening Stream

THE YEARS from 1930 to 1935, like his Harvard years, were filled with movement and action, in which La Farge seemed intent on proving himself in a variety of roles, of which uppermost was the role of the well-rounded gentleman.

He kept no established place of residence, but followed a circuit that included an apartment in the East Sixties in New York; the home at Saunderstown; Colorado Springs, where his wife's family had acquired a cattle ranch; and Santa Fe, New Mexico. He had a brief fling at Hollywood, where he tried out for the lead role in a screen adaptation of *Laughing Boy*. He conducted an ethnological expedition to western Guatemala for Columbia University, accompanied by Tom Dozier and, for part of the trip, by his wife. He continued to edit manuscripts on Mayan linguistics for the University of Pennsylvania. He became more deeply involved in the politics of Indian affairs with his election to the presidency of the Eastern Association. And all through the period he wrote assiduously, publishing two novels and at least twenty-five short stories, reviews, and articles. He wrote rapidly—2,000 and 3,000 words a day, he told an interviewer—and rewrote extensively.

Involvement in Indian affairs now became a serious matter, hardly a gentleman's pastime. This he discovered on the eve of the coming of the Roosevelt New Deal. The Coolidge-Hoover succession in government had threatened the Indians with ultimate disaster on many fronts, which the corrective efforts of the humane Commissioners, Rhoads and Scattergood, had only partially averted. They had not been able to salvage the wreckage of Indian land holdings, and they had not faced down the hard-shelled missionaries who were bent on destroying native religious practices. Some missionaries even contended that the guarantee of religious freedom in the United States Constitution applied only to Christian worship; all other religions were beyond the pale.

A question had also arisen as to whether Rhoads and Scattergood were not improperly protecting the tenure of Herbert A. Hagerman, a major field official originally appointed by the corrupt Secretary Fall of the Interior Department. Hagerman's competence, not his integrity, was at issue. Lengthy, at times heated, hearings took place in a United States Senate Committee room in January 1931, and in the clash of testimonies La Farge found himself caught in a crossfire. His Eastern Association on Indian Affairs had come to the support of Hagerman, of Commissioner Rhoads really, and was interrogated by irate senators from one side and by John Collier and his Indian Defense Association from the other side. La Farge was obviously the Senators' favorite target because of his youth, his brashness in attacking Senator Frazier (a member of the club) in a letter to the *New York Times,* his pencil-line mustache, and his upper class bearing. When Assistant Commissioner Scattergood tried to blunt the attack by reminding the senators that La Farge was a Pulitzer Prize winner, the silence was eloquent. Perhaps the senators had never heard of the prize.

The experience was distressing for another reason. It was readily apparent as the hearing proceeded that the association witnesses were ill-prepared, and as a consequence they fell easy victims to the senatorial onslaughts. They were amateurs competing with professionals and coming out plucked and all trussed up. By contrast, Collier, who at the request of the Senate committee had made a thorough study of Hagerman's record, seemed to have an inexhaustible supply of documents which he pulled out of a battered briefcase.

Dr. Spinden, who led off for the association, seemed especially inept, a stereotype of the bumbling, absent-minded professor whom the interrogators delighted in gaffing. When he explained that he was an anthropologist who had devoted his life to the study of Indians, a senator asked: "Do you study the Indians like a scientist studies a bug, or do you study them as a human being?" Spinden did not know what salary was paid to the demonstration field nurses maintained by the association, although the nursing program had been the major activity of the association from its first years, and he was not quite sure of the organization's annual budget. Less defensible were his attempts to slander John Collier by charging that he organized the Pueblo Indians into "mischief-making bodies" and "counseled disobedience to the government." In the course of his accusations Spinden made statements about the nature of Pueblo social organization which, as a scientist, he must have known were not true.

When Collier testified a few days later, he quite thoroughly demolished the doctor's anthropology, while frankly admitting that he had encouraged the Indians in 1924 to disobey the Commissioner's order directed at suppressing their religions. He told the committee, "I advised those Indians to be locked up and stay in jail, rather than to have their religious liberties suspended by a fanatical Commissioner of Indian Affairs." The Committee seemed sympathetic.

A few years later, La Farge was collaborating with Collier, then commissioner, in drafting a proclamation for the Secretary of the Interior requiring "Respect for Indian culture and religious freedom," which was directed to all Indian Bureau employees. Before that occurred, however, several events intervened, including the 1932 election. It was perhaps a surprising collaboration, in view of what had gone before.

In the circles La Farge frequented at that time, the approaching election and the prospects of Roosevelt's victory brought spasms of fear and recrimination. Oliver did not indulge himself in the emotional outbursts which flared after some of Roosevelt's campaign speeches, but he did reflect the sympathies of his environment. Thus he wrote from his father-in-law's ranch near Colorado Springs in July, just after the 1932 Chicago Democratic Convention, "We are all sick over the Roosevelt nomination, and at a loss what to do." He said he was thinking seriously of voting for Norman Thomas, the Socialist candidate, as some of his Harvard classmates were urging, but in his case it was no more than momentary pique. The La Farges had never been politically active. Their associations with the Cabot Lodges, the Henry Stimsons, the Theodore Roosevelts, as with scores of other public men, were at the family and social level. They did not aspire to political power and engaged in public service only in a specific cause for the satisfaction of performing a duty. At a calmer moment in his career, Oliver wrote, in *Raw Material:* "The strength of this [upper] class lay, and lies, in its control of money. . . .But the great men of our kind were financiers, and they, realists to the core, knew that their power was stabler and more enduring than ever-shifting political power. In the long run money could outlast and wear down any popular movement, with a concession here and there."

The La Farges did not have money, but through their associations and ties they shared, at least marginally, the security of status attached to wealth. The practical effect of these interrelated associations, just then, was to provide Grant La Farge, Oliver's aging father, with a livelihood, reduced but honorable. The depression had left his architectural practice of fifty years in ruins, and would have wiped out any investments he had made against retirement, except that he had always consumed his income and was actually in debt. What might have been an awkward time for him was eased gracefully. President Conant of Harvard brought him in as a consultant to the School of Architecture, and Nicholas Murray Butler, at Columbia, engaged him in a similar capacity. In addition, Columbia, in collaboration with the Metropolitan Museum of Art, arranged a series of public lectures and granted him a traveling fellowship to spend time in Europe gathering material for the series. The lectures, of course, were excellent and the institutions honored themselves.

They were not a political family, but they were concerned and informed about public affairs. Oliver's mother, past seventy and still an omnivorous reader, kept abreast of the news and saw the shape of events with remarkable clarity. In midsummer 1935, with the nominating conventions still a year away, she speculated: "My guess is that the best thing and the probable thing will be Roosevelt in the saddle for another term, but with a wobbling toward safer ways and a certain number of good things done. What we need is a man who can grasp the way to get us on our feet and also put in certain needed reforms without giving up the essential things that a democracy demands."

It was not the politics of the 1932 election, at least not the national politics, about which Oliver was concerned, but the fate of the reforms initiated by Rhoads and Scattergood. He had been taken into the confidence of these men and he knew them to be devoted to the task of improving the lot of the Indian people. They faced an unfriendly Congress, on the whole, in spite of which they had made what he considered impressive gains. In the single field of education, they succeeded in increasing the annual appropriation from $3 million in 1929 to more than $12 million in 1932, and they repudiated the old Bureau policy of forcefully removing Indian children from their families and shipping them to far-off boarding schools.

The Democratic victory meant these men would be replaced. Presently rumors spread that either Harold Ickes, who had worked with the Chicago branch of Collier's American Indian Defense Association, or John Collier himself would be named for commissioner. It was likely that if either were chosen the Eastern Association would be out in the cold. The rivalry between these organizations had grown especially acute since the 1931 hearings, in the course of which Collier had been sharply critical of the Eastern group.

It has always been remarkable how little brotherly love is shared by citizen groups competing for the love of the Indian people. For La Farge, the situation was personally embarrassing. He had told his Indian friends that he thought Collier would be a bad commissioner and he would try to block the appointment—a promise he had not been able to keep. In the spring of 1933, after the appointment, he found himself writing to his Santa Clara Pueblo friend, Vidal Gutierrez:

> Well, Mr. Collier has been made Commissioner after all, and so now there's nothing we can do about it. What we are all going to do is we are going to watch him pretty close. We are not going to let anything bad for the Indians happen without putting up a fight. Remember that Mr. Collier is in a different position now that he is Commissioner. Before he was on the outside and all he had to do was criticize. . . . Now he is on the inside and he is the person who has to do it. . . . He has sent me a telegram saying that he wants to be friends with me and my Association.

A serious consequence of Collier's appointment was the crisis within the Eastern Association. Some members of the Board of Directors were pessimistic about the prospect of working effectively with the new administration. They seemed to expect that Collier would be vindictive, or perhaps they were tired after ten years of struggle. Dr. Spinden found more pressing matters claiming his attention and asked to be relieved of the presidency. Others, for variously stated reasons, proposed that the Eastern Association be dissolved.

La Farge was shocked, he wrote later, when the proposal was seriously advanced at an emergency meeting of the directors. He put up the counter argument that the association had an obligation to remain active and alert and to raise a hue and cry if conditions worsened. A bad commissioner called for strong opposition groups, and no one could say that Collier would be a bad commissioner until he had had a chance to act.

He might have anticipated what would happen next: he was elected president. He described the situation in which he then found himself, in an early history of the association:

> I was quite unaware of one vital factor: the half-dozen "angels" . . . who supported the Eastern Association, regarded it as their property. They dominated it almost totally. Hence they discouraged membership. In January 1933, the Eastern Association

had just eighteen members, six less than the members on its Board of Directors. The controlling group, having handed a dying organization to an innocent young man, then became resentful and suspicious when this intruder took over the reins. The resentment sharpened when he refused to attack the new Commissioner until that official had had a chance to prove himself; and when the Association adopted a policy of cooperation with the Commissioner, their support was ended forever.

The withdrawal of this support almost finished the association. The field nurse program was suspended, the craftwork demonstrations halted, and the two field representatives at Santa Fe, for lack of salary, were "raising rabbits, oats, and corn" to support themselves.

Having been challenged, La Farge would not back down; he had never refused a challenge. Thus the "pet charity" of his flippant reference became the demanding mistress consuming time and substance, and in the end shaping his career.

Within a single year after taking over the presidency, he increased the membership from 18 to 180, and raised a small budget sufficient to reinstate the field nursing program and support the field representatives. (During this period he wrote Christopher: "Isn't it damnable what a genius we have for doing things that don't pay. Unable to coin a story for love or (love of) money, I have: raised about five hundred dollars for Indian affairs, written a remarkable thesis for the commissioner on how to handle Hopis, and finished several chapters on my Guatemala report, with one very elaborate map.")

Also in that year 1933, the Eastern Association changed its name to the National Association on Indian Affairs, to get away from an implied sectionalism. Corresponding branches were established in Washington, D.C., Boston, Colorado Springs, and Lewistown, Montana.

In his report at the end of that first year, La Farge observed, "Having dealt with Republicans throughout our entire existence, we feared that the cooperation with the Indian Bureau, which had been one of our greatest sources of strength, might not be allowed to continue." Happily, he could report: "The new Commissioner met us better than half way, and indeed, in the atmosphere of the New Deal we're enjoying as much authority in Indian affairs as we have ever had, perhaps more. This authority is based, not on influence or politics, but our demonstrated ability to help."

La Farge had not realized until he went down to Washington to meet the new commissioner that he and Collier shared an identical concern in making practical application of social science to the problems of Indian affairs administration. La Farge was particularly pleased to discover this mutual interest. He had been trying to persuade the Rhoads administration to negotiate a working relationship with the Bureau of American Ethnology, a division within the Smithsonian Institution, which since the 1880's had been gathering field data on prehistoric and modern Indians. Rhoads evidently failed to see the immediate value of such cooperation and did not pursue the matter. Collier on his own began at once to consult with anthropologists and sociologists, and within a year he had the nucleus of an anthropological unit within the Bureau. La Farge was among the first of these scientists to whom Collier turned. This also came as a surprise, since Oliver had used abusive language in a personal attack he had made against the appointment. Collier acted as if he were not aware of the attack and thus saved embarrassment to both.

Because of his knowledge of the Southwestern tribes, and of the Navajos in particular, La Farge conducted investigations and worked on assignments in that area. One very practical result of his collaboration was the development of a written form of the Navajo language designed to be transcribed with a standard typewriter keyboard. Various linguists, including Father Berard of the Franciscan Order, had previously devised a written version of the language, but they employed phonetic symbols and this limited its use to professionally trained linguists. La Farge worked with John Harrington of the Smithsonian Institution, and their method allowed any skilled typist to write the language. William Morgan and Robert W. Young further refined it and shortly a Navajo newspaper and a number of English-Navajo reading texts were published. For the first time in their history, Navajos were able to read and write in their own language.

In that same first year of La Farge's presidency, Secretary of the Interior Ickes appointed La Farge to a special advisory committee to study Indian arts and crafts, including their economic potential and marketing problems, and to make recommendations for policy and action. From the work of this committee came legislation creating the United States Indian Arts and Crafts Board.

La Farge's problem now was to find time for the increasing responsibilities he was assuming. He and his fellow directors of the National Association on Indian Affairs should have launched a money-raising effort to finance investigations and field programs, but none of them could devote time to this task. Looking back on that period later, La Farge was struck by the amateurishness of their efforts. The tasks they set for themselves were modest enough, and even so they never succeeded in raising enough money. They fielded one nurse, La Farge reported in 1935, when they could easily have employed twelve to handle the need. They confined their studies and investigations to the Southwest, although they knew that conditions in Oklahoma, in northern Nevada, and among the Seminoles of Florida were wretched and should have been brought to public attention. They tried to publish a regular newsletter on Indian affairs and special bulletins to present the findings of their field workers, but they were chronically short of publication funds. And all through those first years, the office of the association was in La Farge's study, where he also tried to write for a living.

As is often the case with highly devoted but understaffed charitable organizations, the directors watched their pennies, everybody contributed time and pocket money, and they were fearful of using donated funds for money-raising purposes. Not until 1939, and then only after anguished debate, were the directors willing to purchase a mailing list. It seemed a great risk, considering the unpredictability of their income.

Collier's Indian Defense Association was experiencing similar financial problems which became acute when he was appointed commissioner. The membership, which had supported him loyally since the fight against the Bursum Pueblo Lands Bill, was ready to pack up and go home, satisfied that the job of reforming Indian affairs had been completed. Collier, of course, knew that this was untrue. He knew a strong citizen interest was vital, either to support the efforts of a constructive administration, or to oppose any return to the ruinous policies of the past.

Who first proposed a merger of the two organizations is not clear, but the two men, to their mutual surprise, found themselves sharing for their respective organizations a large number of common objectives; it was inevitable that they should join forces. The merger took place formally in June 1937, with the name American Association on Indian Affairs, in 1946 changed to the more logical eponym, Association on American Indian Affairs, which placed the emphasis where it belonged. La Farge' situation did not ease, if that had been his hope. He wrote: "Much to my dismay, I was made president of the new Association. It was also dismaying to find that the former American Indian Defense Association could add almost nothing to our income, financially strong though it once had been. . . . Without training or qualification, I tried to carry out the functions of an Executive Director."

These professional and civic responsibilities now began to make serious demands upon his private life. Two children, a boy and a girl, were born in 1931 and 1933, respectively. When the household moved from Colorado Springs to Santa Fe in the fall of 1934, it included his wife, two infants, one nurse who had just been delivered of a baby of her own, now part of the entourage, one horse, and one German shepherd puppy. "All we lacked," he wrote Christopher, "are goldfish and potted plants."

In that same letter, written at the end of September, he confided: "I finished one good story a few days ago, but that's the total since May." Therein lay the problem, actually a more serious problem than the lack of current literary sales.

Oliver had placed his earnings from *Laughing Boy* and other sales in a family trust, which had fallen precipitously in the downward spiraling securities market of the early thirties. Even so, since he owned 57 percent of the shares in the family trust, he should have derived enough income to meet a major part of his household expenses. But this he denied himself, in order to pay off debts owed by his father. Resort to bankruptcy for his father was not even discussed.

The strain of these efforts and sacrifices soon affected Oliver's marriage. He resisted the temptation to write potboilers, which might have relieved the financial tension. He realized what any serious writer discovers, that time and effort, as well as talent, are invested in producing literary trash, and the ones who achieve memorable success are the few who withhold effort until time and theme make a piece of writing inevitable.

Oliver's wife was growing restive. She was contributing a major share of the household maintenance, and perhaps she failed to see anything wrong in writing saleable stories.

His mother, as might be expected, encouraged Oliver's attitude. She wrote in the spring of 1935: "I am delighted with your writing. Take time out for the moment—don't do potboilers. You need no practice. What you need is leisure time to expand and change a conception, to complete and fulfill it, so it is not sketchy. To write another *Laughing Boy,* you must write from a full mind."

The effect of this, of course, showed in what he wrote Christopher toward the end of that year—"My finances are wretched, and they have been all year. Now I am getting into the quality magazines, so I suppose the big money days are over. One never knows, of course, but writing has been full of reputation recently and low on cash."

To relieve these tensions he decided early in 1936 to accept a temporary appointment with the Bureau of Indian Affairs to work with the Hopi Indians.

❖ IX ❖

Contrary Currents

Wᴛʜɪɴ ᴛᴡᴏ ʏᴇᴀʀs of publication, foreign publishing rights to *Laughing Boy* had been sold in Holland, Sweden, Norway, Germany, France, and Poland. The book also reached the theater and movie screen, where it experienced several false starts but no successes. Before his death in 1931, David Belasco was planning a stage production of the book, for which a dramatic version was prepared by Otis Chatfield-Taylor. That version was brought to New Orleans and produced at Le Petit Théâtre du Vieux Carré, in January 1932. Frans Blom helped with the staging, and the producers attempted to find Navajos for the key roles, but recruiting suitable talent was difficult. It was a social success, since many of Oliver's friends still lived in New Orleans, but as a dramatic event it was disappointing. A further effort was made that year to bring the play to Broadway, where the Group Theatre was enthusiastic, until the producer tried to find a suitable leading woman to play the character of Slim Girl.

Universal Pictures, which purchased the film rights in 1931, at one point brought Oliver to Hollywood for a tryout in the lead role. Oliver had a pleasant expenses-paid trip, but no contract materialized. Hollywood seemed unbelievable. "Everybody calls everybody by their first name," he reported to Christopher.

> Thus Wyler [William Wyler, the producer] says to his secretary, a young woman called Nora, "Call up Junior" [Carl Laemmele, Jr.], or, more likely, "See if you can contact Junior." She then telephones Laemmele's office on the internal phone and passing through several secretaries eventually "contacts" him. It is rather

surprising to hear the director's secretary saying to the president of an enormous organization, "Hello, Junior, this is Nora. Willie wants to speak to you. . . ." Whether I liked it or not, I became Oliver immediately and a horrible tendency towards Ollie was cropping up when I departed.

Eventually the story was filmed on location in Arizona, with Ramon Navarro and Lupe Velez and Navajos in the background, but it never caught on as a boxoffice attraction.

In those years he received other recognition unexpectedly. His story "Haunted Ground" was awarded the O. Henry Prize for the best short story in 1931, and when Brown University granted him an honorary Master of Arts degree in 1932—the youngest man ever so honored by the university—he was cited for his interest in "sometimes neglected racial groups in our national life."

The stories in the collection *All the Young Men* (1935), written during that period, draw almost exclusively upon Indian material—Navajo, Apache, or Central America. The two exceptions in that first collection were the macabre "Haunted Ground," with Narragansett Bay as the background, and "No More Bohemia," a New Orleans tale. The Indian stories came directly out of personal experience, what he had heard, seen, or studied. Some of the stories were cuttings and trimmings left over from the writing of *Laughing Boy*. This is especially suggested by the story, "Higher Education," in which the girl, Lucille, is a faded copy of Slim Girl. Both characters are the victims of the old type of government boarding school, which removed Indian children from their families, forcefully if necessary, and destroyed their capacity to live in their own or any other society. What is notable in this and other early stories is not characterization or plot or story art generally, but La Farge's blistering anger. Of the title story "All the Young Men," he told Christopher: "It was a cry from the soul, as far as I was concerned, a statement of my feeling of the tragic loss of beauty in Indian life, thoroughly romantic and sentimental, which rises up occasionally all the more violently because it is an attitude which I must sternly repress in dealing with the grim realities of Indian affairs."

"Hard Winter" is an excoriation of Eastern women who, out of idleness or a frustrated ego, attach themselves to artless but virile Indian men. He likely had a general type in mind, but in one scene the entrance gate to Mabel Dodge Lujan's house at Taos is described rather explicitly. His narrative often swept forward with broad, general strokes, only nodding at reality in its swift passage. In the more polished stories, for example, "Camping on My Trail," he was painstaking in his attention to sensory detail. The Central American jungle, which is the setting, with its sounds and smells and night terrors, floods the imagination and the reader is carried along a flowing tide of suspense. The detail here is from personal experience, as it is also in the short piece, "A Family Affair," which is built upon an incident reported in *The Year Bearer's People*. In these latter stories, La Farge skillfully selects and highlights details from which the narrative emerges. As he matured this style, his stories achieved extraordinary power, as in such creations as "Old Century's River" and most of the pieces in the posthumous collection, *The Door in the Wall*.

Already in those first years of professional writing he recognized that he was becoming typed as a writer of Indian stories. He protested in various ways against this narrowing of his field of vision, complaining at one time to the book review editor of the New York *Herald-Tribune* that nobody ever sent anything but Indian stories for him to review or to write blurbs for. He also tried to write from his experiences away from the Indian country, as in the New Orleans story, "No More Bohemia." But this only proved that he wrote best when he dealt with an Indian theme and with Indian characters. The white people who appear in his Indian narratives, even in the anthropological stories in which living Indians have no active part, are interesting primarily as observers and interpreters of Indian life of contemporary times or of the archaeological past. White people by themselves, as in "No More Bohemia," are apt to remain stylized symbols, not people one might expect to encounter walking down the street.

In a major effort to break free of the stereotype, he turned to Central America for the background of *Sparks Fly Upward*.

This was still *preeminently* an Indian story, but it dealt with social issues leading to armed revolution, which set it apart from the individual tragedies that characterized his previous Indian stories.

The novel was started in March 1930, just as he was becoming involved in Indian affairs politics and planning to take his bride to the Indian country. When he found time to write is a mystery, as he was more or less camping out until late that summer and was socially active when he returned with his wife to New York in the fall. That winter and the following spring he was fulfilling assignments for the Pennsylvania Museum and absorbing bruises in a Senate committee room. Still, he finished it and the manuscript of the novel was delivered to the publisher in time for late fall publication in 1931.

The momentum generated by *Laughing Boy* carried over to *Sparks Fly Upward*, which moved into the best-seller lists in New York, Boston, Philadelphia, Pittsburgh, Cleveland, and on across the country. It was at best, however, a qualified success, as it fell victim to two publishing hazards. The subject matter was Indians, about which there was ignorance and indifference, and the setting was Latin America, about which ignorance and indifference were colossal. This was reflected in the reviews, which noted "his tendency to romanticize his native Indian characters" and to write about matters which seemed "a little too remote from present day concerns."

One reviewer recognized La Farge's growth as a writer—Herschel Brickell in his column "The Literary Landscape," in the *North American Review* for January 1932. Brickell remarked: "There is power in the book, and it is well written—indeed, it seems to *The Landscaper* a good deal more important novel than *Laughing Boy*—but it will not be so popular as its far more romantic predecessor. There are few other American novels of the year worth singling out." He was speaking of the year in which Pearl Buck's *The Good Earth* and Willa Cather's *Shadows on the Rock* were published.

What was not apparent to the reviewers of the period but seems

obvious now is that La Farge wrote with knowledge and understanding about the Indians who derived directly from the lost
Mayan glory. That this now seems obvious is partly because of
La Farge's own published researches in this field, which of course
are but minor contributions to the massive literature that has built
up since the 1930's. He knew the languages native to the region—
what he later described as "a compound of western Guatemala
and the state of Chiapas in Mexico," where he conducted his 1927
field work—and he knew the history of the people and the cultural
sequences through which they passed from the time of the Conquest. The reader who does not share this knowledge and understanding, and this would include the reviewers of 1932, might pass
it off as a romance, relating events of no "present day concern,"
but this is to miss La Farge's insight into what was then happening among native peoples around the colonial world and specifically in the Americas.

When Esteban, the hero, son of an Indian mother and a peon
soldier who is all but a fraction Indian, decides to throw in his
lot with the Indians who are fighting for land and liberty, thereby
renouncing the Patrón in whose household he was reared, he puts
himself on the side of history. Throughout the Americas, certainly for at least the past hundred years, the Indians of the two
continents have been insisting that they are entitled to an Indian
future. Since the Revolution of 1910 Mexico has proclaimed herself a "Mestizo Nation," a nation in which the Indian heritage
runs deep. It was with this perception and understanding that La
Farge wrote.

In technical skill the novel shows marked improvement over
Laughing Boy. La Farge tells his story and gets his effects without
lecturing the reader on the esoterica of Indian life. He has learned
to let events proceed on their own toward an inevitable and heroic
conclusion. He still takes some liberties with credibility, as in
the scenes in which Esteban ropes a running pig from horseback,
or with a flip of the wrist skewers with his trusty knife the villain
who has just tried to blow him apart with a musket ball. These are
trappings of the romantic tradition in storytelling, and the reader

may accept them as such. What is important about the book is the author's ideological involvement with the fate of the despised and exploited Indian population.

It is understandable that in later years La Farge became impatient with the well-meaning strangers who shook his hand and congratulated him for writing *Laughing Boy,* seemingly unaware that he had ever written anything else. He was painfully aware of that first novel's shortcomings and expressed his wish to destroy the publisher's plates and rewrite the text. Something of this is suggested in the "Foreword" he prepared for the 1957 reissue of the novel.

Still hoping to escape the stereotype which threatened like inevitable fate, he turned completely away from Indians and ethnology and wrote *Long Pennant.* The setting is Narragansett Bay, the high seas, and New Orleans, during the privateering days of the War of 1812.

To write the novel he again had to juggle blocks of time, as various commitments filled his days. He started it in Rhode Island in the late summer of 1932 and worked at it through the winter. In mid-December 1932 he wrote to Christopher, then in England, "Did I tell you I had a novel started?" By early April 1933 he wrote: "I am now about half way through the typed rewriting of the book—and it will not be much over a month before I dust my hands and say 'thar she lies.' " He had returned the previous summer from his third Guatemalan expedition, and in addition to the novel he had a report to prepare. The latter, as it turned out, got sidetracked and did not appear until 1947.

Christopher, in England, was writing the first of his verse-novels, *Hoxie Sells His Acres,* which is also set in Narragansett Bay. The brothers were playing a game, referring to identical landscape features, describing them faithfully, but attaching variant names and moving them apart in space. They wondered whether readers would identify the geography. Christopher had written, upon receiving word that Oliver had started the novel, "It's really about time you (and I) wrote something about Rhode Island. So much to write! The funny little place is chock full of its own kind

of atmosphere and tradition and style, and thar she lies, a virgin!"
As he was about to finish his novel, Oliver commented: "Your
lines on Chog's Cove Harbor are perfect. I think that we are going
to achieve just what I indicated in my last letter, which is a confusion between our two imaginary sections such that nobody can
identify them. Between us we have taken Wickford and smeared it
up and down about ten miles of Narragansett Bay, which certainly ought to keep the identifiers guessing."

Writing to a correspondent about the novel in 1954, Oliver
explained:

> The thing started from remarks of the master under whom I
> studied Greek at school about the cycle of the *Nostoi,* that is,
> "The Homecomers," of which the *Odyssey* was only one. He . . .
> developed various ideas about the cycle, including some thoughts
> about homesickness as a theme. . . .
>
> Later, during my years in New Orleans and Central America,
> I learned more about the nature of homesickness, and with this
> began developing the Homecomer theme. I thought of it in terms
> of my own part of Rhode Island. . . . I had meantime been in-
> trigued by the characters of Samuel Hall and Ephraim Brown
> from two ancient and rather dirty songs. The song about Ephraim
> Brown is also known as "Rollicking Bill the Sailor."
>
> When it came to the actual writing, another influence en-
> tered. . . . I wanted to experiment, and had developed certain
> ideas about the internal monologue-stream of consciousness
> method. Particularly I wanted to play with the idea that a man's
> action at any given moment is governed by the sum of the ex-
> periences of his entire past life. This is almost impossible to han-
> dle in narrative prose for technical reasons.

The book did not sell well, in spite of the publisher's enthusiasm. Ferris Greenslet wrote, after receiving the completed manuscript at the end of April: "It seems to me without question the
best work that you have done. It is singularly Objective and singularly Inward—objective by reason of your real imaginative
grasp of the subject matter and inward through the exceedingly
skillful use of the memory flashback. . . . It ought, it seems to me,

greatly to solidify your position among the few contemporary American novelists who really count."

But, in fact, writers of that period were finding it difficult to sell their wares, and Oliver shared their fate. The depression years provided a shrinking market for literary sales, and many young writers, as well as artists, musicians, dramatists, and other creative workers competed for manual labor jobs or took cattle boats to Europe where living was cheap. The creation of the Works Progress Administration with its special programs for practitioners of the arts salvaged many careers in the mid-thirties. But that was no recourse for a writer in La Farge's situation.

In later correspondence Christopher alludes to a problem which for the fiction writer is often crucial. The writing of a novel allows no freedom for anything else, and meantime the need to eat does not diminish. If the writer puts the novel aside to write short pieces for the pot, he may find himself in trouble of a different sort. Christopher explains about himself: "I don't know how it affects you, but if I try to do a novel and also write short stories, I tend to use up the material I'd put in the novel."

This describes a situation that closed in on Oliver, alarmingly, in the succeeding years. He wrote only two major novels after *Long Pennant,* and yet he went on writing steadily—stories, articles, a newspaper column, juveniles, scientific papers, a war history, miscellanea. The time came when he could not afford the time and energy to write a full-length novel.

The Enemy Gods, however, was a novel he had to write. Brushing aside his reluctance to limit himself to Indian material, he turned again to his Navajo experiences to mount a devastating attack on the ignorance, stupidity, and brazen racism of government officials, politicians, and missionaries. His attack on missionaries was especially sharp, for while the official and the politician were primarily interested in robbing the Indian of property, the proselytizing missionary seemed determined to destroy the Indian as a person, in the name of Christian goodness.

A first outline of the book was sketched in December 1935. "The novel progresses in my head," he wrote his mother in January; and then it languished, as other priorities claimed his time. He accomplished some writing in the early spring months, but in the summer he was fully occupied with work in the Hopi villages. In spite of these distractions and accumulating personal problems, he completed a first draft of the novel before the end of September 1936. "I work in the assurance that I shall have to rework, revise, rearrange, and cut out, as I have never done before," he had remarked during an early spurt of work. And that turned out to be the case. Sections of the manuscript were being revised until late in June 1937, for publication that fall.

The novel catalogs all the vicious practices, the inhumanities, the stupidities, the outright thievery that had thrived in Indian affairs through three administrations, and what he described were not generalizations but conditions he had himself witnessed or had gleaned from official reports. He had seen boarding schools so overcrowded that children were required to sleep two to a bed in buildings that were extreme fire hazards. He had seen the child labor euphemistically referred to as manual or industrial training which actually maintained a school plant in the absence of adequate maintenance funds. From investigations of the Senate committee confirmed by the Brookings Institution's study, he knew that children in these boarding schools were fed a diet that cost the government eleven cents a day per child. When this food allowance was raised to thirty-six cents per child, it was counted a major victory.

In his visits to reservations in the Southwest, at his own initiative or on official business, he talked with callous and incompetent doctors and nurses and inspected intolerable medical facilities. He had conversations of a sort with salvation preaching missionaries who expressed only contempt for the human worth of the Indians they sought to convert. He made himself familiar with the attitudes and activities of the cattle and sheep growers, the mining companies, and their political henchmen who planned and sometimes succeeded in carrying out massive raids on Indian lands or other property.

The novel contains it all, at once a tract and a plea for cultural pluralism. In form it borrows from Greek drama, with the Twin Gods of Navajo mythology contemplating the earth scene, while at intervals other characters plan their strategies and set in motion the events of the story. The scenes in which these characters appear—the characters are as faceless as the members of a Greek chorus—bear various labels: the office of the Commissioner of Indian Affairs, a gathering of missionaries, a conference of livestock men and their banker. The story is not concerned with the lives of these faceless ones and no attempt is made to round them into people. Like the classical chorus, they give the argument which is acted out in the lives of the protagonists.

It is the story of the Navajo people in modern times, and more generally the story of the American Indian. In his first encounters with Indians, Oliver had accepted the notion then prevailing that the Indians would disappear culturally, and perhaps biologically as well. Then, at Jicarilla, as he listened to the singing voices of the Apaches, he came to realize that while biological extinction might indeed be their fate, the quality of Indianness would remain until the last singing voice was silenced.

And this is the theme of *The Enemy Gods*. The hero, Myron Begay—*Seeing Warrior* his people named him—had been taken from home as a small boy and shipped off to school. Because he was bright and responsive, he was encouraged by a well-meaning religious teacher at the school. He stayed in school when other classmates escaped, his missionary friend obtained scholarship assistance for him, and he trained for the ministry to work among his own people. But while he seemed to work with clear purpose, within himself he was filled with doubt and unanswered questions. On the few occasions he returned home, the ways of his people appealed to him strongly, although he really knew nothing about them, except that in Christian eyes they were ignorant and superstitious. His old uncle, a religious man in his own way, disturbed him when he said, "You have never heard anything but the Jesus talk. What you believe, you will have to settle for yourself. But you can't disbelieve something you're never heard of."

His break from Christianity and his return to his people did not occur, however, until after he had killed a man, a drunken Mexican who had insulted his Indianness. In running from that scene, he ran deep into the backwoods of the Navajo country and deep into the mysteries of Navajo religious experience. Finally there he caught up with himself, and with a Navajo girl, who earlier had spurned him for being a "mixed-up" boy. During their reconciliation she asked him whether he would become a medicine man like his uncle, with whom he was going to live. His answer is La Farge's theme:

"Our world is changed; that is no longer the way for me. . . . We have to give up a lot of little ideas because they were the best we knew. If we want to save ourselves, we have to learn to use the white man's knowledge, his weapons, his machines—and still be Navajos."

The Burden

As COMMISSIONER OF INDIAN AFFAIRS, John Collier made a determined effort to bring social scientists into the policy-making process of his administration. He sought the advice of such men as William Duncan Strong of the Bureau of American Ethnology, John Harrington of the Smithsonian Institution, Fred Eggan of the University of Chicago, among others, in selecting field workers and defining problems for study. By 1936, he had brought H. Scudder Mekeel to Washington to head up an anthropological unit, which at different times included young men who later became leaders in their special fields: Julian H. Steward, Oscar Lewis, Morris Opler, Edward Kennard, David Rodnick, Charles Wisdom, and Gordon Macgregor. This was the first attempt by a government agency to involve social scientists in administration. When certain cave dwellers in Congress discovered that Collier was trying to bring scientific methods into a branch of government that had always been ruled by collusion and petty politics, the anthropological unit was abolished.

Collier and La Farge, meanwhile, had discovered their mutual interest in applied social science, and this very quickly ripened into mutual respect. In the summer of 1934, La Farge, acting for the newly formed National Association on Indian Affairs, conducted an investigation at the Hopi reservation in Arizona, and on the basis of his finding the bureau was persuaded to revise regulations with respect to Hopi custom marriage. There were other instances of close cooperation between the national association and the bureau, leading finally to Collier's request that Oliver accept a temporary appointment to work with the Hopi villages in formalizing a tribal government under the Indian Reorganization Act. It was an extraordinary conceit.

The Indian Reorganization Act of 1934, the most significant piece of Indian legislation since the Allotment Act of 1887, directed the Secretary of the Interior to assist Indian tribes in adopting appropriate constitutions and charters. Previously, the federal courts had recognized the tribal right of self-government, but the executive branch had largely ignored the courts and in many instances had usurped tribal authority to legislate.

Collier visited the Hopi villages soon after the passage of this legislation and talked to the people about proceeding under the new law to protect their institutions and customs against possible attack from future administrators. How much of Collier's proposal the Hopis understood is not clear. They were prepared to trust John Collier because of the fight he had made in behalf of the Rio Grande Pueblos, and this persuaded him of their willingness to work toward establishing a tribal government. He realized that the task would be complex and to carry it off successfully he needed a field worker from outside the bureau, for the Hopis had no reason to trust a bureau man.

As it happened, Collier turned to La Farge at a moment when his stories were not selling, and Oliver agreed to take on the assignment. The decision, of course, did not turn on the prospect of earning a temporary income; he was intrigued by the opportunity to apply himself to a specific problem in social change. Even so, his acceptance was phrased cautiously, as he wrote Collier in April 1936: "I do not wish to assume the task of pushing the Hopis toward an organization which does not interest them. . . . If it should develop that they really do not want organization, I reserve the right to consider the entire matter afresh." He added subsequently: "I warn you that my early progress will be very slow."

The congressional act specified that Indian *tribes* might organize and adopt a written constitution, but the Hopi Indians did not constitute a tribe and never had. They spoke a common language, but lived in ten separate villages which could not even be described as an alliance. One additional village consisted of Tewa Indian refugees from the Rio Grande Valley who fled their homeland after the Pueblo Rebellion of 1680. Only once in Hopi history, so far as that history is known, had these independent villages acted together in common cause; that was in 1710, when they destroyed the village of Awatobi, one of their own, for seeming to encourage the return of the Spanish.

The history of separatism is ancient and probably traces back to the origins of these mesa-dwelling people. The population was built up by a process of accretion as people moved into the area over a long period of time, some of them possibly from the cliff-dwelling communities to the north and west. In characterizing them in his *Notes for Hopi Administrators,* La Farge wrote this commentary:

> The major group gives the impression of having been conditioned by generations of struggle for a living under the doubtful conditions of desert farming. The fear of drought, the fear of the future, the desire for security through material possessions are deep in their natures. Warfare is obviously undesirable, since the best that one can achieve is to inflict such damage on the enemy that in the future he will leave one alone. . . . Among the Hopis the cult of peace reaches an extreme, and all personal violence is looked upon with horror. With this comes an attitude of smug superiority towards all who fight, including the white man whose weapons stand between the Hopis and the dreaded Navajos. . . . Unwilling to settle a matter by force, they talk and remember it for years, and it is virtually impossible for a man to live down an unfortunate action once performed or to go back upon a position which he has once taken. . . . It may be said in general that the Hopi looks upon himself as a chosen vessel containing the true religion by means of which the welfare of the whole world is maintained. Furthermore, all the world between the two oceans is his by aboriginal right.

On another occasion he observed: "Entirely governed by their religion, they are magnificently stubborn in their determination to live according to the Hopi path, and will face death and destruction, imprisonment, anything to stand by their ideals and their gods. Through this they achieve real sincerity and strength."

Altogether, a difficult people: "The name Hopi means peaceful. They abhor war and physical violence, wherefore they quarrel constantly and the talking never ceases. . . . They fight with words and sheer endurance."

These were the people the white man, using his own formal procedures and instruments, proposed to organize. The fact that there existed no overriding centralized structure of authority did not mean that the people were lawless. On the contrary, they were highly organized, deriving their institutions from history and tradition, although in forms not readily translatable into concepts of majority rule, parliamentary procedure, and committees within the whole.

Not only were they traditionally organized, but they were guided, and in a sense compelled, in their acting and thinking by a millenial prophecy. Like all prophecies, the Hopi account of the world to come could be invoked either to support or to oppose a course of action.

La Farge described the Hopi government in his *Notes for Hopi Administrators.*

The system is roughly that of the Pueblos prior to the coming of the Spaniards, slightly broken down by American Governmental interference. It is, of course, a pure theocracy. The controlling group is made up of so-called chiefs, who are each the head of a particular line of ceremony. They are succeeded by an individual chosen by them from among their sisters' sons. At the head stands the Kikmongwi—literally "house chief." All these ceremonial lines lead into him, and he has true authority in the villages, but like the cacique in the Pueblos [of the Rio Grande], it is not proper for such an individual to be mixed up in ordinary quarrels. Somebody might speak insultingly to him or he might be forced to perform some violent or unworthy action. . . . Therefore, he must be protected from unpleasant contacts. Several well meaning attempts by the Indian Service to give authority to chiefs have failed because they forced them into public activities of a profane nature, inconsistent with their religious position.

Yet there is no question of the ultimate authority of these men in most of the villages. Their authority is exercised through persuasion and the influence of the general reverence for the Kikmongwi. He must not be ignored but he must be approached with great caution, and anyone dealing with him must remember that he is absolutely bound by the dictates of his religion.

This description defined the problem. The purpose of encouraging the Hopis to formalize their social relations by writing and adopting a political document might be laudable; it would help to protect and perpetuate the kind of society they wanted. But the Hopis faced a dilemma. Their principal men would be required to demean themselves by taking secular action, action which would threaten the very society they wanted to perpetuate. If leaders of lesser rank took on the burden of advocating the political instrument, they would almost certainly be disavowed by the top men, and as a matter of respect no one would undertake such a course.

The practical alternative for the federal government was direct action without regard for indigenous practices, but this would block any hope of local initiative. Colonial governments invariably have pursued such a course "for the good" of the native community; and as La Farge noted, Hopi administrators not only ignored the local leaders but were unaware that such leaders existed. Needless to say, historical colonialism, if pursued here, would have violated the philosophy of the Collier administration.

This left as the only choice a very slow and tedious process: meeting with individuals and groups in each of the villages, building understanding, and working toward a consensus. La Farge's appointment was for three months, with an extension of the period possible, but he had a novel to complete, a Guatemala report still on his hands, and a domestic crisis in the making. He was determined to complete the task in the time allotted.

Between the end of May and the end of August he covered 5,800 miles in a government car, and most of that mileage represented travel between the three mesas which lay within 20 and 30 miles of each other. It added up to countless short trips over washed-out roads or no roads at all, meetings that lasted into the morning hours, gallons of coffee, missed meals, weariness, and doubt. In the middle of June, he wrote in his *Running Narrative:* "I still do not know if it is the right thing for these people to organize. I see a protection for them, I see a means of strengthening Hopi values, while opening the way for progress, for the more intelligent selection of the good things of each culture. But do I *know* that? No. I only think, and that as a white man, studying from the outside. What wreckage may not the alien structure cause?"

The letter from his mother which arrived during those days failed to convey the assurance which was always intended. "If you can do the thing you are trying to do, it will lay the foundation . . . for many years to come," she wrote. But she was writing from a world that was receding for him and that existed only as a threatening shadow for the Hopi people. Here and now, he was really on his own, with no guidelines from the world of Saunderstown—a lone Yankee.

Toward the end of the period, when the impossible consensus he sought was becoming a probability, he wrote: "I really think I'd recommend that the whole matter be dropped for a generation." It was asking too much. From their first contact with the white man the Hopis had never been given choices. They had been under constant pressure to abandon what they called the Hopi way, and the pressure had driven them ever deeper into themselves, into the refuge of their "prophecy." Their ability to choose had atrophied, while the impulse to reject had become a habit.

La Farge told them repeatedly: "The Hopis must do this. It is not something the white man can do for them. It is a power that is offered, an authority. It is laid down here. But the Hopis must pick it up, if it is suited to them."

After the first six weeks of effort, he remarked: "The general attitude, amusingly enough, is this: the old men understand about organization. It is in their tradition, they have long been waiting for it to happen. They are competent to judge this thing. The younger men are trying to judge it by the light of a little schooling, and of course they don't understand."

In the end, it was the old men who decided the issue. A committee to prepare a draft constitution was created early in June, consisting of leaders from First Mesa. In Hopi tradition, First Mesa is the outpost, the place where new things are tried and then passed on to the other villages, and so it was appropriate that the constitution be written by the leaders there. They completed the task at the end of the first week in July, and from then until the end of August the document was carried from village to village, to meeting after meeting. At last an agreement was reached—not a consensus, but agreement to submit the question to a vote of all the people.

The document the committee prepared was a skillful blending of tradition and white man's legalisms. A Tribal Council with limited and specified powers was created, but representatives to the council would be chosen by each village in accordance with its own rules. In the traditional villages, the Kikmongwi would appoint one or more representatives, based on population, to speak for him and to be responsible to him; in the predominantly Christian or "progressive villages," the representatives might be elected. The Tribal Council would have no voice in strictly village matters, and the villages would follow their own preferences in regulating internal affairs. Quarrels between villages, as in land disputes, could be referred to the council to arbitrate. The council would also represent all the Hopi people in dealings with the outside world. The committee meticulously phrased and polished each of these points.

Balloting took place October 26, 1936, weeks after La Farge had left the Hopi country and returned to New York. The vote was 651 in favor of the constitution and 104 against it, with many irreconcilables abstaining. One of these, the leader at the village of Hotevilla, announced publicly that he would be away from the village, working in his corn field, so that his abstention would not influence others. They could vote, or not, and he would not be watching. Very few voted in that village. Even with these holdouts, more than 50 percent of the eligible voters participated.

La Farge prepared two documents from his work with the Hopi people—a journal, which he referred to as a *Running Narrative,* intended primarily for Commissioner Collier, and *Notes for Hopi Administrators,* which, as the title suggests, was intended to provide background information for government workers. One of his initial problems when he arrived among the Hopis was to learn who the leaders were in the several villages; bureau employees did not know and did not seem interested in finding out. The *Notes* spelled out who these leaders were, their powers and limitations, and their positions within Hopi social structure. These documents have not been published. The *Running Narrative,* copies of which are in the bureau archives, is especially interesting as an ethnological working paper.

When he had traveled the last mile, adjourned the last meeting, and shipped the document off to Washington for review and ultimate approval before the tribal election, La Farge sat in the cool evening at Polacca nursing a strong drink of prohibited whiskey. He was aware of a sense of both accomplishment and frustration. He had performed what students of the Hopi people had deemed impossible, but he knew that nothing had been changed, really. It was even questionable whether this was the first step in a new direction.

He reflected, glass in hand:

I have thought often [about "the white man's burden"] in the past fifteen years, in different ways. It is a snare and a delusion, it is also a reality and something not to be ducked. . . . The Hopis are going to organize, first, because John Collier and a number of other people decided to put through a new Indian law, the Reorganization Act. The Indians didn't think this up. We did. . . . We came among these people, they didn't ask us, and as a result, they are our wards. It's not any inherent lack of capacity, it's the cold fact of cultural adjustment. . . . I said all the right things—"This is your decision, it is up to you"—but my manner was paternal and authoritarian. . . . We bring to these Indians a question which their experience cannot comprehend, a question which includes a world view and a grasp of that utterly alien, mind-wracking concept, Anglo-Saxon rule by majority vote, with everything that follows in the train of that. . . . I knew that I was robbing these people of their alibi, of their grievance, and I knew the hell that will be to pay when they realize that they have accepted responsibility as well as power. . . . But I made up my mind that this was right. I took up this burden on my tump line [like the Indians of Guatemala] and carried it to where it should go. That is the white man's burden: to undo, despite the lack of comprehension of his wards, the harm that he himself has done.

What he anticipated in that hour of reflection, was remarkably prophetic. There was "hell to pay" when the Hopis realized what had happened to them. But it was hell in the Hopi sense—no skull-cracking, nothing burned down or blown up. Only much bitter talk.

In 1950 La Farge wrote a brief postscript to his *Running Narrative,* remarking:

The pattern of Tribal Council, decisive action, minority self-subordination, etc., simply did not suit them. Dan Kachongeva [one of the intransigent traditionalists] was brilliant in using the council as a sounding board, and in making the maximum of irritation through it. Otto Lomavitu [one of the "Christian progressives"] and his ilk talked too much. The council stopped meeting, no new representatives were chosen, the constitution went into abeyance. Above all, no village, I think, was prepared to surrender any part of its sovereignty, or to lay aside any of its quarrels with other villages.

He touches on another matter in that 1950 postscript. Commenting on the subjectivity of certain passages in the *Running Narrative,* he noted: "In extenuation, I would explain that this work was done during a time of intense personal emotional stress. My marriage broke up less than three months later, the breakup was coming on then."

His wife, Wanden, had spent a week with him midway through the Hopi tour, but in the press of constant meetings and travel, they had had little occasion for talk, certainly not for reconciliation. That unsatisfactory visit was probably decisive; their divorce followed a year later.

One matter, unmentioned in the *Running Narrative,* augmented the "emotional stress" of that summer. Oliver had been in the Hopi country only a few weeks when he received word that his father had suffered a heart attack. It was not fatal, his father lived for another two years. Only after some years beyond that was he able to express the sentiment that had attached him to his father—a controlled sentiment, as described in *Old Man Facing Death.* But that summer, in the Hopi country where Grant La Farge was still remembered, the sudden news brought private grief.

❖ XI ❖

A New Beginning

IN PURSUING his plan to encourage the development of a science of Indian affairs administration, La Farge sought like-minded individuals and persuaded them to accept membership on the Board of Directors of the expanded Association on American Indian Affairs. Dr. Haven Emerson, a public health authority, came to the association when it merged with John Collier's Indian Defense group, and in the next few years the list included Dr. Charles Russell of the American Museum of Natural History; Professor Eduard C. Lindeman of Columbia University; Professor E. Adamson Hoebel, then at the University of Utah; Dr. Harry Shapiro, Columbia University; and Professor Clyde Kluckhohn of Harvard. Other professional people were added in later years.

La Farge credited Dr. Manuel Gamio of Mexico with persuading him to use the scientific method on problems of assimilation and culture change. Gamio, a leading archaeologist in the New World, excavator of the great Pyramid of the Sun at Teotihuacan, was interested in contemporary Indian life throughout the hemisphere. With John Collier and other Indianists he was responsible for the first Inter-American Congress on Indian Life at Patzcuaro, Mexico, in 1940. Representatives of all the American republics with Indian populations participated. The Congress adopted a convention creating the Inter-American Indian Institute, which is now a permanent component body of the Organization of American States. It sponsors various programs of research and technical assistance among its member nations and meets every four years to review developments in the hemisphere.

The Association on American Indian Affairs, stimulated by the Patzcuaro meeting, in early March of the following year conducted an institute on the future of the American Indian, to which it invited Dr. Daniel F. R. de la Borbolla, a participant at Patzcuaro. La Farge had been an interested observer of Indian affairs administration in Mexico since his field studies in that country, and he asked Borbolla to speak specifically on Mexico's experimental schools.

These schools had been training native rural teachers and developing teaching materials prepared in an alphabetized form of the native languages. This had markedly increased the Indians' interest in formal education and consequently brought an increase in literacy. Previously, Borbolla pointed out, the Indian had resisted "the education which for four centuries we have tried to impose and which he so wisely and intelligently had been able to reject." Indian attitudes had the unfortunate effect of denying the Indian population the benefits of national development. As Borbolla explained: "Western civilization completed the physical conquest of the American continent four centuries ago. But that conquest did not succeed in assimilating the native population into the concepts of Western thought. Today, more than thirty-million natives of the American continent live as foreigners in the land which is theirs by right and by inheritance. Four centuries of Western domination have not been able to open the door of our culture to those thirty million Indians."

The papers of the conference, subsequently published as the volume *The Changing Indian* (1942), covered a wide spectrum of problems and speculations involving the future of the native American. As the editor, writing a *Foreword* to the volume, La Farge made a strong plea for a science of administration, remarking:

In this country and abroad, medicine, anthropology, education, sociology, psychology, changed the whole thinking of civilized mankind, but the Indian Bureau ignored them all. The United States became a leader in many lines of knowledge and practice which bore directly upon the Indian problem—in public health, social service, education, and anthropology, to name a few. Bureaus dealing with all of these existed in our government. But it was a startling thing in the early 1920's to see how utterly the Indian Bureau remained insulated against all this, to see how it continued to exist and work not even in the nineteenth but in the eighteenth century.

Then, after reviewing what had been happening more recently, he added: "We, the United States, have undertaken a serious experiment. Belatedly, we have set out to help some four hundred thousand people—reared in a totally different culture under utterly different circumstances, the remnant that has survived our aggression—to adapt themselves to our culture with benefit to themselves and to us."

While some of the papers in *The Changing Indian* are dated, hence now of only historical interest, as a group they represent the first serious attempt to view all aspects of Indian life—population trends, health factors, land use, education, social and economic adaptation, religion—through a conceptual framework supplied by social science. The Meriam survey report mentioned earlier was packed with statistical findings, and at the time of its publication it was hailed as a carefully documented exposure of the conditions of Indian life. But, significantly, the report contained no discussion of the role of culture in determining those conditions. The term "culture," in fact, is not even entered in the fairly detailed index. In a brief passage devoted to "community life" the only forms of indigenous social action encountered by the field investigators, it would seem, were "the native ceremonies, such as celebrations, dances, games, and races."

Only fifteen years separated the two publications, but obviously new methods and new concepts were being applied to analyze and describe the status of Indians in American society. It was this development, this furthering of a science of human affairs, that La Farge saw as important—not just reformism, but changes in the way of thinking about people of another race or another culture.

While plans to enlarge the scope of the association and for its first national conference progressed, La Farge was, as always, meeting writing deadlines and casting manuscripts upon the trade waters, praying for a return.

In the middle of July 1938 he wrote Christopher: "I've written four stories in the last thirty days, most of them completely written twice, but none of them carries any conviction. I'm sending one out today, more out of impatience than anything else. I've sold one story, written in May, to *Esquire,* which has chosen this moment to reduce its already low rate of pay."

And on the last day of December 1939 he again wrote to Christopher. "I have contracted to write a 25,000-word text for a photographic book on the Indians. It is to be a study of the realities of Indian affairs and the Indian problem, a social document, and the possibilities excite me. But the deadline is January 10, and I am now about two-thirds through the first draft. So you see, among other things, I am rushed."

The work in progress was the documentary *As Long as the Grass Shall Grow,* for which Helen M. Post supplied some magnificent photographs. In writing captions for the concluding series of illustrations, Miss Post took her text straight from Myron Begay, the hero of *The Enemy Gods:* "We have to learn to use the white man's knowledge, his weapons, his machines—and still be Indians."

Meantime, the association was not prospering. Its efforts as a fact-gathering and technical advisory citizen group were continually hampered by lack of operating funds. The situation worsened with stepped-up attacks on the Roosevelt New Deal and John Collier's administration. While the country generally still staggered from the impact of the depression, upper class patrons who in other years had contributed to Indian work as a preferred charity had a particular grievance. The New Deal programs threatened the secure world they had known, and it was reported in some quarters that the new Indian program was promoting dangerous ideas —common ownership of land, tolerance for pagan rites, and protection for tax-exempt Indian lands. Not only were they not supporting La Farge's association as they had supported its predecessors, but some of these patrons sympathized with the attacks being made on Collier's reforms. And these reforms, on the whole, were vigorously endorsed and promoted by the Association on American Indian Affairs.

It was an awkward situation for La Farge, since his advocacy conflicted with the sympathies of his social world. Clearly the association would have to draw support from a broader segment of the general population, if it expected to shape public policy. But this was not accomplished until after the World War.

Events at Pearl Harbor brought the activities of the association to a virtual standstill, like those of most civilian establishments. Members of the Board of Directors scattered to wartime assignments. Moris Burge, who had been with the association or its predecessors as field representative and just recently as executive director, was co-opted by the War Relocation Authority administering Japanese centers. La Farge was soon commissioned in the Air Transport Command as historical officer. Dr. Haven Emerson, who had been president of the American Indian Defense Association, took over for La Farge and served as president until after the war.

The entire Indian endeavor went into eclipse. Money for land purchases, one of the most hopeful of the New Deal Indian programs, dried up at once. Credit funds for reservation enterprises evaporated. More than thirty thousand Indian men and women went into the armed services or into wartime employment across the country. At the very end of the war, in 1945, after twelve years of tireless, innovative accomplishment, John Collier resigned as Commissioner. And thereafter, wolves were in the land.

War's end and economic retrenchment after the war brought acute distress to many Indian communities, most sharply felt perhaps by the Navajo people, simply because they were the largest tribal group and their resources in greatest imbalance. On top of this the Navajo country suffered an extremely severe winter in 1948–49, with deep snow, sharp winds, and persistent cold. Thousands of sheep starved, unable to break through the wind-crusted snow to reach feed, or they simply froze to death.

Emergency brought the Association on American Indian Affairs back into action and to a reappraisal of its organizational needs and methods. La Farge returned to civilian life in the summer of 1946 and, although he did not resume the presidency of the association until 1948, when Dr. Emerson retired, he began at once to build a new program. In previous years volunteer workers had carried on staff work on a part-time or intermittent arrangement.

As the first step in postwar reorganization, the association employed Dr. Alexander Lesser, an established anthropologist, as a full-time executive director. A year later the position of legal counsel was created and filled by Felix S. Cohen, who for fourteen years had been associate and acting solicitor of the Interior Department. In those positions he had been responsible for a complete overhaul of the government's legal policy in handling Indian matters. In his *Handbook of Federal Indian Law* (1940), he traced out the historical framework within which the United States had dealt with the aboriginal population. Cohen's appointment was followed in 1950 by the creation of a legal committee under the chairmanship of Charles L. Black, Jr., associate professor of law at Columbia University. This committee quickly embarked on a full program to define and defend Indian civil and constitutional rights —in the courts, before administrative bodies, and in congressional committees.

The association resumed its original role of field research, investigation and study, and publication. Study committees were established in law, education, health, and economic adjustment, and reports were published dealing with the Navajo Indians (1945–46), California Indian communities (1948), advanced education opportunities for Indians (1949), living conditions in the Southwest (1948–50), Indian adjustment in urban New York (1949–50).

An Institute on the Navajo Indian, in 1947, in which Navajo leaders, government officials, anthropologists, and citizen groups participated, contributed to legislation that Congress ultimately adopted (in 1950) as the Navajo-Hopi Rehabilitation Act, discussed below. Following this model of public discussion organized around formal position papers, institutes were devoted to American Indian Self-Government, 1949, and American Indian Assimilation, 1952.

From its first years the association had emphasized publication of background material in the belief that an informed public was the best ally that Indians could have. In keeping with this policy, it pursued a vigorous publications program in the postwar years. *The American Indian,* a 32-page quarterly, was launched in 1947 and very soon almost doubled in size, while circulation increased from 1,200 to 8,000 copies. It was a semiprofessional journal to which established writers contributed, as did administrators and students of subject fields. La Farge regularly wrote the editorial or the lead article. Contributors of course were not compensated. A newsletter, *Indian Affairs,* appearing monthly, reported on proceedings in Congress and current happenings in the Indian country. It, too, found an expanding circle of readers.

All of this activity demanded a larger income than the association had enjoyed in earlier years and required it to move beyond the scope of a volunteer society and engage in fund raising and program management. The first such effort, mentioned earlier, was the association's reluctant purchase in 1939 of a mailing list. The results were so meager as to reaffirm for the doubters the inadvisability of spending money to make money. Now, with less hesitancy, the association in 1948 contracted for the services of a professional fund-raising organization. In the first year of the contract, the annual receipts almost doubled those of the previous year, and a year later the increase was a further 85 percent. Within six years, the 1945 income of $6,000 had been increased ninefold. The new funds were derived not only from a greatly increased dues-paying membership but from foundation grants to support designated projects. It was finally possible for the association to operate at a professional level. Only La Farge maintained his volunteer status. He refused to accept a salary from the association, however grievously its affairs encroached on his time. A self-imposed rule of limiting himself to not more than two days a week on Indian work was never self-enforcing, unfortunately, and entire weeks would go by when nothing but Indian work crossed his desk.

The maturity of planning and execution that characterized the work of the association in the postwar years was a direct reflection of La Farge's own maturation. Whereas before he had worked alone, by preference, and had resisted any arrangement which saddled him with continuing responsibility for the actions of others —the basis of management—he now found himself bringing together a variety of talents to perform office routine or to function in a committee. He was skillful in delegating responsibility and in precisely defining the responsibility. He maintained control at the policy level. Board members carefully reviewed every major publication or position statement the association issued, but in the end they bore La Farge's imprint. His leadership was never questioned, but neither was it doggedly asserted. It resulted from his obvious ability and experience.

The war contributed to La Farge's maturity, as he frequently acknowledged, but in a second marriage he achieved a more inward balance and poise—and confidence—and that he also acknowledged, with surprised exultation. These changes in himself, these discoveries and renewals, prepared him for the battles that were already building.

❖ XII ❖

The Breakaway

L‌A FARGE did not contest Wanden's complaint for the divorce. His lawyer's letter informed him simply, "On August 27, 1937, a decree of divorce was entered by the District Court of the State of Nevada in favor of your former wife. The decree ratifies and confirms the appropriate provisions of the separation agreement." The agreement awarded the children to the mother, with the usual visiting privileges, a provision that brought Oliver much anguish in later years. It was the usual judicial marital settlement that settles nothing. The son, Oliver Albee (who later assumed the name Peter), and the daughter, Povy, were soon strangers to Oliver, a development which distressed him greatly. Only after they had become young adults was there a reconciliation.

Christopher once chided his brother, in the summer of 1948, "What bothers me is a suspicion that you are tending to harbor your grievances and your sorrows and disappointments too long, too hard, too well."

The failure of his marriage and the loss of the children were, indeed, grievous hurts. When divorce proved unavoidable, however, it came as a great relief. Oliver explained to Christopher soon after it occurred: "Shocking and upsetting to fixed ideas as it was, [the divorce] has been the shedding of an incubus, the end of years of struggling against a steady resistance."

A basic incompatibility had always existed. Although obscured in the first years by the enthusiasms of success, it came sharply into view when success receded and the drudgery of a writer's life remained. If he had been willing or constitutionally inclined to seek full-time employment, or if he had consented to pursue success as measured by literary sales, their marriage might have lasted longer. The incompatibility might have been smothered. In referring once to John P. Marquand's novels, Oliver commented: "One of the things about his books is the profound realization of escape they give me. When I study his wives and environments, I wind up re-membering, like waking up from a bad dream—that I'm out of all that."

He hurried out of the East late that summer and reached Santa Fe in time for the annual Fiesta over the Labor Day weekend. Fiesta time in Santa Fe, as Oliver wrote about it in his column for the *Santa Fe New Mexican,*

> is the season when the inhabitants of this Ancient City and envi-rons let down their hair and act completely natural (i.e. slightly looney), just like the City Council. . . . Now the weather-beaten men come down from Chimayo and Trampas to sell cucumbers and chili verde. . . . The number of Indians under the portal of the Palace of the Governors increases. . . . The hotels fill up, and the costumes of the visitors become ever more curious. You would not, in this season, be surprised to encounter a laughing horse or a talking dog. It is obvious that something is going to pop, and so it is fitting that at the end of summer, and not at any other time, comes the outburst of Fiesta.

Fittingly, the festivities are touched off when a torch is applied to the towering figure of Zozobra, a grotesque of Old Man Gloom. After that a madness falls upon the population, only slightly chan-neled into costumed parades, candlelight processions, and Indian dancing. Sidewalk vendors purvey tamales and Indian craftwork, and every bar in town promotes a fellowship in spirits.

For some years, whenever he had been in the Southwest, Oliver had made a point of getting to Santa Fe at Fiesta time, and in the autumn of 1937 it seemed especially important to be there. The skylarking fun was the tonic he needed, but besides, he wanted to renew an acquaintance.

The year before at Fiesta, he had met Consuelo Otille Baca and in the interim they had corresponded some. He was giving a course in creative writing at Columbia University that fall of 1936, and his letters were mostly about students who, for lack of anything better to do with their time, were trying to write a novel. It was unrewarding, in terms of talent discovery, but it brought him needed income.

Years later, Oliver described Consuelo Baca's early life in the collection of tales that make up *Behind the Mountains*. She was one of the three little sisters growing up in Rociada who each carried a doll and a lunch when they went out to play and always bargained for a proper wage when they rockered their older brother's illicit moonshine on the front porch of the family's mountain valley home or trampled silage for their father, Don José de Baca, Lieutenant Governor of the State of New Mexico.

These details were not known to Oliver in the fall of 1937, but he carried from the first encounter a vivid impression of Consuelo's beauty and dark-eyed vivaciousness. Fiesta was a fitting time to meet again and to discover mutual interests. He realized that she liked to ride and was in fact a good horsewoman, a grace acquired in childhood—an auspicious beginning. Then and later he also came to realize that she had many friends among the artists and writers in Santa Fe and had a sound understanding of the artists' craft, though she was not formally trained. Of more importance to him at the moment was her awareness of the stresses and disappointments of creative effort, as she had observed times of crisis among her friends. She accepted these without dismay, as part of the cost of producing creditable work. It was, he thought, a wonderful quality in her.

Before he left Santa Fe, they had an understanding that she might come to New York, where an older sister was living, and if she did she would let him know. She wanted to visit her sister, had in fact been planning it before Oliver appeared, and had only held off for lack of money. The family had once been modestly prosperous, until the sudden death of her father and disastrous losses in the livestock market in the early depression years. Now that the eastern trip had an added significance, Consuelo set out in her own way to solve the money problem. Late that fall and into the winter she traveled through the mountain valleys of northern New Mexico buying up firewood and green chili which she then sold under contract to a wholesale merchant. In Santa Fe everybody eats chili and everybody burns piñon wood in the fireplace; marketing was no problem.

A friend wrote her from New York late that fall: "I hear that it is cold in Santa Fe. Wood and chilies must be selling, so I'll be expecting you soon, in sables."

Miss Baca arrived after the first of the year, not in sables, but with enough money to travel comfortably and to move around after she reached the city—the theater, the ballet, museums, concerts, all the exciting places and events that had beckoned from beyond the horizon. It was some weeks before Oliver learned through various intermediaries that she was in the city. What did he expect! After that, he courted her with great diligence and fervor, and when Consuelo returned to Santa Fe in June, a commitment had passed between them.

A long summer followed. He had promised to join her in Santa Fe as soon as he sold some stories, and that was a summer when nothing sold. A letter to Christopher in mid-July expresses his frustration: "I want to get out West so bad my teeth hurt. . . . Right now I'm feeling far from fit. Largely mental, I am sure, because of uncertainty, and not liking being unable to do just as I please, but some of it is hard work, plus heat, plus a slight tummy upset. New Mexico looks like heaven at the moment, and I wouldn't refuse a good offer for a weekend in Kamchatka." Christopher, of course, thought only that New Mexico meant mountains and Indians.

Altogether, it was a depressing summer for Oliver, divided between New York, where the writing went poorly, and Saunderstown, where his ailing father awaited an expected end. Oliver described it for Consuelo.

The family picture here is rather grim, as father has an attack of neuritis, which has stopped all his progress and he is naturally depressed by it. I go up at regular intervals and converse with him. I must say, he's game as the dickens. . . .

My God, this place is certainly family. I forget about it until I see the look of bewilderment crossing Oliver's [his son's] face as yet one more individual is introduced to him as a cousin or an aunt, and he finds cousins who are old and grey-haired, as well as contemporaries, and so forth. He has two great aunts here right now, one aunt and one uncle, two first cousins, four first cousins once removed, five second cousins, two more firsts once removed due over the weekend, and three elderly cousins whom I'm not savvy enough to classify.

That was the nature of a La Farge summer.

Finally his plans worked out. He made his sales and went west, and the two went to the Hopi country together. Later, Consuelo was in the East again, this time working for a literary agent, and Oliver brought her to Saunderstown to meet his mother and others of that multitudinous La Farge family. The commitment deepened.

That was also the summer at the end of which came the horrendous New England hurricane, which Oliver described with such breath-catching detail in *Raw Material:* the dinner "with boiled lobster" served by the family cook at nine o'clock after they had all escaped from the house as it seemed on the point of collapse. Part of the miracle of that escape was the rescue of Oliver's father, immobilized with heart disease, who had to be carried out of the house to a waiting car, then driven through lashing winds and toppling trees to a place of safety. As the car shuddered through the gale, Grant La Farge remarked with proper irony that his doctor had promised him he might go for a ride when the weather was suitable.

He survived that crisis, but a month later, in October 1938, Christopher Grant La Farge was dead, victim of his failing heart. In a marvelously evocative piece, Oliver wrote of his father's last days, "Old Man Facing Death," which he also included in *Raw Material.* The writing is stripped of sentiment, so that nothing stands between the word picture and the reader's perception, and the impact of a total sentiment comes through all the more sharply.

Of the piece, Christopher wrote: "I think it is an absolutely first-class job of work, moving, clear, honest, and altogether fine. I couldn't like it better."

The Baca family in Santa Fe was almost as numerous as, and in any case more voluble than, the Yankee La Farges. When Consuelo announced to her family in August 1939 that she and Oliver were to be married, she reported to him, "I broke the news last night—and such an explosion! Everyone had something to say and they all said it at the same time. . . . Mother, of course, is distressed about the Church business but she likes you so much that I hardly think it matters too awfully much."

The Bacas were Catholic, while Oliver, born in a part Catholic family, seems to have been baptized an Episcopalian.

He, meantime, had a different situation in which to maneuver. Telegrams began coming from Santa Fe, and Oliver had to send Consuelo a cease-and-desist request. He explained, "At present . . . the place [Saunderstown] is a madhouse. I am not going to spring the news on mother until some [of the guests] clear out, which will be at the end of this week. So until then, please tell people to send no more telegrams. Telegrams are taken down by whoever answers the phone, usually wrong, handed to mother or stuck on the mantelpiece, and become public property."

The quiet moment came, after a few days, and he reported that his mother was "not in the least surprised." Oliver's attentions obviously had not gone unnoticed by a watchful mother when Consuelo was a house guest at Saunderstown. "I think she rather enjoys its being a secret, and was very cute about it when we were alone." His postscript to that letter bespoke another era and a different style of life: "In writing to Mother, the address on the envelope should be Mrs. La Farge, with no first name. It's a very small matter, an English custom, but it pleases her."

The small private wedding took place in October, and Oliver moved out of the silk-stocking district where he and members of his family normally resided. Taking an apartment in Greenwich Village was dictated first by economy, since rentals were relatively cheap and his sales were still lagging. Of more importance, however, was the psychological release triggered by the decision. It was a first step in physically separating himself from a society with which he had a steadily diminishing correspondence—a step he had tried to take on previous occasions, only to haul back. Now, with a bride from a strong countering world, whom he deeply respected and loved, it seemed possible that he might find his own way. Anything seemed possible in the hazy sun of that New York October.

The wonder of that marriage grew steadily in his mind as the next years passed. He wrote to Christopher just after Pearl Harbor: "Consuelo is a swell wife for an artist. . . . She has a quick grasp of a sound general conception of work, and she would rather see me put out good stuff than make money on poorer stuff or in a regular job. And this is quite realistic in her, [since] our non-making of money has direct effects upon her—she cannot get a dress, she runs short on stockings, she does the cooking, our Christmas is run on a shoestring."

Actually, the second marriage did not come easily, for all the pleasantries leading up to it. The disastrous first marriage left him with disturbing doubts about himself, doubts which were reflected in his continuing failure to write pieces acceptable either to himself or to publishers. A full year went by between the time of their coming to an understanding and the marriage ceremony. The sense of wonder came after that.

On his fortieth birthday (1941), answering Christopher's congratulatory message (the three brothers were faithful in their remembrances), Oliver responded: "Had this birthday come three years ago I'd have been in a slough of despond. But now I'm in such a flood of beginnings and new ventures that my only worry is whether there'll be time for all of them before the joints stiffen or, more important, the mind sets. I have every reason to be grateful. . . . I have at last married the woman I ought to have married. . . ."

In that same letter, he announced: "I have a book in Houghton-Mifflin's hands, another one-third done in first draft, another under contract, another under discussion. How does that sound? I have been able to advise Columbia that I shall not teach there next year."

Renouncing the part-time teaching position at Columbia brought a special relief. He had taken the position in the hope of saving his marriage. But it proved nothing—teaching only took up time, on which he had prior demands, and the money he earned did not compensate for the time it took from writing. Resigning from Columbia was the final break from an experience that had fostered a sense of failure and self-doubt.

A Guggenheim Fellowship he won early in 1941 made the break possible, and almost immediately he and Consuelo were on their way west. He had been moving westward for a long time, since his first trip to the Navajo country, but only now did he fully realize how his bearings had shifted.

He wrote of his feeling about the West a few years later in a letter to Consuelo, during a train trip while on military duty:

> At Cheyenne it was very early morning—faint streaks of light— about four-thirty, and you could recognize the Western air and the hour when you stir in your bedroll and wonder if you should get up and light the fire. I thought of camps and of catching the horses, and longing filled me. The sunrise was over true mountains—peaks and snow and canyons and pine and aspen. We stopped at a little place on Bitter Creek to refuel, more mountains after that, then Utah with its mesas and canyons, and one stop in Nevada in desert country right under the mountains. It was still cold but the air was so clear and dry, and it was all *home,* all of it.

In the first enthusiasm of the move to the West, Oliver seriously considered becoming a rancher, or buying ranch property, which would have meant selling land he still held in Rhode Island. He wrote Francis, to whom he always turned for financial advice.

> I find [that] $7500 would install us very comfortably on a good productive farm, including ample allowance for incidental costs. . . . The more I look at the future, the more this seems like a good move to me. I seriously doubt that writing will support life in the

near future. The next solution is a Government job, but the land looks like the long term one. . . . Remember that irrigated land here is ridiculously fertile and easy to farm, and labor almost indecently cheap. Share arrangements are common and easily made.

Writing to Christopher in the same vein, he noted: "Since we must make up our minds to live in one place only, New Mexico is the place."

Meantime, they found a small house in Tesuque, just north of Santa Fe, and Oliver settled down to write. The elation born of a new beginning, a new freedom, caught him up and swept him along.

Ever since writing the story "No More Bohemia" in 1935, he had harbored the idea of expanding the action of that story into a full novel. He had made a start in 1938, but nothing much came of it. Between that year and 1941, in fact, he completed only five poorly contrived chapters. That was part of the frustration of those years. Now he took the story in hand and by October completed the first draft of *The Copper Pot*. He wrote with an urgency he had never known before as, with war coming closer, he sensed that the time was near when the pursuit of individual goals and careers would be sharply curtailed. His letters of the period reflect a growing awareness of what lay below the horizon.

Writing the novel also carried a sense of breaking away from the past. He had resisted being typed as a writer of Indian stories and at times complained about editors and publishers who seemed to solicit his reviewer's judgment exclusively for literary products in the Indian field. But in fact, for all his protests and complaints, his stories invariably turned out to be Indian stories; either Indians became involved in the action, or the plot turned on a character who was knowledgeable about Indians. As he said on one occasion, "Indians had got to me."

Now, at last, he had a theme without Indians. He informed Christopher: "My novel moves right along, and I'm having a world of fun with it. It is an enormous pleasure to write about contemporary white people out of my own knowledge. I thought it was going to be short, but it is turning out fairly long, partly because I know so much about my characters."

Later, after the manuscript had been delivered to the publisher at the end of 1941, he explained, "The book . . . is in many respects a 'first novel.' I believe it will show the faults that go with that. I've done my best to make a professional job, but I am so definitely shifting my bases and interests that young faults are bound to appear and I not spot them." In this, he seemed to be saying that, despite his voiced protests, he felt less comfortable, less in command, when he was not writing about Indians. They really had become part of the fabric of his intellectual life.

What is probably most remarkable about *The Copper Pot* is what it reveals about Oliver La Farge. The portrait of Tom Hartshorn, young painter making a start in New Orleans, a Yankee out of New England and Harvard, dreaming of the time when he will win the big prize and make it back to New York where success counts—all this closely parallels the course of La Farge's early life. The details differ and, in any case, are immaterial. He is looking at himself from a later perspective, explaining, in part excusing, but most emphatically condemning the inherited and acquired traits which led him finally to a disastrous personal decision. The references to Tom Hartshorn's experiences at prep school, which conditioned the growing boy to despise the "slack" life and "self-indulgence," are reminiscent of La Farge's Groton days; Chog's Cove, used also in *Long Pennant,* is the fictive name for Wickford on Narragansett Bay, near Saunderstown; and the Goldwater Prize, of course, has its counterpart in the Pulitzer Prize. The events in the book that correspond to La Farge's experiences are numerous, and they are often symbolically revealing.

There was a notable difference between Hartshorn's decision after initial success came his way and the real choice made by La Farge. Hartshorn did not marry the rich girl and entangle himself in the strands of proper social behavior. Rather, he first made that choice, then realized in a moment of great stress that the girl and her family offered only what he had always had, shelter: the shelter of a good school and college, a solid New England family, an allowance which made possible his Bohemian fling in New Orleans. To go through with the marriage was to destroy himself, or what through his own effort he might become.

The Frances Warren who comes between him and the rich girl and who may elude him in the end, is not just "the most beautiful woman in New Orleans"—she represents what Hartshorn most wants in life: success as a creative and effective human being. With that certainty fixed he sees no way out except to break his engagement—and all the while the unsuspecting fiancée is in New York with her mother, buying a trousseau.

"It wasn't Yankeeism I was against," Oliver explained to Christopher, "it was the idea that the purpose of [the artist's] work should be to maintain him in a certain style, whereas the purpose should be, of course, the work itself."

That was 1941—a year of freedom in which to write. He was finishing the second draft of *The Copper Pot* when the bombs fell on Pearl Harbor. What came after that led him to new discoveries about himself, to finding inner resources he had been unaware he possessed.

❖ XIII ❖

In Military Dress

THE BLOODY REALITY of the war hit New Mexico in the spring of 1942, when so many of her young men were killed or captured in the Japanese conquest of the Philippines. They were members of the 200th Coast Artillery (anti-aircraft) Regiment, originally New Mexico's National Guard Cavalry Unit. The personnel consisted of Spanish- and Anglo-Americans and some Indians. The Regiment was on Bataan in December 1941, and by April 1942 the war was over for the men in it.

Oliver wrote Christopher that spring: "So many men from New Mexico were caught in Bataan, that the news from there has crowded everything else to one side [in local newspapers]. The population of New Mexico is less than Rhode Island's, and having two thousand men in a body caught in that collapse involves pretty much everybody."

That same spring he went east, hoping "to get hooked up with useful war activity." Someone had suggested that he try for a place with Nelson Rockefeller's Office of Coordinator of Commercial and Cultural Relations Between the American Republics, but he was dubious. His comment to Christopher was: "There seems to be about the whole program a taint of innocent, Anglo-Saxon condescension and lack of grasp of the Latin American point of view." He preferred the State Department which, he thought, "knows its stuff in that line," and he explored that possibility.

In Washington in May he made the rounds of various military commands as well as the State Department and finally decided to apply to the Air Force, where he found encouragement. He was sent out to Bolling Field for his physical examination and there he was introduced to military procedure.

"I waited around there from twelve-thirty, and from two til four, stood around naked with a lot of other guys, getting one thing examined, then a long wait, then another, and finally staggered out, half-starved and weary, at four. Followed all the application papers, two sets of triplicates, and I was damned near dizzy by the time I got to some food at six-thirty."

He and Consuelo stayed in his brother's New York house in the East Sixties during part of that trip east. Christopher, who was out of town at the moment, had been an Air Warden for his block, and this brought Oliver to report: "I am causing considerable confusion on this block, as apparently people can't make out that this is their former and justly popular Air Warden only he shrunk, or just an unfortunate coincidence. They're always starting to speak to me and changing their minds. If the two of us get into uniform do let's take a stroll together. Consuelo says no, you should walk around the block and I walk about half a block behind you, and get people really confused."

The resemblance between these brothers was striking—in build, facial expression, and movement. There is a "La Farge physique" which has persisted through the generations, at least from John the grandfather. The salient features are a long narrow face, high-crowned head, long upper lip, and joints that seem to be wired together loosely. At age forty-four, Oliver stood five foot ten-and-a-half inches and weighed a hundred fifty pounds, about what he weighed when he rowed with the Harvard hundred fifty-pound varsity crew. The La Farges typically stayed lean and bony.

Oliver and Consuelo returned to Sante Fe to await his promised commission, and to fill in the time Oliver trained as a first aid instructor. Then, toward the end of June, he got the shocking news from the Adjutant General that he was "ineligible for miltary service, including limited service, because of old milinary type tuberculosis, pulmonary."

He told Christopher "As you can imagine, I leapt into the air like a scared duck, and came down running for the doctor. I felt pretty goddamned sick in several different ways and meanings."

Examined by a local tuberculosis specialist (New Mexico has always had good pulmonary men, because so many TB victims have gone to the Southwest to recuperate), he was told that he probably had had the disease in childhood. His lungs, as he said, looked "as if someone had stood off at extreme range and fired a load of number ten shot into them."

The verdict of the local experts, in consultation with the Army Surgeon in Albuquerque, was that he was completely cured and was physically fit for regular duty, including flying. The problem after that was to persuade the Adjutant General to modify his finding, and that took most of the summer. When a friend expressed surprise that he was not satisfied to be classified 4H, he exploded: "Can you see me coming home from deer hunting in the mountains next fall, or riding in the Apache country, and telling people that the reason I'm free to do these things is that I'm 4H? Jesus!"

He obtained the medical clearance, only to be delayed while the necessary papers were processed through the Air Transport Corps. What came through finally at the end of August was an offer of a temporary civilian appointment, "pending action on your application" for a commission, if he would pay his own way to Washington, "but without prejudice to payment therefore when ordered to active military duty." The wonderfully ambiguous Army language was signed by "Arnold, Commanding General, Army Air Force." Oliver informed his mother and, by round robin, the family. "It's a dream job, if they do finally give me the assignment originally planned; that is, writing the Air Transport Corps' own history for its own records. It will mean that I will visit their bases all over the world."

And so he went to Washington and into the horrors of finding bed and board and public transportation. The Bureau of Indian Affairs moved out to Chicago and other civilian agencies scattered to other localities, while thousands of hapless new employees of wartime agencies crossed and recrossed the city in search of living space. Oliver landed in one of the oldest and least habitable hotels in the city—a hotel which he said "would be considered a credit to Tierra Amarilla, New Mexico—however the coffee is good, the sheets are clean, and I am lucky to have found it."

By October he was reporting,

> The evolution of this command from two officers and a secretary fifteen months ago has been spectacular, and until my assignment started no single, coherent record of it existed. . . . Everyone is most cooperative, the atmosphere here is utterly informal, energetic, and marked by great pride in the Command's achievements. We believe that military history was made here last week. A dynamo of a Lieutenant Colonel had a job to do for which he needed a good writing man. He was assigned a former Washington correspondent, now a buck private on account of the draft, but far and away the best man for the job. Well, it was clear that he needed a helper, so the Colonel put a Lieutenant *under* him, to answer the phone and to run errands. Which everyone has taken calmly.

His captain's commission was not cleared until March 1943, which meant that for five months he sat in suspense, with no clear authority or responsibility, no travel orders—an idling civilian cog carried along by a driving military machine. As soon as the commission came through, however, things happened. He was sent at once to Officer's Training School at Miami Beach; he and his fellow candidates were housed at the Roney Plaza Hotel.

Oliver underwent an interesting transformation then. From school days on into adulthood, he had resisted regimentation. He had always been his own man, displaying a fine scorn for individuals who had no will and no passions of their own. Now, this quintessential individual found himself enjoying the marching around, singing in stride, drinking beer with his campmates. He wrote Consuelo: "Actually, this life is tough, but no tougher than lots I've done. I am making new friends, eating lots, drinking next to nothing, and while I expect that at times it will get awfully long and dragging and I expect to be tired plenty, I also expect to continue enjoying it. I wish you could see us marching when we're in the groove, it's not a bad sight. When I'm through this I shall honestly feel like a soldier."

Another day, he wrote:

> It's a man's life, man's jokes and kidding and fun, and while we have a normal percentage of sons-of-bitches in a group of some five hundred men, in the main it's a grand bunch.
>
> The other day we were coming down the street, singing, and a man and wife and six- or eight-year old girl were on the curb, new to Miami, I guess. As we went by the little girl cried out, and she was jumping with excitement, "Oh, daddy, isn't it wonderful!" And we all green and raw and our ranks out of order. I got a kick out of it. And also when at the end of a hard day the instructor says, "Gentlemen, if Squadron B does not win the ribbons for the guidon, it will not be the fault of Flight 3 (ours)."

It gave him particular pleasure to discover that he was in better physical shape than other men his own age or younger. It was hard work, but not nearly so hard as hunting in the New Mexico mountains at an altitude of eight to ten thousand feet. Certainly he was feeling self-satisfied when he wrote, "I thank God for my physical inheritance. When I see not only the men in my own over-40 group, but the younger ones stripped, I'm horrified. It makes me ashamed to be rated by age with these old ducks; I find them all so much older than I."

He also discovered, perhaps unexpectedly, that he got along with men whom he would not have met in ordinary circumstances, many of them men he would have avoided. The scuttlebutt as it reached him gave him points because he did not use his outside reputation to get special consideration. All in all, the atmosphere was good. "The ones I like, like me, and we go around together, which is very pleasant," he told Consuelo. Some months later, he was traveling by train with a fellow officer and a party of sailors. He remarked on the camaraderie, "the freedom of contact and the great friendliness between all men in uniform. It's all smiles and casual jokes and ready conversation." These were new experiences in a world of fresh discovery.

As an officer, finally, he could carry out his assignment. This involved traveling to all theaters where the Air Transport Command maintained stations for servicing aircraft in transit. He had to arrange for information to be sent back to headquarters in Washington, where it was abstracted and collated for use by the Command. He wrote *A Running Narrative* as well as special reports and established archives. As historian of the ATC, when finally staffed, La Farge was responsible for organizing and directing the work of some 250 men scattered all over the world.

A passage in *The Eagle in the Egg,* which is his account of the establishment and growth of the Air Transport Command, describes vividly the nature of that service and the men who served.

> These were not combat troops. . . . They were the pioneers and forerunners who, beginning as soon as hostilities started, prepared the way through new wildernesses for the fighting men. They worked in every variety of climate, under every imaginable discomfort, with little in the way of equipment, and with vast ingenuity, cloaked by secrecy then, forgotten later, lonely, weary, exposed to all the world's ills from those of the Arctic to those of the Equatorial jungles, and always game. They were exasperated by the unreality of some of the directions they received from Headquarters; they sometimes exasperated desperately busy men in Headquarters, trying to juggle the four corners of the world, by their irregularities. The books did not apply, so they threw them away. It could happen that, as they progressed from trial to error to knowledge, what began as a courageous violation of a regulation ended as standard operating procedure, ordained by regulation.

When he looked back on his own personal involvement in the war, he wrote:

> The important thing was the total change. Writers and scientists are solitary workers. They are inclined to associate principally with their own kind. They control their own hours and methods

of work. The Army Air Force provided a violent contrast. I was a member of a large headquarters, I had to learn to play on the team. I had to learn to work with men from totally alien backgrounds, and had the delight of becoming fast friends with many of them. Aviation had never interested me; it was essential that I become something of an expert on it. I had to become an administrator, an organizer, and something of a politician. . . . Nothing better, I think, could happen to a man in his forties.

In becoming a soldier, and an efficient one, he remained what he was, however—a sensitive observer of the world around him, and he wrote about it in non-military language. One imagines that army headquarters received few reports like La Farge's about Georgetown, Guiana, where he was inspecting a field installation: "The trip up-river was very lovely, with the water glassy and a double sunset, east and west, sending a dramatic streak of blue shadow radiating towards the center of the sky like an aurora borealis. . . . At two A.M., the cold woke me. I got up and put on pajamas, and was struck by the white brilliance of moonlight, and the sound of massed insects, which I had not heard in years. The moonlight in the tropics is a cold, white liquid fire filling the air and coating everything it touches." By contrast, his comments on the officers and personnel who manned these stations, the physical arrangements, the efficiency of operations were factual, balanced, properly military. No moonshine.

Wartime promotions came painlessly and promptly. By January 1944 Oliver made Major and reported to Christopher: "I am really very pleased about it, especially as, by special request of General George [his Commanding Officer], I was promoted when I was still two months short of the length of service in grade usually required."

When he was promoted to Lieutenant Colonel in August 1945, he wrote both his brothers. "As you boys have known me all your lives, pretty near, and as I am a democratic man at heart, under my rough, military exterior, you may in informal moments address me as plain Colonel, or occasionally, Col." He added, "This is kind of a consolation prize, as a matter of fact, for it looks as if

I might be a long time getting out of the army. They are not letting historical officers go at present."

It was July 1946 before he started terminal leave, and before that he remarked: "There's a curious letdown to being in uniform once the shooting's stopped. You begin to wonder when people will start asking you why you aren't doing something useful." During those earlier months, while Oliver waited to learn what the military would decide to do with him, he began a series of articles, partly reminiscent, partly as commentary on the sphere in which he had moved. With war overreaching all else, it seemed likely that life in America—especially in that segment in which he had grown up—would not return to what it had been. The transformation would be too deep and too inclusive. When he looked back on the experiences that had shaped his learning, he was not at all dismayed by the prospect of change. He had already rejected much of that learning.

The articles, as put together finally in *Raw Material* at the close of the war, are autobiographical in detail, but their intrinsic interest is the intellectual process they detail. Oliver's rejection of the past is stated with particular sharpness—almost savageness—in the pieces on Groton. The sketch of his father, "Old Man Facing Death," by contrast, is a graceful recognition of the love and wisdom which also dwelt in the house of his youth.

Back in civilian life, he at first found it difficult to demilitarize himself. He explained to Christopher, "In the army one is not self-starting; either one is told what to do, or the situations as they arise or the mail coming in have the same effect. I found myself terrified at the thought of sitting down with nothing before me but time and blank paper and proceeding to make something all on my own."

First he picked up the threads of his old Mayan research and the report that had remained unfinished since the 1932 expedition. Robert Redfield and Sol Tax of the University of Chicago anthropology faculty had seen the report in rough draft and they urged La Farge to prepare it for publication by the University of Chicago Press. Oliver was still in the army when he wrote Consuelo, in August 1944, "Redfield, of the University of Chicago, writes enthusiastically about my manuscript. 'I am very happy to see it again and to experience again an appreciation of its high merit.' " Dr. Melvin Tumin of the same faculty assisted with the final editing, and *Santa Eulalia: The Religion of a Cuchumatan Indian Town* was issued in 1947. "There will be no money in it," he told Christopher, "but a strong boost to my scientific standing, I think."

Dr. A. V. Kidder, with whom Oliver had studied anthropology at Harvard, had also seen a draft of the report in 1939, and had written, "I think you have done a bully job, and your interpretation of Indian character and life is remarkably penetrating. Hereafter I shall always look at these people with a more understanding eye."

At this time he also resumed correspondence with the University of Pennsylvania Museum and made plans to complete the editing of certain eighteenth century manuscripts containing Spanish and Mayan texts. Work on this material in the early 1930's had stopped before publication when museum funds ran short.

Oliver's military experience did not recede easily into the past. It was hard to believe, as the weeks passed in the fall of 1946, that he would not be returning to Washington—hard to believe "that I shan't be back in that grimy building tomorrow, and that C-54's, when I see one at all, will be merely a big thing passing high over head." Before it all got away, he undertook to write the history of the Air Transport Command from its first days as the Air Corps Ferrying Command, with the support of a second Guggenheim fellowship.

The creation of the Command, and its achievements, were among the truly remarkable developments of the war years. Before 1942, flights across the oceans of the world were still uncommon enough to be viewed as feats of daring. By the middle of 1945, the Air Transport Command operated twenty-six flights daily each way across the Atlantic and thirty-eight two-way crossings of the Pacific. In that same year, 71,000 tons of supplies were flown from India to China in a single month. The network of routes embraced the world. Between May and September 1945, some 160,000 men were flown to the United States from Europe, after Germany's defeat. From a handful of aircraft, none built specifically for cargo lift, the Command in the three-year span built up a fleet of a thousand four-engine and two thousand two-engine transport planes. The experience of those years made possible the Berlin airlift which saved free Berlin a few years later from capitulating to Communist demands.

In writing *The Eagle in the Egg,* which tells the story of the Command, La Farge's problem was to write something for a public "which, by the time it comes out, will have no use at all for war books." To avoid this difficulty he put the development of air transport in a broader context than immediate military experiences. He used those experiences rather to illustrate the evolution of a system of transportation for which there were no models. He attempted to write the military history, but with an analysis of factors—plane design, in-course services, pilot training—that could be applied in the future.

The war experience brought him a deepening awareness of himself and his relationship to his times and his society, which is what he wrote about in *Raw Material*—that often anguished reappraisal of his own development. His mother's death in September 1944, and the funeral which he could not attend because of war's urgency, made him realize how far he had traveled from the security of a Saunderstown childhood. He wrote Consuelo on September 20, "Mother will be buried today. I'm sorry not to be there." The past which his mother represented was forever gone. "The only place where I can carry my childhood is in me, the rest is fantasy. New Mexico is my home."

The loss, indeed, would have been more deeply mourned, more shattering—his mother, after all, had been the deepest influence in determining the climate of growth—had he not traveled that distance. The depth of feeling was there, but now it was tempered by the events and the passions of other times and other places.

A direct and simple affirmation of what he had achieved, more telling than anything he stated in *Raw Material,* is in a letter he wrote Christopher while he was still in uniform.

I'm coming more and more to think that the two best things which have happened to me since *Laughing Boy* are marrying Consuelo and entering the army. Consuelo has given me contentment, which it has taken me a long time to realize and get used to, and both she and the army have given me self-confidence. The army has given me something else, a perception of internal disorderliness—that's not right, I don't know just how to say it, but I look back upon myself in recent civilian life and I look messy, unkempt, and dandruffy to myself. I don't mean physically, but in my *Modus Operandi.* I certainly hope I never again have to be a cog in a huge organization, and even more that never again shall I have to run an organization of many people, but I'm deeply grateful for the experience.

❖ XIV ❖

Embattled Citizens

INDIANS RETURNING to their home communities from war service too often found those communities shattered by the effects of the economic pressure of the war years. The various relief and rehabilitation programs which operated prior to the war and provided work in road construction, range improvement, irrigation projects, timber management, family housing, and dozens of related activities gave way to the war effort. This caused no hardship in the war period, since the families of servicemen received monthly cash allowances, and war industries and agriculture provided jobs for those who were not in uniform. War's end brought this to a crashing halt. The sons and fathers who had been contributing to family support from their military pay went jobless. The war workers also streamed back as industry shut down.

Not only were the prewar, depression-spawned programs gone, but the federal Indian service had been nearly dismantled during the war. Most reservations lacked personnel to operate schools and hospitals and the various resource development activities which provided jobs. Operating funds had been reduced to a minimum and would not regain lost ground for several years. The land acquisition program which, before the war, was gradually restoring the resource base for a number of tribes was discontinued, and there were no credit funds to invest in family rehabilitation. Both had been major economic booster programs initiated by the Indian Reorganization Act.

Returning Indians soon noticed other problems. There was a growing demand, among the western states primarily, that Indian lands be made taxable or that federal monies be paid to the states in lieu of taxes. These states through their congressional and other leaders complained that large percentages of land within their boundaries were federally owned—in this, they lumped Indian lands with federal lands—and therefore exempt from state taxation. For the first time, upon the insistence of some states, language was inserted in the Interior Department Appropriation Act prohibiting the purchase of land for Indians which would further reduce the tax base. As a corollary to this demand, the cry was raised, to become quite shrill in a few years, that the government divest itself of trust responsibility for Indian property and "get out of the Indian business." Not only would Indian lands then become taxable—and available for purchase or acquisition by whatever means—but government costs would be reduced by some insignificant amount.

When La Farge resumed active participation in the Association on American Indian Affairs—he was reelected president in 1948 —these issues were coming into focus and would soon be a central part of the government-Indian relationship. The lines of conflict would not always be expressed in terms of taxation and trusteeship, but would break out at any point where Indian interests were vulnerable to attack. Very quickly La Farge and the association were fighting skirmishes and major battles on many fronts. In the heat of these conflicts, the association came of age as an effective and respected citizen force.

The first major encounter of the postwar period occurred in the course of enacting legislation to rescue the Navajo Indians from disaster. Conditions among the Navajos had been progressively worsening since the 1930's, when it was first realized that runaway population growth had already exceeded physical resources. As a result of overuse of the grazing land on which the Navajo economy depended, the resources were deteriorating. Deterioration in this case meant severe erosion of surface acreage and a consequent further loss of carrying capacity. Various agencies had studied the problem and reported on it, including the National Association on Indian Affairs in 1937.

After the war, with servicemen and war workers returning and begetting more children, the threat of actual starvation came close to many families. The Red Cross and various private charities averted ultimate disaster on several occasions. As the crisis deepened, action was still delayed, while further reports were written—a Bureau report in 1947, one by Charles Collier in 1948, and in the same year a survey of educational needs by Dr. George I. Sanchez, the latter two at the request of the Secretary of the Interior. Then the Secretary, also in 1948, published his own report and recommendations—*A Long Range Program for Navajo Rehabilitation* —on which a number of experts collaborated.

How much longer action might have been delayed can only be conjectured, but in February 1949 a harsh winter brought matters to a head and forced decisions. One of the worst blizzards in local history struck the high plateau country where the Navajos live. The Air Force, the Navy, and National Guard units had to fly emergency supplies to the snowbound people and their livestock and news of the Navajo plight reached the front pages of newspapers all across the country. The Hearst Press, which was opposed to the Marshall Plan for rescuing a bankrupt Europe, used the Navajo tragedy as a club to belabor the national administration. One picture magazine sent a team to the scene and posed a Navajo child weeping in a snow bank dressed only in an undershirt. A mercy plane flying low over a hogan dropped a sack of canned milk which crushed a woman's skull. As it happened, the woman's husband had just struggled through the snow from a trading post, fifteen miles away, on horseback, laden with groceries.

What emerged in 1949 was a legislative proposal "to promote the rehabilitation of the Navajo and Hopi tribes of Indians." The Hopis were included since their reservation exists as an island completely surrounded by Navajos and was subject to the same economic factors that brought ruin to the Navajos, but all the publicity had centered on the latter. The proposed legislation had actually been introduced in the House and Senate in 1948; hearings had been held in the spring of that year, at which massive testimony in favor of the proposal was offered by Navajo and Hopi representatives and by numerous organizations, including the Association on American Indian Affairs, but no action was taken by either house. The next winter's tragedy succeeded in bringing the proposed legislation out of committee the following spring—but then it met unexpected trouble.

The bill provided for a ten-year program, of which resource conservation and management, irrigation works, school and hospital construction, roads, credit financing, and domestic and stock water development were the principal features, with an authorization of $88,570,000 to be appropriated over the ten-year period.

When the bill reached the House, a congressman from New Mexico, Antonio Fernandez, threw out a challenge. He insisted upon an amendment providing that henceforth the Navajo and Hopi Indians would be subject to state law and state courts, while federal law along with tribal customary law would apply in other instances. But that was not all. The amendment would also require the federal Social Security Administration to pay 80 percent of the state's share of the cost of providing assistance to old people, dependent children, and the blind.

La Farge discussed the amendment in his weekly column for the *Santa Fe New Mexican* in August 1949, expressing surprise that the newspapers of the state showed so little interest in the legislation. He chided them for thinking of Indian affairs as "something remote" and of no common concern, then pointed out: "If it [the rehabilitation bill] becomes law, and if Congress then makes the appropriations it authorizes, close to $90 million will be spent in Arizona and New Mexico. That's a nice piece of change. It means more than that: By setting the Navajos and Hopis on their feet, it will give us 65,000 good customers in our own backyard. There are other advantages in wiping out illiteracy, disease, and crime within our borders. By and large, you'd think that the papers would follow the course of this bill fairly closely."

Next he turned to the amendment and raised some questions

about extending state law to some of "the biggest, wildest, most roadless Indian area in the country." He noted:

> The existing federal laws are not repealed, the tribal ordinances remain in existence, and so does tribal "customary law," the ancient laws which remain in effect whenever federal law or tribal ordinances have not replaced them. . . . This is really going to be fun for the judges. If a homicide occurs, is it to be considered a federal homicide, a New Mexico one, or an old tribal custom? What is a judge going to do with a countersuit against a tribal custom divorce? Under Navajo tribal custom, if, for instance, the wife puts the husband's goods out of the hogan, the marriage is ended. Suppose the husband countersues?"

What he was pointing out, without saying it bluntly (after all, Fernandez was a New Mexican with whom he had to live), was the folly of using an urgent human appeal as a means of serving a wholly unrelated interest. Extending state law to these reservations would ultimately have resulted in a state tax levy against Indian lands to finance the cost of law enforcement.

The proposal to excuse Arizona and New Mexico from a substantial social security payment aroused protests all across the country, since it threatened segregated treatment for all Indian tribes and, indeed, other minority groups, ethnic or otherwise. Some members of Congress served notice that if the provision became law, they would insist on similar treatment for their own states. The bill passed the House with the Fernandez amendment, emerged intact from a conference of House and Senate members, and was laid before President Truman for signature.

The subsequent emergency meeting of the Navajo Tribal Council in October 1949 was conducted in bitterness and in confusion. A previous meeting had given unanimous approval to the pending legislation, and even after the Fernandez amendment was adopted the tribal leaders were at first willing to agree, rather than risk defeat if they expressed disapproval.

Then in the fall, when former Commissioner John Collier urged them to voice objection, and when their friend Oliver La

Farge suggested that their tribal land and water rights might be jeopardized if they came under state law, the leaders were deeply disturbed. One council member, who was also a medicine man and later would be a tribal judge, expressed what might have been in many minds as the Navajos contemplated the coming of state law to the reservation. He declared: "I feel that, with this amendment, our ceremonialism would not last long. And we are dependent upon these ceremonies to save us and cure us. By carefully carrying out these ceremonies we are saved from danger, and we manage to continue living as a group."

On October 13, after two days of strenuous discussion, the council voted to renounce its previous endorsement and asked the President to veto the measure. President Truman accepted this recommendation reluctantly, he told Congress. He wrote in his veto message: "In reaching my decision I have been greatly influenced by the attitude of the Navajo Indians. . . . They greatly favor the long-range rehabilitation program which the bill proposes but much as they favor the constructive provisions of the bill, they fear section nine [the Fernandez amendment] more."

It was a signal occasion. Presidents have not been known to override Congress at the request of a tribe of Indians. The upshot of the congressional maneuver was to delay until April 19, 1950, some six months, the adoption of a program to relieve distress among a suffering people.

While the problems of the Navajo and Hopi Indians were being discussed in and out of Congress, the association joined a struggle to extend the franchise to the Indians of Arizona and New Mexico, the only states that as late as 1948 denied Indians the right to vote. All Indians born in the United States were made citizens by act of Congress in 1924—the Indians did not request this, and some tribes actively opposed the beneficent gesture, thinking it might somehow reduce their sovereignty—but in the matter of voting, each state sets forth its own qualifications, within the terms of the Constitution.

A report of the President's Committee on Civil Rights, *To Secure These Rights,* issued in 1947, called attention to the disfranchisement of Arizona and New Mexico Indians. The report noted, "These states have constitutional provisions which have been used to disfranchise Indians. In New Mexico, the Constitution should be amended to remove the bar against voting by 'Indians not taxed.' This may not be necessary in Arizona where the Constitution excludes from the ballot 'persons under guardianship.'"

Calling public attention to the problem served a good purpose, but it was unlikely that either state would act voluntarily to change its basic law or the attitudes that validated the law. In New Mexico in 1948, the majority party held a margin of 8,000 votes, and an estimated 20,000 Indians of voting age, if enfranchised, might make the mistake of voting for the other party. What was needed in each state were Indians willing to come forward and challenge the political order.

It was not an easy task for an Indian to assume. In the past, a friendly lawyer would initiate a law suit only to have the Indian in whose name the action was brought withdraw, out of fear of reprisal. The reprisal might, indeed, come from the Indian Pueblo or tribe. The elders in most southwestern Indian communities were strongly opposed to voting in white men's elections, because they did not want white politicians electioneering in the community. They also feared that the vote would somehow lead to taxation of their lands and to forced tax sales.

Returning war veterans, however, fresh from the experience of being treated as equals by their comrades in arms, objected to discrimination at the polls and were not inhibited by the warnings of their elders. In both Arizona and New Mexico, action was initiated by former servicemen—the New Mexico plaintiff was a discharged Marine sergeant and candidate for a master's degree at the University of New Mexico.

Felix S. Cohen, who, as mentioned above, became counsel for the Association on American Indian Affairs in May 1948, represented the association in filing briefs *amici curiae* in each case.

In reversing the trial court which had denied the Indian petition for a writ requiring a county elections board to register

Indians, the Arizona Supreme Court declared that it found no evidence to indicate that the framers of the state constitution intended to include Indians in the category "persons under guardianship," from whom the franchise should be withheld. It was not a legislative barrier, the court held, but "a tortuous construction by the judicial branch" which had enabled discrimination against Indians.

In demolishing this "tortuous construction," the state supreme court declared:

> No superintendent or other official or employee of the United States has custody of the person of the plaintiffs. They are not confined to the reservation and may leave it at any time they so desire. The plaintiffs are under no duty to follow the advice or instructions of any federal officials in selecting a place to live. The power of the Commissioner of Indian Affairs, or of the local superintendent, to decide what people might visit an Indian reservation and meet the Indians thereon was abolished in 1934. The plaintiffs have full and untrammeled right to utilize their own property (except their interest in land or other property to which the federal government has a trustee's title) as they see fit and to receive and expend income therefrom without federal interference. . . .

In New Mexico, a special federal panel of three judges heard the Indian plea and ruled that the state constitutional provision disqualifying "Indians not taxed" was in conflict with the Fifteenth Amendment, and that in fact Indians pay income taxes, sales taxes, excise taxes, and are exempt only from *ad valorem* taxes on real estate held in trust for them by the government. The constitutional provision was ruled void and the court declared that "No Indian shall hereafter be disqualified from voting on the ground that he is an 'Indian not taxed.' "

That was in 1948. Early the following year the New Mexico legislature attempted to circumvent the court's ruling by adopting legislation specifically aimed at denying the ballot to Indians. La Farge reported to the association:

> The bill took us completely by surprise. Within five days the governor of the state was required either to sign it or kill it by pocket

veto. The pressure on him to sign was strong. Your Association sent out a flood of telegrams to people of prominence and conscience throughout the country, asking them to wire the governor. . . . The governor was astounded by the wires pouring in upon him, and I am in a position to know that it was these wires which decided him finally to kill the bill—an act of political courage, incidentally, for which Governor Mabry deserves real credit."

While these legal actions were proceeding, the association joined battle with the same two states over their refusal to include Indians in the social security benefits paid to all other citizens. In a petition addressed to the President, the Administrator of Social Security, and the Secretary of the Interior, the association reminded these officials that the Social Security Act required that public assistance be rendered "without discrimination because of race or color," in spite of which the Indians of Arizona and New Mexico were excluded.

The petition continued:

This callous denial of rights guaranteed by national law has intensified suffering among American Indian people in New Mexico and Arizona for the past fourteen years. These people are among the most deprived of our country. The 61,000 Navajos, for example, are without adequate education, without adequate medical care, and without an adequate economic base for minimal standards of living. Yet thousands of such Indian families, themselves impoverished, have had to bear the added burden of indigent helpless and dependent relatives who are being denied the federal assistance which is their statutory right. It is estimated that not less than 10,000 members of the Navajo tribe are eligible for social security benefits. . . .

The two states had pleaded their own poverty as justification for the policy they had pursued; if benefits were paid to Indian as well as non-Indian claimants, all would receive smaller payments. The association's answer was blunt. "In explaining their practice of racial discrimination, these two states assert the justice of such discrimination! For on what other basis can it be claimed that those of Indian ancestry shall be sentenced to starvation and death so that those of other racial origins may have greater benefits?" As it happened, the two states were rescued by the Congress, which allowed to pass into law that part of the Fernandez Amendment requiring the federal government to refund an amount up to 80 percent of the state's share of social security payments to Indian beneficiaries.

Discrimination against Indians at times could best be characterized as mere heedlessness not related to motives of spoliation, a reflection of local folk ways rather than a premeditated attack. This was the case when four Indian young men for whom the association waged a successful legal defense, were arrested in Moscow, Idaho, for sheep stealing.

The four men, none older than twenty-one, while on a drinking bout to celebrate the fact that one of them had just become a father, picked up a sheep which ambled down the road in front of their car. They caught the sheep, put it in the trunk of the car, then forgot about it as they continued to drink to the health of the new father. Eventually their behavior attracted the attention of a law officer in the little Idaho town and they were arrested and discovered to have the sheep. When they came before the local district court, charged with grand larceny, the county prosecutor advised them to plead guilty as the judge was known to be lenient and would probably let them off with a light sentence. The judge's leniency seemed to extend only to white offenders, not to Indians. The four defendants were given the maximum penalty of fourteen years in prison.

Only then did the Indians seek legal assistance. A local attorney in their behalf appealed to the court to set aside the sentence and allow the four defendants to plead not guilty and stand trial. The court, presided over by the same trial judge, refused the appeal.

The case reached the newspapers then because of what seemed "cruel and unusual punishment," and the association, represented by Felix Cohen, joined the local attorney in carrying the appeal to the Idaho Supreme Court. Two points were raised: the Indians had not been advised of their rights or of the meaning of a plea of guilty to a charge of grand larceny; and they had not been told that they were entitled to be represented by legal counsel. On the latter point the trial judge said ingenuously: "If they had made up their minds that they didn't want an attorney, certainly I was not going to employ one for them."

The state supreme court heard the case in June 1950 and agreed that the rights of the Indians had not been properly safeguarded, as argued. By unanimous decision the court set aside the lower court verdict, whereupon a prosecuting attorney observed: "I'm pretty well convinced that the people of this part of the state of Idaho don't want these Indians prosecuted further." The newspapers of Idaho, stimulated by unfavorable press comment from as far away as Boston and New York, had become sharply critical of the handling of the case. The Lewiston, Idaho, *Morning Tribune's* comment reflected the common feeling in the region: "A light sentence is frequently promised in return for guilty pleas. Indians, who feel the cards are stacked against them, give in. The four Indians at Moscow shuffled into court with this attitude. But when the judge decreed fourteen years and the citizens of the Moscow region protested, the defendants elected to fight it out."

In its various efforts to win justice and fair dealing for the Indians in these controversies, the association rarely had to act alone, although it was willing to do so. Usually, however, in any major conflict involving a clash of moral or legal principles, the association happily found itself joined by other aroused citizens and official agencies. This was notably the case when the Native Village of Karluk, an Alaskan village of Aleut fishermen, appeared before the United States Supreme Court in defense of its traditional fishing grounds. Here the villagers' representatives were joined by the Alaskan Native Brotherhood, representing all Alaska Indians, The National Congress of American Indians, representing the Indians of the United States and Alaska, the American Civil Liberties Union, and the Association on American Indian Affairs. At issue was the right of a native village, and the Secretary of the

Interior acting in behalf of the village, to protect its livelihood against the invasion of powerful commercial fishing companies.

The action was initiated in June 1946 by seven major fish packing companies, who sought an injunction to set aside Department of Interior regulations protecting the off-shore waters adjacent to the village of Karluk. Earlier, in May 1943, the Secretary had established a reservation for the natives of this village, under authority vested in him by the Alaska Indian Welfare Act of 1936. The natives had requested the reservation, had marked the boundaries of the lands and waters they traditionally occupied and used, and then—after the Secretary issued a public land order proclaiming the fact—had voted affirmatively to accept the reservation. This was the procedure prescribed by the 1936 Act, and it was intended to provide a means by which the natives of Alaska might gain title to "any lands actually in their use or occupation or now claimed by them."

The land surface claimed by the natives was accepted by the Secretary, after the proper field investigation, and he then extended the boundaries 3,000 feet offshore—in accordance with an earlier Supreme Court decision as a precedent. The village of Karluk, located at the mouth of a small river, was the site of an extremely large and valuable salmon run—so valuable that commercial fishing and canning companies had been encroaching upon the area for some years and crowding the natives into less productive locations. This encroachment had continued until the village's total income was jeopardized. To protect the native waters, the Alaska fishing regulations for the 1946 season included for the first time a prohibition against commercial fishing in Karluk Reservation waters, except as individual operators might be authorized and licensed by the village.

The legal action instituted by the big companies was not directed at the village of Karluk, as that might have brought before the court the history of how the companies had exploited the native resources. Instead, action was confined to the single issue of the 1946 fishing regulations, which the companies argued were discriminatory and therefore illegal. Thus, the case *Grimes* v. *Hynes* was, superficially, a contest between Grimes Packing Company and Frank Hynes, Regional Director of the Fish and Wildlife Service of the Department of the Interior. The village of Karluk was not represented when the case went to trial. The federal district court in Alaska even ruled out information intended to explain why the Karluk Reservation had been created and why the natives had been protected in their fishing rights. The court admitted none of this in issuing the injunction requested by the companies. The Circuit Court of Appeals in San Francisco affirmed the findings of the lower court in 1947, and the case was carried by the government to the Supreme Court.

In this appeal the government was allowed to present the larger issue, namely, the power of the Secretary of the Interior to grant title to lands occupied by natives of Alaska, with adjacent waters, and to provide for their protection against trespass. Also the village of Karluk and the private organizations mentioned above were permitted to file briefs as friends of the court.

The brief submitted by the association stated: "What is at stake in this case is not an ancient wrong to ancestors of those who now seek redress; it is a present assault, recently initiated and not yet fully consummated, against the basic human rights of the Karluk natives."

Thus the record which the canning industry had tried to keep out of court came under judicial review. On May 31, 1949, the Supreme Court reversed the lower court and confirmed the rights of the natives in their traditional lands and waters as well as the authority of the Secretary to protect those rights.

The fight did not end there, however; it was carried into Congress, and in time the Secretary was stripped of his authority under the 1936 Alaska Native Welfare Act to reserve for exclusive native use lands which natives had occupied since before the coming of the white men.

The closing years of the long Democratic control in Washington began to cast shadows across the Indian future and to obscure some of the gains that had been achieved in the early enthusiasm of the Roosevelt era. One of the most disturbing counterthrusts against the progress of those years was an attempt by the new Commissioner of Indian Affairs, Dillon S. Myer, to place severe limitations on the freedom of Indian tribes to contract with attorneys of their own choice. Evidently annoyed with attorneys who counseled their tribal clients to challenge actions taken or proposed by him, the Commissioner in November 1950 issued a "circular letter" to field officials and to tribes, stating in minute detail the conditions which future tribal attorney contracts must satisfy. A committee of the American Bar Association, together with the American Civil Liberties Union, the National Congress of American Indians, and the Association on American Indian Affairs all joined in issuing a *Memorandum on the Indians' Right to Counsel,* which attacked the commissioner's "circular letter" on grounds of law and public policy.

Congress in 1872 had given the Secretary of the Interior practically unlimited discretionary power over tribal contracts, and the Secretary in recent years had delegated his authority to the commissioner. The Indian Reorganization Act of 1934 circumscribed this bureaucratic control. For tribes that accepted the Act, discretionary power was limited to "choice of counsel and fixing of fees." What incensed civil liberties groups as well as private attorneys was that the commissioner's "circular letter," under the guise of establishing guidelines for "choice of counsel," had set forth a schedule of requirements relating to length of term of a contract, procedure for terminating a contract, and for reporting (to the commissioner, not to the Indians), which clearly exceeded the purpose of the liberalizing 1934 Act.

Charles L. Black, Jr., Professor of Law at Columbia University and chairman of the association's legal committee, wrote of these requirements:

> They reverse as sharply as possible a trend which everyone had previously assumed to be entirely desirable and quite irreversible. For the first time probably within living memory, the Indian is being subjected, in a matter of major importance, to more rather

than less Bureau control. The Bureau may sometimes have failed to do all it could to help the Indian advance; it may even on rare occasions have retarded his progress; but it has been a long time since it pushed him back. What a proud achievement for an Indian administration in mid-Twentieth Century!

Of more serious consequence, Black wrote of the *Rules* presently issued, based on the terms of the "circular letter:"

> They force the wishes, the conveniences, the particular circumstances of the real parties at interest (the tribe and the attorney) into the mold of Bureau desire. They embarrass Indians in hiring the lawyer they want, and in making with him the arrangements they want; they hamstring the lawyer in normal dealings with the tribe, and will undoubtedly tend toward making him feel, unless he is unusually strongminded, that he is really working for the Bureau, with the tribe as nominal client; indeed, the better lawyer, accustomed to normal conditions of practice, will think long before he takes on an unheard of amount of supervision and harassment. They confer upon the Commissioner (most improperly, since his Bureau often stands in a position legally adverse to that of a tribe) multifarious and hazy powers exercisable at discretion over the inception, the performance, and the termination of contracts between other people. They nibble away, section by section, the Indians' right to counsel, the key to all other rights under law.

The *Rules* were published in the *Federal Register,* without provision for a public hearing. The outcry across the country was so articulate and came from so many quarters, however, that the Secretary of the Interior announced a public hearing for January 1952. The association reported, "The resultant attendance was dramatic and inspiring. Indian delegates from tribes, and from regional and national inter-tribal organizations, whose members total three hundred thousand, traveled thousands of miles to offer testimony. To this was added protests by spokesmen for national civic, welfare, labor, and legal groups." In response to such universal disapproval, the Secretary withdrew the proposed *Rules,* but without proposing substitute measures. For the time being, the situation was left unresolved—a condition not uncharacteristic of Indian affairs administration.

The years of Democratic control were coming to a close and a new administration would take command in 1953. If the years just passed had seemed at times to diminish the Indians' status and to threaten tribes with ultimate dispersal, what waited just over the horizon was a holocaust in the making.

✤ XV ✤

The Rumble and the Roar

As THE NEW ADMINISTRATION moved into Washington in 1953, La Farge was frankly optimistic that the recent deterioration in the management of Indian affairs would be reversed. The long Democratic administration, he felt, had become tired and inflexible. "What began with new thinking and fundamental reforms had developed the common phenomena of fixed thinking and of commitments to policies, breeding rigidity and excessive conservatism."

Thinking no doubt of the struggles over attorney contracts and a dozen other clashes with the bureaucracy, he wrote in his annual report, in the spring of 1953: "In the last years, the administration even swung back towards outright reaction with a regrettable revival of the archaic concept of 'wardship,' the false myth as to the Indians' status that has been used for more than a century to excuse dominating their daily lives."

His understanding of the Indian situation had been sharpened greatly by those encounters and by his close association with students of law and administration. What had become quite clear was that basic to the disabilities which complicate the lives of Indians —now withholding the right to vote, at another time denying social security benefits, and at still other times impeding their freedom to contract for services—was the mistaken notion that Indians are not whole persons, that they are wards of a benevolent nation and incapable of acting responsibly for themselves. Under the guise of this supposition, states refuse to provide free schooling for Indians, for example, holding that that is federal responsibility; and the federal government pursues a policy of colonial administration within an Indian reservation, because the Indians are in a "state of tutelage." The fact that the states refuse free education and that the federal government acts as decision-maker seems to confirm for everyone the conclusion that Indians are not legally competent. From this supposition and its corollaries flowed a wide range of consequences through the years. "Wardship" became a magic word, as Felix Cohen observed.

Writing in *The American Indian* (summer of 1953), Cohen noted:

> Over the years, any order or command or sale or lease for which no justification could be found in any treaty or act of Congress came to be justified by [Indian agents and Indian commissioners] as an act of "guardianship," and every denial of civil, political, or economic rights to Indians came to be blamed on their alleged "wardship." Under the reign of these magic words nothing Indian was safe. The Indian's hair was cut, his dances were forbidden, his oil lands, timberlands, and grazing lands were disposed of, by Indian agents and Indian Commissioners for whom the magic word "wardship" always made up for any lack of statutory authority. Through constant repetition of that phrase by the persons having greatest influence in shaping public opinion, the idea of wardship under a "Great White Father" became firmly fixed in the popular imagination.

Cohen remarked on "the tendency of non-lawyers to confuse two very different legal relationships—trusteeship and guardianship. Guardianship is a relation that limits the personal rights of a ward. Trusteeship is a relation that limits the property rights of a trustee and makes the trustee the servant of the trust beneficiary." Indians are beneficiaries of a trust—not wards under a guardian.

The tendency to revert to these harsh practices would be renounced, La Farge reassured the 1953 meeting. "The administration has been deeply pledged by the President to operate in consultation with Indians and fully to respect the status of the

Indians as American citizens. There is every indication that the Secretary of the Interior [Douglas McKay] and his principal subordinates subscribe to this commitment. They are sincere and well-intentioned officials."

Exactly a year later, again reporting to the membership of the association in a speech entitled "Freedom, Equality, Brotherhood," La Farge was thoroughly disillusioned and caustic in his observations. "The first two words of the title of this article are being cynically debauched today to mask the most wholesale and heartless attack upon the surviving Indians of the United States that has occurred in the entire history of the Republic." Obviously events during that interval had completely altered the outlook. The 1954 report sketched out in bold, at times brutal, terms what had happened to bring about so remarkable a change.

La Farge began his outline of those events by pointing out that "wardship," which suggests limitations on personal freedom and citizenship, lends itself to the manipulations of those who would plunder the Indians. He noted:

> In the desert lands of the Navajos are oil, helium, uranium, and vanadium. Certain Alaskan tribes lay claim to the best salmon areas. Here are millions of feet of the finest timber, here is the best grazing in the northern plains, and here, having been restored by careful use since the tribe took the range over for itself, is priceless cattle country in the arid Southwest—and all in the hands of Indians, all protected!
>
> The loot is rich indeed. How to get at it? The men of greed put their heads together. It is really quite simple. . . . On the one hand they have the impatient ones, on the other the ignorant well-intentioned. The same slogans will capture both groups. . . .

Two actions in the Eighty-third Congress (1953–54) gave rise to La Farge's pessimism. Public Law 280 extended state law to the Indians of five states, at the request of the Indians of those states, but it also authorized any state in which reservations were located to assume civil and criminal jurisdiction without consulting the Indians. The other was the adoption of House Concurrent Resolution 108 (both of these enactments came in the month of August, 1953), which expressed it as "the sense of Congress" that "as rapidly as possible" the special legal status of all Indians was to be terminated, and the Secretary of the Interior was directed to recommend legislation carrying out this general policy. These actions, in La Farge's view—a view shared by Indian leaders all across the country, by many lawyers, and even by some Congressmen—if not viciously intended, readily lent themselves to vicious purposes.

> There are two principal ends to be reached: Destroy tribal corporate existence, and, with that, corporate ownership of property, and terminate the trust status of property. The organized tribes are not only becoming annoyingly able competitors in the exploitation of their own assets, but they are too effective in defending themselves and in making themselves heard. . . . You do not, of course, introduce a bill to break up tribal organizations. What you do is enact a bill enabling any state to extend civil and criminal jurisdiction over the Indians within its borders any time it chooses. Where that occurs, most of the authorities of tribal government are automatically terminated, since they are based on Indian and Federal jurisdiction.
>
> You allege that this bill will give the Indians "equality," and thus you get the well-intentioned to go along with it. . . . In California, where state jurisdiction became effective immediately, the authorities promptly started arresting Indians for exercising their ancient right of hunting and fishing on their own land. It happens that these Indians control some very fine hunting and fishing areas, which they reserve for their own use. But they are equal now, and they will shortly learn better.

House Concurrent Resolution 108 authorized a more direct attack, and from it resulted a number of bills, two of which were directed at the Klamath tribe of Oregon and the Menominees of Wisconsin, owners of valuable timberlands. These bills, as La Farge pointed out, abolished tribal government and tribal or group business corporations, and ended the trust. "They terminate all Indian rights. In fact, if enacted, then the members of the tribe concerned will no longer be Indians! The powers of Congress are truly remarkable."

> No legislation of the sort just described can get anywhere when the Department of the Interior is worth its salt. No Secretary of the Interior since Albert B. Fall [who was convicted of misusing his office and served a prison term] has tolerated legislation of this sort, and none has found it difficult to rally men of good will in both houses of Congress to defeat similar measures. Sad to relate, the present Department is not only tolerating it, but collaborating in it. The President, whose interest in Indian Affairs is so genuine and whose pledges to the Indians had been so definite, is simply being ignored.

La Farge's keenest disappointment was in the President. During the 1952 campaign Eisenhower had stopped over in Albuquerque. Consuelo's mother sat on the platform with him when he spoke there and campaigned for him through the mountain villages of New Mexico. Eisenhower as President was of a different order. In October 1953, Oliver wrote to Christopher, describing his frustration:

> I regret to say that the present administration seems to be bent upon wiping the Indian out; we have never seen anything so grave. We are desperately trying to get through to the President, who is clearly a man of good will, and explicitly so in regard to Indians, but it is most difficult. I hear from many sources that he does not like to read, goes in heavily for verbal briefing, and does not seriously read the newspapers. The result is, as nearly as we can see, that he is somewhat of a captive of his advisors, and, in the Department of the Interior, he has very bad advisors—men who have shown themselves prepared to misrepresent situations to him to obtain their ends, which is plain disloyalty. At this juncture, Felix Cohen, our attorney, and attorney for a number of tribes, has just recently died. It's like losing your only good fullback, and an outstanding star, in the first quarter of your hardest game.

The loss of Felix Cohen, indeed, was mourned all through the Indian country. Son of Morris L. Cohen, the philosopher, Felix had joined the solicitor's office of the Department of the Interior early in the New Deal, coming fresh from a term as law clerk for Felix Frankfurter. He was a principal draftsman of the Indian Reorganization Act and the Indian Claims Commission Act, and editor of the *Handbook of Federal Indian Law* (1940), a monumental, annotated compilation of statutory law, court decisions, administrative and judicial rulings, and case listings dealing with the legal status of Indians. His *Powers of Indian Tribes,* published in 1934 soon after he joined the Interior legal staff when he was still only twenty-seven years old, was the earliest attempt to bring together a coherent statement of the residual powers still attached to original tribal sovereignty. It was the legal base underpinning the Indian Reorganization Act.

The criticism of the President that La Farge so sharply expressed had its source in the disastrous results that flowed from the policies and activities of the new administration. Everything that he and the Association and men like Rhoads and Scattergood, John Collier and Felix Cohen had advocated for so long, and much of what they had achieved, was being swept away. It seemed to signal the end of all hope of bringing Indians into American life as fully functioning participants. The experience of the Klamath Indians of Oregon illustrated in specific detail what could be expected of the new policies.

The Klamath reservation in southern Oregon contained about one million acres and a valuable forest of Ponderosa and other pine species, which had been harvested on a sustained yield basis since 1913. The income from this forest, amounting to about $2 million annually, paid all administrative costs of government operations as well as dividends to tribal members amounting to about $4,000 per family. In addition, many members farmed or ran cattle and some worked in neighboring towns.

The tribe numbered about two thousand, of whom, based on a sampling of the population carried out by the Stanford University Research Center, about one-third had a grammar school education or no education at all, a smaller number had completed one or more years of high school. The tribe had few skilled workmen and no professionally trained individuals. These people were required by Congress, in the legislation adopted in August 1954, to decide how best to dispose of a tribal estate whose value was estimated at in excess of $100 million.

Federal trusteeship over the property would terminate at the end of three years, and within that three-year period the Klamath Indians must either (1) transfer the property to a management corporation or to one or more trustees, in the hope of obtaining benefits equivalent to those they had derived from federal trusteeship, or (2) if they failed or refused to act within the three years, allow the Secretary to sell and distribute the assets. The chairman of the Tribal Council, when the full significance of the legislation struck home, was quoted as saying: "I think the Secretary wants the white man to get our land." The tribe pleaded for more time, more leeway, "on the principle," a spokesman said, "that this is an entirely new departure, not only on the part of ourselves, the Indians, but the state and federal government as well."

What procured the additional time was not the Indian plea but the timber industry and business interests of the Northwest. A timber market already declining in those Eisenhower years was seriously threatened by the time schedule built into the legislation. To liquidate the tribal estate and divide the proceeds, if the Indians or the Secretary chose that alternative, involved the forced sale of some 4 billion board feet of tribally owned timber and an additional 250 million board feet of timber standing on individually owned allotments. Ruination would follow.

One of the leading newspapers of the area, the Portland *Oregonian,* at first an advocate of federal withdrawal (Secretary McKay was an Oregonian), suddenly saw the logic of the Indians' request for more time and urged that the legislation be amended. Some doubt about the wisdom of the legislation itself is suggested in its editorial comment: "We foresee a time when Klamath County's public welfare lists would be burdened with destitute Indians."

The three management specialists appointed by the Secretary to conduct the appraisal of tribal assets and to advise the Indians concluded that the terms of the act could not be carried out in a manner to benefit the Indians and the community. Two members resigned before negotiations were completed.

Finally, members of the Congress realized that the time schedule was unrealistic. By then it was the summer of 1956, when the tribal members were required under the law to choose the irreversible course. At the last moment, a bill was adopted in Congress allowing a "breathing spell," when amendments would be considered and a more equitable formula discovered, not necessarily to benefit the Indians, but to insure that the economy of the region would not be wrecked.

This was accomplished through further amendment, by providing that private buyers must pay not less than the appraised market value and must harvest the timber on a sustained yield basis for at least seventy-five years. If the lands were not all purchased privately by January 1, 1960, the Forest Service of the Department of Agriculture would purchase the remainder, but that Department was not to spend more than $90 million. The government appraisers had placed a value of $121,659,618 on the forest. The prorated shares of each Klamath member was estimated at $59,000—better than a quarter of a million dollars for a family of five. Not unsurprisingly, only 5 percent of the membership voted to retain the tribal estate intact and to continue as a tribe.

The Klamath Indians, like the Menominees of Wisconsin, invited severance from the trust relationship because they were wealthy, in Indian terms. But by such a test it was difficult to understand why some other tribal groups were selected for similar treatment—the Turtle Mountain Chippewa of North Dakota, the Seminoles in Florida, a small Indian community in Texas. These were groups without resources—welfare recipients without a future.

La Farge called particular attention to one such obscure group in his annual report to the association (May 1954) as an example of the lack of rationality that prevailed in the administration. He reported:

> In the state of Utah is some of the most forbidding desert in all of the United States. On portions of that desert are settled small bands of Shoshonean-speaking Indians, mostly of the group called Paiutes, who have always been poor and humble. Simple, peaceful, few in numbers, long before the white men came they were driven into the wastelands by stronger tribes, and learned to wring a tolerable subsistence from the desert. Under our beneficent rule, their condition has deteriorated, and it now appears to be the intention of the United States of America that their lot shall continue to be extreme poverty and wretchedness, with a possible alternative of mere extinction.
>
> There are 358 of these poor people, occupying some 66,000 acres of arid land, the surface of which, at least, is worth very little. The agencies that are supposed to serve them, and admittedly do very little for them, are located at distances ranging from 75 to 450 miles away from the various bands. They are forgotten, neglected, remote [the reservations have such intriguing names as Koosharem, Kanosh, Shivwitz, Goshute, and Skull Valley].
>
> Of these 358 people, five speak no English, thirty-three are illiterate. . . . To get a correct rate, we should deduct the number of children under school age, but I have not that number. Of about forty-eight children of school age, twenty-four are not in school because of "home conditions." Early marriage, staying out of school to work, being unable to go to school because of home conditions, are all familiar parts of the tragic picture of poverty.
>
> There are ninety-eight families. . . . Of these, forty-two earn their own living, while fifty-six are dependent, wholly or partly, on charity and relief. The Department [of the Interior] says that local church and charitable groups are doing more for them than is the Department. . . . The Department further reports that they are ready for termination "as rapidly as possible."
>
> Legislation to terminate their status as Indians, to make them non-Indian by act of Congress, did not originate with the Department but with the Utah delegation in Congress. . . . The argument seems to be that, since the Indians are sadly impoverished

and have been dreadfully neglected, the thing to do is to wash our hands of them altogether. Since their property is worth very little, let them sell it. Since they are as they now stand incapable of earning a decent living, let them go it alone.

Now an interesting item was brought out in the hearings, which is that there are oil structures under some of this worthless seeming land. Apparently the Department did not know about this. Also the record includes a letter from an official of the Triumph Uranium and Oil Company of Fillmore, Utah, setting forth how the Indians want to be set free, and are strongly in favor of the bill. And here is what the superintendent of these Indians has to say about the author of that letter [in testimony before a Senate Committee]: [He] is our enemy, in a way, Sir. He represents some oil company; and he desired to negotiate a lease without going through the usual procedure, which provides that when Indian lands are leased, they are advertised and awarded to the highest bidder. He thought there was a way around that, and that the lands should be leased to him without going through the bidding procedure."

Regardless of the facts I have cited, some of which are rather startling, the Senate Committee approved the bill [during that same summer, the bill cleared both houses of Congress and became law].

It was, as he said, "a year of confusion," with many forces pulling in contrary directions. It was also a year of growing fear and anger. "I have been active in Indian affairs for somewhat over twenty years," La Farge told the members, "and never have I seen the Indians as a whole so hostile to an administration."

A newsletter issued by the association in March 1954 reviewed the situation:

Protests against the current drive to destroy their status as Indians are pouring in to us from tribe after tribe. February 25–28 saw the largest gathering of Indians ever to appear in Washington, representing tribes of twenty-one states and Alaska, come together to speak out against a ruinous policy. [This was the emergency conference called by the all-Indian National Congress of

American Indians, whose membership at that time included more than fifty tribes.]

Tribes not touched by present termination bills are united against them with those affected, since the bills are only part of a larger program.

All over the country, Indians not immediately affected, fearful of the trend, are speaking out.

The program is not, as its sponsors claim, new, nor will it "free" any Indians. It is as old as the discredited notion that determined policy in earlier times—that Indians should stop being Indians. Detribalization and forced assimilation were promoted by the government for a hundred years before the 1930's; they resulted only in demoralizing the Indians and making them into public charges by thousands.

These annual meetings of the association and its news releases generally found a friendly press—not spontaneously, of course, but as the result of careful planning and the cultivation of appropriate news outlets. Department officials and some congressmen at times spoke disparagingly of "that Eastern outfit" or "that Indian Association" which succeeded so frequently in reaching newspapers and magazines with sharply worded statements that punctured the inflated pretensions of the bureaucracy. Official outcries were often the anguished acknowledgment that a well-flung shaft had found its mark.

Oliver was always in good form at these membership meetings. Whatever scurrying, personality clashes, and scenery shifting might have occurred beforehand, the meetings gave the impression of effortless good will. The maturity he had found lacking in the association's early floundering years had been quietly achieved. And this was reflected in the nature of his own remarks. In those early presidential messages he was often only too obviously putting up a good front and spreading cheer when there was little cause for self-congratulation. Now he could talk confidently about accomplishment—about the legal staff's major court cases, about the association's influence on legislative maneuvers, about effective field work with Indian tribes.

While the association had not solved its money problems—no action organization ever does—it was operating on a broader base, offering more services, and rallying public support as never before.

Oliver's speeches were always written in advance, after consultations with staff members, but the writing was his own, and invariably it sparked and snapped. His delivery was relaxed and urbane, his gaunt, loose-jointed frame draped over the lectern—even the dentures he wore in later years which seemed not to fit and clicked and hissed could not lessen the effectiveness of what he was saying.

At the 1955 meeting he was concerned to have the issues of immediate conflict viewed in a larger perspective, as he was well aware that issues get settled, one way or another, or just fade away, but the principles that give rise to issues are the real battleground. He called his speech *Consent of the Governed,* and in it he talked of his conviction.

Working in Indian affairs is a constant process of learning. As we go forward from year to year we see ever more clearly that the solutions we seek lie, not in the remedying of this or that specific trouble, but in extending to all phases of Indian affairs the basic moral and political principles out of which American democracy at its best is made.

The events of the past year have strongly emphasized the essential nature of the principle of government by the consent of the governed. Much of the evil we have had to fight and are still fighting, if not all of it, would be eliminated if men in positions of authority would refuse to do what the Indians object to and would consent to do what the Indians urgently ask for. We have long preached that the time was past—if indeed it ever existed—when we could rightfully say that the American Indians were primitives for whose benefit others, of greater knowledge, should make the decisions. Through the years that attitude has usually resulted in having the white men make the Indians' mistakes for them, and being a highly civilized, advanced people, accustomed to operating on a large scale, the white men's mistakes have been accordingly stupendous.

It is striking how regularly the Indians are right about what is good or bad, just or unjust, for themselves. It is even more striking when we consider that they range, on the whole, from poorly educated to plain uneducated, that a distressingly large proportion of them lack even a real command of the English language, that very few of them get enough schooling to enable them to enter college, or to stay in if they are admitted.

It is these people, half-educated, poverty-stricken, that many now in authority wish to strip of all their rights and protections. That they clamor against this is to be ignored, or—as in the case of the Menominees and Klamaths—they are subjected to quite open, indecent pressures to bribe and frighten them into the appearance of consent.

In his campaign for office, the President promised the Indians that they would be consulted on matters concerning them. I am sure he meant just what he said. . . . But lesser men, notably little men in big shoes, have been busy redefining "consultation." To them it means that I tell you what I'm going to do and then you can go ahead and yell your head off, I'll still do it.

In order to see just what we are doing and what we are up against, let us state some basic principles. One of these is government by consent of the governed. Another is that we, the United States of America, must fulfill our obligation to give the people the training and equipment they must have to live in the manner they choose without further special protection.

These are somewhat abstract. As a practical matter, we know that Indian progress is based on two essential elements, underlying all others, even education. One is keeping the Indian estate—land, resources, funds—intact. The other, closely related to the first, is continuation of their corporate existence. These two things are more fundamental even than education or health service.

It is precisely these two elements that are under the most powerful attack today. Indian corporate existence is troublesome. It takes the form of modern tribal organization, systems of self-government, authorized by the Indian Reorganization Act. These organizations, invested by law with real authority, have given the tribes new vigor and self-confidence. They provide them with a means of voicing their opinions and getting themselves heard. . . . They have revolutionized the Indians' ability to protect and beneficially exploit their property. In modern corporate and municipal organizations holding an undiminished estate we see the perfect means of transition from the Indians' present condition of required protection and special status to a status identical to that of the rest of us.

The principle of Indian consent is alive and vigorous. It is a measure of the genuineness of our own democracy, an element by which the whole world may judge us.

He had moved a long way from the ideas he first had about the future of the Indian people. During the period in which he wrote *Laughing Boy,* the fading away of Indian life, indeed biological extinction, seemed certain and imminent. Perhaps his views were not exclusively those of a brash young man speaking with less knowledge than he would have been willing to admit. What was visible to the surface observer in the 1920's was certainly disquieting. The phrase "vanishing redman" expressed the sentiment of the time.

He had learned otherwise from observing the fiercely independent Bachajon Indians of Chiapas, listening to the ceremonial songs of the Jicarilla Apaches, and in later years working with tribal councils on problems of economic and political development. These experiences and the insights which followed prompted the view he expressed to a correspondent in 1951:

We do not believe that Indians "must be assimilated." We believe that assimilation should be a matter of their own free choice, and it is our observation that these level-headed and practical people, where they have been able to make an intelligent choice, go at the question of what cultural values of their own to retain and what to abandon in favor of ours in a realistic manner. They should be given not only the academic education but the general understanding of our world which will enable them to make these choices soundly.

His scientific colleagues, as it happened, were advocating similar views. A conference of some thirty social scientists held at the University of Chicago in February 1954 dealt with a cluster of assumptions then current in Indian affairs. The most basic of these assumptions, as reported to the conference by John H. Provinse, former Assistant Commissioner of Indian Affairs, a man with training in both law and anthropology, was "the idea that assimilation of the American Indians into the normal stream of American life is inevitable, that Indian tribes and communities will disappear."

The conferring anthropologists and sociologists, nearly without exception, had all worked in Indian communities and spoke from direct field observation. The conference concluded

> There was complete agreement on the part of the discussants that this prediction is unwarranted. Most Indian groups in the United States, after more than one hundred years of Euro-American contact and in spite of strong external pressures, both direct and fortuitous, have not yet become assimilated in the sense of loss of community identity and the full acceptance of American habits of thought and conduct. Nor can one expect such group assimilation within any short, predictable time period, say, one to four generations. The urge to retain tribal identity is strong, and operates powerfully for many Indian groups. . . .
>
> Despite external pressures, and internal change, most of the present identifiable Indian groups . . . will continue indefinitely as distinct social units, preserving their basic values, personality, and Indian way of life, while making continual adjustments, often superficial in nature, to the economic and political demands of the larger society.

When the Eighty-third Congress finally adjourned in the fall of 1954, leaving behind a wreckage of tribal programs and tribal hopes, La Farge looked to the White House. He was still confident that President Eisenhower, if he could be reached, would redeem his campaign pledge of consulting with the Indian people.

⁂ XVI ⁂

A Letter to the President

In spite of what he told his brother Christopher in 1953, that President Eisenhower was said to read almost nothing, Oliver in the summer of 1955 was trying to find a way to get a letter to the President under circumstances that would compel a reading. It seemed to be the only way to circumvent the conspiracy that kept the President in ignorance.

The working executive staff of the association at that time consisted of William Zimmerman, Jr., Assistant Commissioner during the Collier years and for a while Acting Commissioner (until Dillon S. Myer succeeded in moving him out of the Indian service), who now served the association as a kind of general liaison officer; La Verne Madigan, executive director; and Alden Stevens, secretary. All helped in preparing the letter, the original rough draft of which seems to have been prepared by Zimmerman. All shared the cautious optimism that they could reach the President if they picked the right strategy. The outcome is of interest, since it demonstrates the care with which the association planned its moves, and the extent to which La Farge involved himself in the planning.

From the outset, they agreed that a delegation of some kind should call at the White House, bearing the letter, rather than send it through the mail. As Miss Madigan observed at one point during the discussion, "a picture of the mailman wouldn't do us much good" for publicity purposes.

La Farge wrote Zimmerman, July 15, 1955: "I don't think there's much point in trying to get an appointment to deliver the

letter by hand unless we can form an extremely strong committee. . . . As you point out, even to form a strong committee would
require a great deal of delay." Delay, however, was inevitable, as
at that moment Eisenhower took off for Geneva and the summit
conference that was to deal with Southeast Asia. This almost ruled
out the possibility of getting access to the President during the
summer and forced the association to revise its plans. Oliver observed: "I think the letter should not be sent until after the President has returned from Geneva and has had time to work off the
publicity deriving from that trip. Prior to then, unquestionably, his
mind will be taken up by the forthcoming meeting as well as with
the legislation he wants to get through before Congress adjourns.
With that over and Congress gone home, things will be quieter, it
will be easier to get his attention, and easier to get space in the
newspapers."

In early August, La Farge wrote Zimmerman: "I am still sitting
on the draft of the President's letter, waiting for a copy of your
revisions and cuts. . . . It is my impression that the President is
going to continue wrapped up in foreign affairs, and content with
his performance in office on that basis. I suspect that it will be
quite difficult to get his ear on Indian affairs by whatever means."

When Zimmerman next wrote, toward the end of August, the
President had returned from Geneva and gone off to Colorado for
a vacation. He and Miss Madigan, in New York, discussed the
new situation. "La Verne's first inclination," he wrote Oliver, "was
to put off the release of the letter until Thanksgiving, but this
seemed to be too far away unless our conclusion is that the letter
would be most useful at that time as a fund-raiser. Finally, we
agreed that the text of the letter should be finished and approved
at once with the understanding that additional material would be
added if the letter is to be released to meet a special incident or
situation."

Late in September the strategy was still not final. Oliver informed Miss Madigan: "None of the people to whom I wrote
about possible channels of reaching the President have even

bothered to answer, and yet I wonder whether we should not make some further effort honestly to reach him, rather than merely resigning ourselves to a public education stunt. Of course, it is not quite as bad as that, but it partakes of that nature."

The next complication occurred September 24, when the President suffered a heart attack and had to be rushed to Fitzsimmons Army Hospital in Denver. During the next weeks the association strategists, as well as the rest of the country, wondered whether Mr. Nixon would be named Acting President or retain his constitutional role as Vice President, serving without clear authority in the absence of the President.

Miss Madigan wrote Oliver: "Since the President cannot be active again in the near future, we must decide whether to address ourselves to Nixon when and if he is designated Acting President, whether to send a revised form of the letter to Mr. McKay as member of the cabinet and 'team' to which Republican leaders are referring as being well equipped to run the country in the President's absence, or whether to abandon the whole idea."

La Farge clung to his image of Eisenhower as a man who would make good on his word to the Indian people, if he could be reached. He returned again and again to this idea, and he wrote his executive director at the end of September, "One of the things that makes a letter to Eisenhower effective is the almost universal feeling that he is a man of good will and integrity, so that appealing to him as we have planned to do will strike most people as a natural and sensible step."

He was willing, however, to yield to expediency and follow a lesser tactic, namely to

> revise and shorten the present letter to make it suitable as a general statement of protest to the Secretary of the Interior. It should not be hostile in tone, although it is difficult to avoid hostility in the content. . . . It should be on the face of it a letter to the top man in Indian matters written to call his close attention to what his subordinates are doing. . . . The fact that we have communicated with the Secretary and not in a combative tone, and that this has proven

fruitless [no one expected positive or even friendly action from the Secretary], will give us a much greater justification for appealing to the President.

Eventually, the President provided the occasion which the association capitalized on to send the letter forward—it went through the mails, after all, with various White House aides and others urged to bring it to attention. The event was Eisenhower's announcement to the press toward the end of October, while still hospitalized, of his intention to ask Congress to authorize a program of technical assistance to economically depressed areas in the United States—what was immediately described as a domestic Point Four program.

Miss Madigan conveyed her enthusiasm to Oliver (October 26): "The *New York Times* story got me so excited that I had to borrow a pencil from the man sitting next to me [she commuted on the New Haven train from Connecticut] so I could jot down thoughts. It seemed to me that the Point 4 angle gives us a much more positive, challenging issue on which to hang our resounding appeal for Indian rights. . . . After all, Point 4 is modern America at its best. Development of economic opportunity for the Indians in the areas where they live is exactly what we want."

It answered those in the Department of the Interior and in Congress who were pursuing a course of dismantling reservation communities and dispersing the Indian population into urban areas. Understandably, it was an exciting moment for the association. The letter, after reposing for months on Oliver's desk in Santa Fe, was quickly recast to tie it to the Point Four philosophy, and on November 10 it was sent.

It was a strong letter, succinct, and yet conveying the complex legal, economic, and cultural situation of the Indian people, and conveying also, in respectful language, frank criticism of the administration's Indian policies. After urging the President that he "explicitly include in that [domestic Point Four] program areas occupied by the American Indians, who are certainly as chronically depressed as any group in the country," La Farge added, "I address you with the more confidence, because your own statements during the last presidential campaign and on several later occasions have shown real interest in our Indian fellow citizens and a humane desire for their advancement."

The next paragraph established the battle line, as he wrote:

We believe that your subordinates have not advised you of the present state of Indian opinion and its causes. We hope that you will inform yourself of what is in their minds, and we are sure that you will find that what they are protesting and what they have been vainly recommending are essential to the requirements of a Point 4 type of program.

Courageously imagined and implemented in good faith, an American Indian Point 4 program would halt, before it is too late, the present administrative tendency to see the solution to the Indian problem in the dispersal of Indian communities. It would reveal the solution to lie, rather, in the elevation of Indian communities to the level of health and well-being enjoyed by other communities in our country.

The years of paternalism and mismanagement have left the Indians of the United States trapped between a shattered economy and a grievous lack of education. Two-thirds of their once adequate estate have been dissipated, and they have nothing to show for it. Your administration has done much to alleviate the educational lack, particularly for the great Navajo tribe, so long grossly neglected. On the contrary, in regard to their economy and the well springs of Indian initiative, your administration's present policies tend to worsen the situation.

In three succeeding paragraphs the letter politely instructed the President in some elementary facts pertaining to Indians, about which the chief executive had seemed confused when he had answered questions in an earlier press interview. The letter itemized: (1) Indians are citizens and voters, (2) Indians retain limited rights of self-government, and (3) Indian lands are held in trust and tax-exempt, as part compensation for the vast areas they ceded to the United States by treaty.

La Farge cited religious sanction for the Indians: "I urgently call to your attention the recent statement of the National Council of Churches, wherein it is said, 'We recognize that America has been enriched by the Indian cultural heritage and that the values thus brought into our society should be conserved. We therefore affirm the necessity for assuring to each Indian tribe or band the right to preserve, to the extent consistent with the general welfare, its own cultural identity.' "

The main argument of the letter centered on four controversial points:

(1) While Indian tribes were in desperate need of capital funds for economic development, the Commissioner of Indian Affairs, a banker before he became commissioner, refused to grant loans from a cash balance of $6 million in a revolving loan fund previously established by Congress and insisted instead that Indians avail themselves of commercial credit sources, as a way of learning "standard banking practices."

(2) A departmental regulation dating from the Collier regime required that an individual might not sell his land until it had been determined that other holders of allotments would not be damaged. Previously, a land buyer might induce an Indian, whose land contained a valuable source of water, to sell; then by closing the water source to surrounding Indian land holders, the buyer could induce the Indians to sell at a price he stipulated. A memorandum the commissioner issued in May 1955 nullified the Collier regulation, and Indian land sales accelerated at a rate to endanger the economy of some reservations.

(3) During the depression years, large acreages of submarginal lands adjoining Indian reservations were acquired by the federal government as a soil conservation measure. The lands were to be transferred to the Indians after they were restored to productivity. Income from leases or other uses was held in a special deposit, to be transferred, along with the land, as a capital fund to assist in further development. In August 1955 the Secretary of the Interior deposited the funds in the United States Treasury, and at the same time he opposed legislation to transfer the land itself in certain cases then pending.

(4) When the President in 1953 had approved Public Law 280, the law authorizing a state to extend its civil and criminal laws over Indian reservations without first seeking Indian agreement, he had expressed "grave doubt" and recommended that a future Congress amend the law to provide for Indian consent. Such an amendment was before Congress, and the President was asked to instruct his Secretary of the Interior to support the amendment.

The paragraph discussing this matter concluded: "Government by consent of the governed is not an alien doctrine. It is a measure of the genuineness of our democracy. It is at the heart of the many issues which the American Indians face, and is an element by which the whole world will judge us."

After one of the several drafts of this letter had been completed, Oliver mentioned in a letter to Christopher: "I finished final revision of a letter to the President about the busy things that are going on behind his back. It is a good letter, a remarkable letter, the work of a number of able people. . . . The trouble is . . . the odds are ten to one that he will not see it. If he did, it would probably jolt him." Evidently the President never saw the letter, or if he saw it, he was not jolted.

The White House staff shunted the letter over to the Department of the Interior for handling. The bureaucratic maze provides two courses for disposing of communications from a concerned public. If the communication is considered important enough for the President to see it with the response, the official preparing the reply is instructed to return it for signature. If the matter does not merit such treatment, the department may answer as it pleases. This decision is not made by the President, but by a staff person exercising his own judgment, presumably a person who knows the chief executive well enough to act as he would.

That does not describe the full bureaucratic process, however. At the Department of Interior, in this case, a mail clerk, or equivalent, decides whether the head of the department shall respond to the communication personally or whether to send it down the line to a bureau chief. The bureau chief, however, does not write the letter—he may be a thousand miles away and may not know enough to write about the subject anyway. What finally emerges from this slide down the ladder is a letter prepared by a junior civil service employee. The employee knows the facts, but he also has his future in mind and inevitably he cites the facts in a manner calculated to demonstrate the wisdom of his superiors. Such a letter must never admit that the concerned public has established a *prima facie* case against the bureau or has even a plausible complaint. The civil servant who made such a concession would be instructed to try again.

That was the fate of the association's letter to the President— a letter inspired by La Farge's faith in President Eisenhower. The answer signed by Secretary McKay was made up of quibbles ("I am not sure whether any single individual is really qualified to speak on behalf of a majority of 400,000 or so Indian people"), distortion of actual events, irrelevant responses to questions that were not raised, misconstruction of passages in the association's letter to facilitate a simplistic response—in short, a whitewash of the actions of Commissioner of Indian Affairs Glenn L. Emmons and his administration.

By the end of 1955, the results of the first termination acts began to appear. The Klamath and the Menominee time schedules were running into difficulties and Congress was being called upon to salvage the Indian situation, or at least the surrounding economy, as in the case of the Northwest timber industry. By then citizen groups, church organizations—the do-gooders, as they are called when they are in opposition—were voicing protests and writing letters to congressmen. Termination bills in Congress at the close of Eisenhower's first term quietly expired in committee.

Change came, although not suddenly and drastically, and not until midway through Eisenhower's second term. And before that occurred, Oliver faced a crisis of his own that immobilized him at the time and left aftereffects from which he never entirely recovered.

He returned to Santa Fe in November 1956, after a meeting of the association's board of directors, complaining of fatigue. For many years he had been subject to chills and fevers which his doctors attributed to recurrences of the malaria he had contracted in Central America. He was hospitalized during the winter and a more thorough examination revealed that he was in fact suffering from emphysema. He returned home from the hospital feeling stronger—perhaps the definite medical finding and setting up of a regimen to deal with it restored his spirits—and then he collapsed. He was rushed back to the hospital, where chest surgery was performed. His right lung failed to reinflate, and a section had to be removed. His doctors anticipated he would need a long convalescence, so in February he reported to his board that he was forced to take a leave of absence.

He wrote to La Verne Madigan, "I shall spare all concerned the personal details of why this is the case [Miss Madigan, of course, and a few others knew the details]. I trust that at the end of six months, my physical and financial health will be so restored as to permit my resuming normal presidential duties, if this is desired."

She replied, "I told the Executive Committee your story and shall summarize it for the Board. The committee does not want any other president and will collectively carry your responsibilities as long as necessary."

In April, he underwent a second lung operation, from which he recovered well. Later, when he could travel, he went to Santa Barbara to convalesce.

To one friend he summed up the experiences of that year as if it had been rather a lark, explaining, "I spent the first half of this year hopping in and out of hospitals with bouts of pneumonia, and these resulted in the collapse of a lung on account of which it was necessary to carve and stitch me up in a very large way."

He had difficulty accepting disability, and within ten days of that last operation he was writing to Miss Madigan, catching up on association news—the annual meeting seemed to have gone well, there were good news stories resulting from it. He concluded,

This whole business of my physical troubles came about so strangely and by such a curious series of gradations that it has taken me some time to realize that I have been through major surgery and apparently at one point had a fairly close call. I judge the latter from the expression of a doctor who is one of my closest personal friends on one occasion and from the tone of satisfaction with which, on two days in succession, the principal surgeon told me I was out of danger. I must now make a series of fundamental readjustments in my plan of life, whole and in detail.

But, of course, that was an intention he would never entirely realize. Shortly before the second operation he prepared his annual report, and it was read for him at the annual meeting in early April. For a man recovering from a lung operation and about to undergo further surgery, writing this report demanded great exertion. In it he commented on a "steadily increasing acceptance . . . of the principle that Indians have the same American right to maintain their communities and group existence as other Americans, and that such communities . . . are the means of successful Indian adjustment to the modern world in an American way, as against the Communist-Fascist way of absorption through the destruction of identities, indeed, of souls."

He told of how "official hostility to the principle of consent of the governed when applied to Indians continues"; of how the commissioner traveled through the West during the previous summer, "where he met with leaders of all tribes at points well away from their reservations . . . and those who asked to bring their attorneys were not allowed to do so. Resolutions prepared in advance were handed to the Indians, thanking the Commissioner and approving his program"; of how "the Indian bureau has been consistently destructive towards going enterprises that served the tribes. It brought about the abandonment of the garment factory at Flandreau [South Dakota], on which the Santee Sioux depended for bare subsistence"; of how "Indian cooperatives have been steadily bludgeoned, many of them nearly to death. In Alaska, official policies are destroying the Indian fishing and cannery cooperatives and . . . everything possible is being done to force them to sell out to non-Indian corporations"; of how "a small factory is being established handy to the reservation of the North Carolina Cherokees, but federal assistance has been withdrawn— on the highly specious plea of 'taking the government out of business' "; of how "in the last four years some 12 percent of Indian allotted land, 1,600,000 acres, has been taken out of trust and is being sold to non-Indians"—it was a long and dreary catalog of confusion and obstruction.

He summarized,

Everything I have so briefly mentioned fits into a single pattern of negation, of destruction. Indians may work in factories owned by others, but they shall be discouraged from maintaining their own enterprises, which increase solidarity and pride in group achievement. They are aided and encouraged to move to distant cities and find work there, but their tribal homes shall be eliminated. They are to be helped, but their opinions, their desires, shall be ignored, their tribal organizations and councils are to be overridden or at least minimized wherever possible. Above all, they must be discouraged and frustrated out of the simple American right to live in communities of their fellows; their tradition must be lost.

While lying in the small hospital at Espanola, New Mexico, after the second operation, he wrote Miss Madigan, "This hospital is sandwiched between Pueblos, even much of the staff is Indian. During my illness, two of all the possible Indians have visited me —Mike Dozier [brother of the Tom and Pete Dozier with whom he had traveled and camped years before], and this morning to my utter astonishment and almost tears, Maria Martinez, the great potter. Of course, she is a very great lady, so it would occur to her to visit the sick, but I had not expected it."

In that same letter, written in May 1957, he began to plan ways of reaching and winning over to the Indian side the new Secretary of the Interior, Fred A. Seaton. Of Glenn L. Emmons, who continued as commissioner, La Farge wrote: "Emmons is unintelligent, unintelligible, unspeakable, and inedible," then he added, "Should we not do our best to keep the Secretary from being maneuvered into a position he has to defend, and show him the way to constructive policies and glory?"

Clearly, he was on the mend.

The association was moving into a larger action sphere and exerting influence within a wider range, thanks to increased financial resources—its 1959 income, including foundation grants, amounted to $222,000. This growth also reflected the energy and managerial skill of the executive director, La Verne Madigan. "Suddenly, from an organization which agitates," Miss Madigan said, "we are emerging as an organization which acts—and whose actions are solicited by Indians and the residents of Indian states who are friendly to them."

It was another sixteen months before Secretary Seaton aired his position on the controversial question of terminating the federal trusteeship, but when he finally spoke on September 18, 1958, at Window Rock, Arizona, headquarters for the Navajo tribe, he made himself quite clear. House Concurrent Resolution 108, the congressional measure which had given rise to bitter opposition among the tribes, he interpreted as "an objective, not an immediate goal."

Then he became specific: "To me it would be incredible, even criminal, to send any Indian tribe out into the mainstream of American life until and unless the educational level of that tribe was one which was equal to the responsibilities which it was shouldering."

He elaborated, "No Indian tribe or group should end its relationship with the federal government unless such tribe or group has clearly demonstrated—first, that it understands the plan under which such a program would go forward, and second, that the tribe or group affected concurs in and supports the plan proposed."

The change of policy, of course, was reflected in the relationship between the association and the department, as revealed in an exchange of correspondence between La Farge and Roger C. Ernst, Assistant Secretary in charge of Indian affairs.

Writing in February 1959, La Farge traced briefly the history of this relationship, pointing out that from its beginning, during the Coolidge administration, the association had

> established a policy of cooperation with the Bureau and the Department. I received my own initiation into Indian affairs directly from Commissioner Charles J. Rhoads in the Hoover administration. We carried this policy over into the Roosevelt administration. Throughout the years we found this relationship by far the most fruitful for the advancement of the Indians. . . . This continued until Mr. Dillon S. Myer became commissioner in the middle of the Truman administration. It was then that the policies of which, I would say, the basic element is hostility to the idea of the survival of Indian communities as such came into effect. The first hard drive towards enforced termination occurred under Commissioner Myer. I would say that Mr. Myer liked administrative privacy. True consultation both with the Indians and with ourselves was ended abruptly.
>
> When the Republicans came into office we had great hopes. . . . Various of us went to Washington, and found, to our distress, that the doors were still closed and that the policy established under the dying Democratic administration was to be vigorously continued.
>
> Now the atmosphere seems to be changing once more.

Ernst's response was prompt. "In all frankness, I admit that before now I did not fully appreciate the size of the arc which the pendulum has described over the years. . . .

"Premature termination is, as the Secretary expressed it, simply unthinkable now. Rule by doctrinaire fiat is also out of the question. We reject the closed door theory and welcome a thorough exposition of principles and programs."

In a newsletter released later that year, the association reported on some of the particulars in this changed atmosphere:

> Most clearly indicative of the Interior Department's new approach are two recommendations made to Congress within recent weeks: (1) to increase the Revolving Fund by $15,000,000, and (2) to convey to eighteen different Indian tribes a total of about 346,000 acres of submarginal lands now owned by the federal government.

Both of these items have long been high on the list of legislation desired by Indians and their friends. To see them sponsored by the Interior Department is most encouraging. . . .

The Department's new proposals mean, essentially, a commitment to the principle of Indian community development. They mean that the Department no longer holds to the view that reservation communities should be ignored, in the hope that they will somehow go away.

Unfortunately, the atmospheric change was more apparent than real; official policy at the departmental level was never translated into action programs at the bureau level. Months after Secretary Seaton made his public statement, one of the assistant commissioners in the bureau confided that the statement had never been discussed within the bureau family, no directives were sent to bureau personnel advising them of the policy change—in fact, any mention of the secretary's statement in staff meetings or at other times was frowningly disregarded. Hence the bureau continued to act negatively on tribal development requests to deny credit loans and to approve ruinous Indian land sales. The problem for this assistant commissioner was to find a channel of communication through to the Secretary of the Interior. The association provided that channel, but too late to effect any major change in the expiring Eisenhower administration.

In February 1961 the quadrennial federal housecleaning had taken place; the perennial American hope that things would improve was in the air. La Farge was again optimistic when he wrote of the Kennedy administration, in the association newsletter *Indian Affairs:*

In this year we look to the future in Indian affairs with the happy assurance that the new administration's approach is governed by sympathetic, hard-headed, practical idealism. The President's repeated statements of policy, the established records of Secretary of the Interior Udall and his Assistant Secretary Carver, and their initial actions, all are guarantees of this approach, an approach which, among other things, outlaws the heartless war against the continued existence of Indian communities waged by a subordinate Indian Bureau in recent years.

This time, however, there was a difference, a sounder base for the optimism. Before assuming the Interior post Stewart Udall had served in Congress, where he was identified with the liberal Western block. This group generally and historically had been friendly to Indian causes and Udall was one of the congressmen with whom the association maintained cooperative relations. The relationship remained close after the new administration took office. When Secretary Udall created a Task Force on Indian Affairs to investigate reservation conditions and make policy and program recommendations, two of the four-member team appointed by the secretary had occupied official positions with the association—William Zimmerman, Jr., as field representative, and Philleo Nash as a member of the board of directors. Soon after the task force submitted its report in July 1961, Mr. Nash, an anthropologist by training, was named Commissioner of Indian Affairs.

The association had traveled a long way from the day in a Senate committee room when the absent-minded Dr. Spinden tripped over his own testimony and an eager but naive La Farge was cuffed about by heavy senatorial hands. It was still "that Eastern outfit" to those who resented Indian survival, but the epithet conveyed an acknowledgment of a worthy adversary. Oliver's personal acquaintanceship with the new secretary encouraged a frankness not usually present in the exchanges between a private citizen and a cabinet officer. His letter to Udall in February 1962, for example, was written as if directed to his own association members: "With the right policies in effect, sufficient funds available to carry them out, and the right people in the Presidentially appointed positions, the job before us is to see that the officialdom down the line understands and carries out those policies. But here is where we face our greatest obstacles. Without making a blanket condemnation, I do not hesitate to say that in the Indian Bureau staff in Washington and in the field there is a dangerous proportion of those who lack . . . feeling for people." Some he declared to be racists, and offered to name them, but a majority were simply individuals who do not particularly "care about Indians" and "might better be working for the Treasury's Bureau of Accounts."

Still writing as if to his own board of directors, he suggested a series of personnel actions which would encourage loyalty to the administration and remove from positions of power those who lacked sympathy or ability. "Such measures," he realized, "may lower the morale of some Bureau employees; to others, they will be like the promise of new life. More important, they would raise the morale of the Indians."

One of the recommendations of the secretary's task force was the creation by law of an advisory board on policy and program development, and Udall expressed the desire that Oliver accept appointment to such a body, when created. To this, however, Oliver would not agree. In explaining his position to his staff, and presumably to the secretary, he wrote: "I absolutely will not become involved in a statutory advisory board. I am in trouble now with my publishers and a good six months behind in my work, partly from sickness and partly from Indian affairs. I desire not to go deeper into Indian affairs but to pull out to some extent if I can manage it." It was an old problem, never solved.

La Farge never lost sight of the proper role of a citizen organization. At about the time he was writing his letter of advice to Secretary Udall, he also wrote to his executive director, "Here is my understanding of our most fundamental policy, underlying all other policies, as it has stood since the 1920's. It is to find the most effective ways of assisting Indians to advance themselves, etc., with a preference for achieving this end through causing the appropriate agencies of the federal government to do everything that they ought to do. Implicit in this latter part of my understanding of our policy is a further preference for working in cooperation with these agencies, and above all with the Bureau of Indian Affairs."

Such was the relationship between the association and the Department of the Interior that, not surprisingly, Roger C. Ernst, after completing his tour as Assistant Secretary at the close of the Eisenhower administration, accepted election to the Board of Directors of the Association on American Indian Affairs. Mr. Ernst, a practicing attorney in Phoenix, Arizona, at once assumed his proper share of association duties, and eventually succeeded to the presidency.

✤ XVII ✤

The Indian and the Land

LA FARGE was a Yankee, and a Yankee is a paradox: proud of who and what he is, with a compulsion to understate it, but capable of deep resentment toward any who accept his understatement at face value. La Farge had expert knowledge and experience, but, though being a Yankee he might understate his expertness, let no one challenge it. It had made him furious that Secretary McKay, a small town man who had reached a President's cabinet, should question his currency in Indian affairs.

But what he was expert about was Indians, and Indians are truly laconic about who and what they are and quite capable of outfacing even an inveterate Yankee in understatement. Being non-paradoxical, they harbor no resentment, only pity for the blundering stranger who fails to detect their deep-seated pride.

La Farge at first did not appreciate this Indian quality. The simplicity of the lives he described in *Laughing Boy* was something he accepted for what it appeared to be—like the white men who, in their encounters with Indians, so often saw them as childlike. La Farge's view changed, and this change was what brought him into conflict with the officials of Eisenhower's administrations. These were men who lived with the stereotype of the immature, improvident, inebriate Indian, and to them it seemed only proper to make decisions without consulting the Indians, who could not be expected to give rational answers.

La Farge's insight began to grow as his work with the association and with Rhoads' administration took him into Indian country as a trained observer looking for the causes of breakdown in Indian society. What he saw required no abstract theoretical base for understanding—Indian communities and the Indian personality were decaying out of sheer idleness. They were in no way involved in the current of life that raced past. Most white men in contact with Indians—administrators, teachers, missionaries, welfare workers—described them as indifferent, apathetic, dependent. But in these judgments the critics were seeing themselves, or their own kind, not Indians. They were saying to themselves, "If I acted like that, that's what I would be—lazy, ambitionless, willing to let somebody else take care of me."

As early as 1933, La Farge saw the dilemma. In a speech before the Boston branch of the old National Association on Indian Affairs, he remarked: "It has been my experience in observing the very curious ways of white people in the presence of Indians, that they never look on the Indian as a human being, but regard him as a curious sort of a phenomenon either admirable or contemptible, but always devoid of the rounded character and complete nature which they ascribe to their fellow whites. I think it can be safely said that the average white person in Indian country never actually sees an Indian, but only the projection of his own preconception."

He also realized early in his observations of Indian communities that it was easy to let oneself be fooled by what one saw, or to report on something other than what one saw. Some observers, including trained ethnographers, saw a vanishing race; some soured welfare workers saw footling clients on perpetual dole. In writing about his ethnological field methods, he alluded to this problem: "You may bathe yourself in this Indian world, but you cannot go on pretending about it. Every factor which forms or malforms its character must be directly and fully faced. In return you acquire a form of power as you achieve a fair degree of knowledge, while retaining a perception which is impossible for the people themselves."

The dilemma of insight lives with us all. The outsider sees the forces at play—historical antecedents which bring on the present, cultural biases which determine present decisions, personality fixes which warp relationships—and falls into the error of assuming that the people under observation are looking through his eyes. If they are not, he thinks, they should be, and then everything would be clear. The outsider does not remind himself that he also is an actor in different context, haunted by history, culturally impelled, wrought upon by the personalities of his circumstances, in which his own role is not always clear. In any case, it is impossible to transpose the social universe of one group onto another and find correspondence at all points. From earliest settlement days, however, the white man has tried to fit his social experience onto the Indian, and to trim and cut the Indian world as need be.

Much of La Farge's writings about Indians, apart from the polemics of policy battles, were attempts to clarify the nature of cultural impact on the individual and the group, to delineate the difficulty in translating the experience of reality across cultural horizons.

In a 1960 speech before the Friends Seminar on Indian affairs in Albuquerque, New Mexico, he mentioned some of the observable conditions of modern Indian life.

We find once solidly united tribes torn by senseless factionalism. We find almost everywhere the distressing phenomenon of rabid drunkenness, and in a few places a horrifying incidence of suicide. These are symptoms. Of what? We do not know. Apparently successful, progressive, prosperous groups may be as badly off in these respects as those in the worst conditions.

All we on the outside can say is that obviously something is wrong, and that this whatever-it-is is creating spiritual destruction. We can lay our fingers on a number of specific things . . . , such as contemptuous treatment, chronic injustice, or the insane vacillations of bureaucracy that would upset almost anyone. Nonetheless, in our thinking about Indians, we are too much inclined to concentrate on what we, the non-Indians, think of as rewards and goals, as the things that make life worth living, stressing the purely material, without trying to find out what it is that actually would make life worth living for the Indian—and Indians, experienced in dealing with white men, have long ago given up trying to explain their own non-material values.

On another occasion, writing in the Methodist family magazine *Together* for June 1958, he looked at these "non-material values," explaining: "We have replaced a rich mode of life with a thin one, although the average Indian today may own many more complex objects than his great-grandfather. It can almost be said that we introduced poverty to the New World. The Indians lived richly with few material possessions; we have shown them our device of living in physical and spiritual poverty with numerous possessions." He went on, "Most Indians, I believe, want to retain their identity. They do not want to be assimilated or to have their tribes and rights as Indians terminated. This desire to continue as Indians does not mean wanting to stay primitive, wear feathers, or live in tents. It is based on the idea that men can be different yet progress equally."

Some misconceptions about Indians are practically imperishable. No matter how often or how thoroughly they are refuted, they reappear down through the years and claim attention all over again. One such is the fatuous notion that an Indian cannot remain Indian in a complex modern world, and from this comes the argument that those who would encourage Indians to retain their identity are closing the door to the future and condemning Indians to the stone age.

In 1924 *Forum Magazine* ran a series of articles by "experts" on Indians of the period, and this was one theme the writers kicked around with gusto. Flora Warren Seymour, one of these "experts" (she was a member of the old Board of Indian Commissioners, a toothless advisory body), declared: "If some sentimentalists had their way, Indians of the younger generation, products of our American education and civilization, would go back to their old picturesque dances and worship." To this Mary Austin, novelist, poet, and Indianist, made a flat rejoinder. "The first thing that appears in Mrs. Seymour's statement is that she is totally uninformed as to the relation of a thinking citizen to the Indian question, and only shallowly acquainted with the Indian himself."

The argument roared on. John Collier, as commissioner, was accused on numerous occasions of wanting to preserve Indians in glass cases as museum specimens.

Behind this fallacy, of course, is a failure to allow for the Indian view of life; or more likely, it is to insist that the Indian view, whatever it is, is unrealistic and must give way to the superior logic of gross numbers. La Farge tried to make something explicit and nonsentimental of this Indian view, which he expressed in the relationship between the Indian and the land, the mother earth. Writing in the magazine *Country Beautiful* in 1962, he spoke of this relationship as a trinity of values—the land is beautiful, the land is holy, and the land is useful. It was a relationship universally misunderstood by incoming Europeans, who saw Indians as perennial nomads, wandering the earth with no fixed place of abode and with no regard for the economic value of the land.

What they were observing and interpreting through their own customs and experiences was the absence of legal, merchantable title. To Indians it was inconceivable that land could be sold, since land was the common mother of all, the giver and sustainer of life. This did not mean, however, as Europeans inferred, that Indians lacked a sense of belonging to a particular geographical locale or that they had no boundaries they would defend against willful intruders.

La Farge cited some of the social conditions under which land was held.

> In the northern part of California, many tribes held to rigid boundaries, punished any trespass, and even maintained permanent border patrols. Farther north along the coast, where the great mountains come steeply down to the sea and in the inlets and river mouths are the fabulously rich fishing grounds that made the complex Northwest Coast culture possible, the competition for territory became intense and cruel. Elsewhere, it was more commonly felt that the living earth could not be precisely marked off. Boundaries were broadly defined, hunting areas might overlap, and

sacred places were shared. A casual stranger or two straying into tribal territory was not resented. . . . Much depended on the adequacy of the food supply; where there was plenty, to hog it all would be contemptible.

More difficult for the incoming European to understand was the spirituality of the relationship between the Indian and his land. The newcomer might refer to this as "nature worship" and thereby relegate it to the irrational, but he could not allow it the status of religion, which took place in a church structure on certain days or hours of the week.

La Farge pointed out, "In the Middle Ages, Europeans understood that their churches were beautiful, that the beauty was an expression of their holiness, and that the holiness was an actively useful thing. The Indians had no elaborate churches, and they extended this threefold understanding to the whole world within which they lived and worshiped."

When Indians moved into new territory, as the Navajo people moved into the Southwest sometime after the twelfth century A.D., they absorbed it emotionally, building a belief system upon it, and filling it with the heroes and adventures of their mythology. The features of the landscape became personalized and engendered anecdotes. Once when driving through the countryside with an Indian companion La Farge had remarked on a particular formation of pink rock and how it always pleased him to view it when he drove by. The Indian's eyes brightened with appreciation. The rock had a name and a history, and for the rest of the journey he pointed to features all across the landscape which were equally part of his living world. It pleased him to find a white man who would notice such things and to see in them something more than real estate.

What gives Indians a kind of homogeneity, in spite of language differences and a variety of cultural dissimilarities, is their common feeling for and hold on the land. "Land means a place where all of a tribe can build homes. From the land, some can wrest a living; others can establish enterprises of many sorts without breaking away from their fellows. Thus it is an essential factor in the continuance of one's ancient community; it is useful, but at its most useful it serves a higher, non-material aim. Over the land lies a special light of ancient memories, beliefs, events, and each bit of territory, whatever its nature, has its beauty."

Perhaps nowhere in modern Indian history is there a clearer case of the Indian attachment to land than that shown by the Taos Pueblo Indians for Blue Lake and the Rio Pueblo watershed— what they call "The Bowl" in their language—above their village in northern New Mexico. They refer to the lake and the surrounding watershed as sacred and, so strong is their sentiment, they have devoted sixty or more years to an unceasing struggle to retain the area in an unspoiled state.

La Farge became personally involved in the case in 1949 and 1950, when the leaders at Taos first requested his help, but the association's precursors had advocated protection of the Pueblo since the 1920's.

The Pueblo has occupied its present site, including the adjoining mountain area, since at least the fourteenth century A.D., by archaeological reckoning. Under Spanish rule, beginning in 1598, the Indians of New Mexico were affirmed in their rights of occupancy and boundaries were delineated for their protection. In 1821, Mexico supplanted Spain's sovereignty but continued unbroken the Spanish policy of recognizing and affirming Indian possessory rights to the lands they occupied. The treaty of Guadalupe-Hidalgo of 1848, by which sovereignty passed from Mexico to the United States, contains specific language guaranteeing all property rights recognized under Spanish and Mexican law. For two hundred fifty years, up to the United States' accession, the Indians had not been disturbed in their land holdings.

After another fifty-plus years, as white ranchers began to encroach on them, the Taos Indians in 1903 requested that the watershed, including Blue Lake, be reserved for their exclusive use. The area was outside the Taos land grant, but it contained the water sources upon which they depended for existence. The request was granted, but in a peculiar manner. A Presidential Proclamation of 1906 added the area to the Carson National Forest, and while this protected the land against settlement, it transferred control to the Department of Agriculture's Forest Service and made Indian use subject to government regulation. The effect of this was to place Taos religion itself under regulation.

The inspector for the Department of Agriculture who visited the area just before it became part of the national forest reported that he was "very much pleased with the natural primitive condition in which the Taos Indians have kept their watershed."

But that was not surprising. For over five hundred years the people had been going to the mountains, following the stream which flowed through their village and sustained the people and the plant and animal life along its course. As a Taos spokesman explained: "The essence of our religion is that Taos Pueblo and the Rio Pueblo watershed form an integral organism of land and water and dependent plant, animal, and human life. Our religious activities encompass the entire area, where our young men receive their religious training and their preparation for manhood, and our religious societies go to perform their sacred duties throughout the year. In this way the people sustain and protect the sanctuary of the watershed, and the sanctuary gives life and meaning to the people."

The intimate association between the people and the land, and the manner in which that association was negated by governmental regulation, was described some years later by an official of the Pueblo who was testifying on pending legislation before a committee of the House of Representatives. It was an extraordinary occasion, since the practices described are almost never talked about outside the Pueblo. The official explained:

> The religious life of Taos Pueblo is organized around religious societies associated with our underground chambers, which are called "kivas." The many religious groups participate in the training of our young men to take their place in our community, and their members conduct religious ceremonies according to an ancient religious calendar throughout the year. Virtually all of those ceremonies are practiced in the Rio Pueblo watershed, but the places, times, and participants are secret. The ritual practices may

involve only one Indian or a group of Indians. The ritual will frequently require a journey at a special time, by a special route, to a special place. The ceremony must be practiced in privacy; it will not be performed if outsiders are present.

Here is where the Forest Service, the recreationalists it invites to the Rio Pueblo watershed, and the trespassers it fails to exclude, interfere with our religious practices. The presence in a part of the watershed of a Forest Service crew, recreationalists, or trespassers will require the Indian group which needs to be in that part of the watershed to detour or to discontinue its ceremony to avoid detection by outsiders. When our people are so interrupted in their religious practices, we do not tell the offenders of that fact; we do not approach them and ask them to leave because of our ceremony. We instead preserve our privacy and the sanctity of the ritual by avoiding contact with the interlopers. . . .

In all of its programs the Forest Service proclaims the supremacy of man over nature; we find this viewpoint contrary to the realities of the natural world and the nature of "conservation."

In the course of their dealings with government agencies and officials, the Taos people experienced a variety of astonishing miscalculations. In seeking protection for their holy land, they managed only to become ensnared by a bureaucracy. In a later attempt to bargain for what they had failed to obtain through petition, they learned another lesson.

The Pueblo Lands Board, created after the defeat of the infamous Bursum Bill to adjudicate title to land claimed by the several Pueblos against adverse possessors, in due course sat to hear claims presented by the Taos Pueblo. Part of the Taos claim included the land on which the town of Fernando de Taos was built —modern Taos, located a few miles south of the Pueblo. This land had simply been preempted, without payment.

In the course of the hearing before the Lands Board, the Taos Indians let it be known that they would renounce their claim to the town land and would not demand compensation, if their watershed lands were returned.

The Lands Board was pleased to receive this offer, and forthwith cancelled the Pueblo claim to the town lands. What the board did not explain to the Indians, however, at least not at that time, was that it had no authority to take land away from Carson National Forest and return it to the Pueblo. Only some years later did the Indians discover the hole in their bargain.

In 1955, La Farge was again called upon by the Taos leaders to help them in their long struggle, and at that time he wrote William Zimmerman, now a staff member of the association, "It may seem peculiar that I should allow myself to be involved in this matter at all, when I'm crying to be let alone. It is partly a matter of Seferino's remarkable personality [Seferino Martinez, then Governor of the Pueblo], partly a matter of not betraying the confidence that the Taos Indians now seem to have in me, and partly that I do not think I shall be required to expend a very great amount of time."

La Farge should have known better. Since 1930 he had been expecting that Indian work would not require too much of him and continually had seen it absorb him, almost to the point of destroying his livelihood.

✦ XVIII ✦

The Reach and the Grasp

LA FARGE's career fell short of expectations. The success of his early years denied him later satisfactions, simply because the promise had been so great. He drank heavily on occasion, with close friends, and the bitterness of those thwarted expectations came to the surface. The fact that he never repeated the success of *Laughing Boy,* and that strangers knew him only as the author of one book, whipped up inner storms. When an editor suggested deleting material in a story, he might accept the suggestion, since he needed to make the sale, but it left him in a rage. He planned his work meticulously and had reasons for the build-up of a story, from word choice to choice of incident. He could defend what he wrote on esthetic grounds—and frequently battled with editors— but he could not argue against the purse.

His failure to grow in stature, or at least in public recognition, brought not only disappointment but a chastened outlook which he was willing to reveal publicly. He chose the Twenty-Fifth Anniversary Report of the Harvard Class of 1924 to acknowledge his discomfiture. He wrote of "the slow but relentless arrival of the realization that . . . one will never be great" as a writer. "The dream one had at the beginning," he confessed, "is achingly real, but it will never be fulfilled."

One expectation with which he had lived a long time, the abandonment of which did not come easily, was the possibility of returning to linguistic research to pursue the comparative calendric studies with which he had become identified. The ambition to do scholarly work he had never dismissed, even as he found himself engulfed in the politics of Indian affairs and absorbed by the tedium of writing for a living. The youthful hope he had expressed in his letter to J. Alden Mason—that literary success would give him the leisure to pursue a scientific career—was demolished by the reality of dwindling literary sales. The ambition remained, however, and after the war when he returned to civilian life with a nest-egg of severance pay, enriched presently by a Guggenheim Fellowship, it seemed possible to pick up the long neglected strands of professional interest.

Accordingly, he arranged with the University of Pennsylvania Museum to resume work on a Quiché manuscript of 1722, which had been badly translated by a German scholar and had remained unpublished. La Farge had become interested in the manuscript during his association with the museum in the 1930's, and now he agreed to prepare a revised Spanish text to accompany an annotated edition of the original manuscript. Very shortly after entering this agreement, however, he found himself and the Association on American Indian Affairs embroiled in a series of critical issues affecting Indians, beginning with the disastrous blizzard in the Navajo country. He never did find the freedom to concentrate on scholarly work, as crisis led to crisis in the growing cynicism of the Truman, then Eisenhower administrations. When he returned the manuscript to Pennsylvania in 1958 he sent with it something akin to his appraisal of his future as a writer—a realization that his achievements would fall short of his hopes.

In his letter to Linton Satterthwaite, Director of the University Museum, he reported, "At the time I took it on, I was still coasting on my military pay and I let myself be deluded that I could take the time required to teach myself Quiché while still supporting myself and family. . . . At the end of 1956 it looked as if the desired situation might develop within the next few months, whereupon I fell gravely ill and all my surplus went to the medical profession."

He tried for several years to encourage the Maryknoll fathers in Guatemala to engage in what he termed "salvage ethnology." In some respects this reflected his continuing interest in field work— a passion or an affliction which lingers on in an ethnographer—but in part also he was trying to awaken in the missionary fathers a sensitivity for the values and beliefs which they were trying in good faith to supplant. It was to this point that he wrote Father James P. La Coste in January 1958.

> The study of your Indians is interesting from two points of view. They are a people in transition—you and your colleagues are one of the powerful transitional forces—and as their religion and other aspects of their culture change, they present a study of considerable interest to anyone concerned with cultural dynamics. Second, they have retained a remarkable amount of the lore of pre-Columbian Mayas, and what we have learned of it so far has helped greatly in reconstructing parts of that ancient civilization.

On a different occasion, writing to one of these padres, he remarked: "In one way or another, the *costumbre* [the native religion, a hybrid of nativism and Christianity] has to go, and personally I prefer to see it go by being replaced with a living belief than merely die away into the common twentieth century vacuum."

He tried to be specific about the kind of information the missionary fathers might look for, as he wrote in the letter to Father La Coste.

> To give you an instance of how the study of people like these can help in the broader study of the whole history of Maya culture, I would take what I got on the calendar during my two visits to the Cuchamatanes in 1927 and 1932. I was struck by the remarkable fact that with but little communication between the pertinent authorities in the different villages and without a system of writing, there was entire agreement as to the Maya date of any given day among people speaking different dialects. In that same period, another scientist came up with a modern Quiche calendar that correlated exactly with the Cuchamatan ones. Starting from there, I worked backward through the existing records of dates in our system that were recorded in Maya Day Name-and-Number to Bishop Landa's first recordings [1566] in Yucatan, then carried over to the Aztec. Out of this I was able to show [*Maya Ethnology:*

The Sequence of Cultures] that, except for a demonstrable error of one day by Bishop Landa, all of these calendars from Mexico City to central Guatemala, over a period of 500 years, had been maintained without the loss of a day. Hence I suggested that any valid correlation of the dates on the ancient Maya monuments with our historical calendar should meet the test of fitting this continuity of Day Names.

The Maryknoll fathers were willing, but their lack of training in the social sciences handicapped their efforts. They did not know what questions to ask, nor of whom to ask them. They seemed unaware of cultural survivals or of accommodations that may have been made between the old ways of belief and the new. Unconsciously, they looked upon Indians as a people without a history—not an unusual attitude among "advanced" people in confronting a preliterate folk people.

La Farge chided the missionaries on occasion, urging them to read the English translation of *Annals of Cakchiquels* and *Titles of the Lords of Totonicapan,* about which he commented: "If you will read these—and I am sure that they will not corrupt your Christianity—you will understand better the significance of the very strange myths about Our Lord in Santa Eulalia, and will be helped in spotting possibly significant material." Correspondence remained friendly and respectful—La Farge collected books for the Maryknoll mission—but it was fruitless as a venture in data collecting.

Inevitably, La Farge found himself outside the brotherhood of social scientists. As in any profession, unless one stays in midstream and rides with the current, he may easily become beached or trapped in slack water. Oliver recognized the justice of this (he referred to himself as "a nonpracticing anthropologist"), but he spoke out, sharply at times, when practitioners in the social sciences tried to dismiss him as a meddling amateur and—further to disqualify him—a fiction writer.

At one time he exchanged polite insults with Dr. Margaret

Mead. In October 1951, when writing Dr. Eliot Chapple to complain about a "Code of Ethics" proposed by the Society for Applied Anthropology, La Farge cited the "weasel-worded, . . . inadequate" style of the paper. "The author, like many other scientists," he wrote, "would come close to intelligibility if he would abandon the Fallacy of the Long Sentence or Dromedary Construction."

Chapple, the editor, executed an agile sidestep and turned the letter over to Dr. Mead, who had served as chairman of the committee which labored and brought forth the misprized statement. In her reply she explained some of the committee's problems, then offered to engage his services: "If this is a case of artistic indigestion, and you are genuinely concerned about the problems raised, will you . . . consider attempting to put our code, to which we have given many years of thought and effort, into a form which will endear it to lovers of the English language."

La Farge replied, "I feel that the applied anthropologist is an individual engaging in one of the most important, dangerous, and potentially beneficial of all possible forms of tinkering with human life. Unless he has deep convictions, genuine courage, a firm code of ethics, and great clarity of thought, he is unfit for any such undertaking. To my mind the Society's present code of ethics demonstrates the absence of all of these qualities. It shows instead self-protectiveness, timidity, and turgidity of mind."

As a proper gentleman, he thought it only fitting to comment: "My very high opinion of yourself as both writer and scientist leaves me all the more surprised that such a document should have been issued when you had a hand in it."

He saw no reason why scientists should not be literate or why they should be allowed to maim and mongrelize the English language in the name of science. "Good scientists write simply and clearly," he insisted and, as well, "the affectation of an esoteric vocabulary is the hallmark of the second-rater."

He was critical of word usage social scientists accepted uncomplainingly. In reviewing the special Southwest issue of the *American Anthropologist* (August 1954), he cited examples.

It is saddening to note that even distinguished anthropologists now confuse "disinterest" and "uninterest." One hates to see so useful a word destroyed. More objectionable is the now strongly established practice of referring to all American Indians in the singular. Anthropologists affect to write, "There are 3400 Hopi" or such combinations as "the Hopi are." They would not write "There are millions of Swede," nor would they dream of saying, "the American are." How this vice started is obscure; it is bad English, and it is semantically dangerous, since it fosters the error of thinking of tribes as monoliths.

He refused to apologize for being a professional writer, not a practicing ethnologist. In writing the Introduction to *Santa Eulalia, the Religion of a Cuchamatan Town,* he warned he would use "a good deal of subjective, even opinionated, writing. This is present partly because the author is an amateur scientist and an ardent professional writer. It is present even more because the writer believes that ethnology is an inexact science, inseparable from subjective, qualitative observations. The opinions and bias of the observers, therefore, are essential data which should be frankly stated. The colorless objectivity affected by many ethnologists is a deception and a suppression of data." A practicing ethnologist might shy from such an admission to maintain his professional standing. In fact, some would quarrel with La Farge, and perhaps take the position that his statement proved what they knew all along—he was no scientist!

The "science of Indian affairs," about which he wrote with some optimism in *The Changing Indian,* never materialized. It never disentangled itself from the maze of civil service requirements, political pressures, and perpetual emergencies that beset Indian life. His being assigned to the Hopi reservation was part of John Collier's strategy to incorporate anthropology into the procedures of the Bureau. The effort was smashed by a suspicious Congress which seemed to resent the idea of applying scientific method to human affairs.

Collier would not accept the verdict and tried again in 1941, when, in collaboration with the Committee on Human Development of the University of Chicago, he established the Indian Education Research Project. The project was a pioneering interdisciplinary venture involving anthropology, psychology, psychiatry, medicine, and human ecology, but it was launched in September 1941, and after Pearl Harbor it lost key personnel to the military build-up of the war. No commissioner after Collier took the view that Indian affairs was a proper field for empirical process.

While La Farge retained the scientist's faith in methodology and generalization distilled from the particular, he found himself caught up in everyday complications. He brought scientifically trained and oriented individuals into the governing board of the Association on American Indian Affairs, but their talents, like his own, were soon dissipated in planning crisis strategems. The only generalizations that emerged were those phrased in his own writings, and these were personal, polemic, and often *parti pris*. It was an area of ambition in which the diminution was grievously felt.

The vision of himself that Oliver carried out of boyhood changed in various ways—diminishing in grandeur, but gaining in firm outline. The transformation was gradual, imperceptible, except when in moments of alcoholic lucidity he saw the dismal road over which he had traveled. His autobiographical *Raw Material* reveals the process of disintegration and reaffirmation through which he lived.

His relationships within the world of Saunderstown and with his brothers, which in the early years were close and warmly supportive, reflect the flow of his concerns. Saunderstown and his relationships there presumed material success and a secure social position. One needed a substantial amount of money to maintain these, and thus money is a constant theme in the letters between the brothers—money to pay living expenses, to provide for the upkeep of a shooting lodge on Narragansett Bay, to maintain club dues. Oliver and Christopher depended on income from literary sales; Francis, partner in a New York investment house, was concerned with the management of family finances. Of the three, Oliver had the rockiest road to travel. Except for the war period, he never escaped the pressure of finances. "I cannot tell you how often between 1936 and 1942 I literally did not know where the next month's rent was coming from," he wrote Christopher in 1948. "It is a wretched way to live."

The tender side of the relationship is revealed in Oliver's story "Thick on the Bay," in the collection *A Pause in the Desert*. It is a story of two brothers trying to make a safe landing in heavy fog. Partway across Narrangansett Bay they become aware of a powerful motor launch bearing down on them—it is Prohibition times, and they suspect a rumrunner taking advantage of the fog to outmaneuver a Coast Guard cutter. In terror, as disaster roars down upon them, the elder brother thinks of his young brother's safety; "I'm master, he must not drown." His own safety does not occur to him.

When they reach shore at last, after escaping an exchange of gunfire between rumrunner and Coast Guard and the expected collision, the younger brother turns sick at the dock and vomits. He is not just relieving his panic—something had happened out there. The elder brother waits not insisting, for him to explain. Then it comes out: the boy had seen a man in the water, probably from the rumrunner, mortally wounded, flop over and go under. After the nausea had passed and he could speak of it, he said simply, "It was bad enough me seeing it, I didn't want you to see it, too."

The intimate exchanges, the companionship, shared weddings and Christmas parties continued through the years, but with the passing of time the inner quality changed. Some of the occasions of family solidarity became a burden and survived as form, if they survived at all. One of the first casualties was the big family gathering at Christmas—the "25 or more" uncles, aunts, cousins, and always the "stray guest," as Christopher described it in a magazine piece. By 1939, after coping with such an affair in his New York flat without help, Oliver declared "I am going to make a serious effort next year to get the dinner permanently called off."

Another early casualty was the relationship between the three brothers and their sister, Margaret. A virulent animosity had developed on Margaret's part toward her mother, and this animus in time cut her off from her brothers. So bitter and unrelenting was the hostility that on the occasion of his mother's funeral in 1944 Oliver wrote Consuelo expressing reget that he could not leave Washington, but he added, "At the same time [I am] glad that I do not have to witness all the nasty tensions which will revolve around Peggy. Fond as people were of my father, it is mother whom Milly, Aunt Frances, Uncle Ben deeply loved, and all of whom are poison to Peggy. . . ."

The pressing need for money at times came close to driving the brothers apart—and it drove Oliver out of Rhode Island. In the first flush of success in 1931, Oliver had purchased 100 acres of land near the La Farge holdings at Saunderstown. The plot was strategically located to block off encroachment by invaders, and at the time of purchase Oliver intended ultimately to build a country place, in the tradition of his family and class.

After he settled in Santa Fe in 1941, the likelihood of ever returning to Rhode Island to live receded into the misty past. And finally a time came when the ownership of that property seemed to him sheer folly. In 1948 he received a generous offer for the property, more than double the price he had paid for it. But to sell meant, in a very practical sense, breaking with his clan. Specifically, the sale would destroy somewhat the value of the neighboring property Christopher owned. And so he wrote to his brother:

I cannot tell you how I long to achieve a situation in which I am sure that at, say, sixty, I can pay the rent and have food to eat if for any reason I should have to stop working. I would like to go beyond that. I'd give anything to get quickly to a position in which Consuelo would feel willing to hire a maid right along. . . . My actions, decisions, and I am sure many details of my behavior of which I am unaware, are strongly influenced by my financial situation and the attendant sense of insecurity. So that in a situation like the present one you get a line of thinking something like this: My present dependable income is about $1,000 a year, if you include royalties on back books. The land costs me $55 a year in taxes. That is sheer extravagance. . . . If I sell this land, then perhaps my dependable income will rise to $100 a month, which will be an important landmark in my project.

Christopher, earlier, had written: "It is difficult for me to advise you what to do about this, as it so very clearly affects the River Farm [Christopher's property]." The prospect, as all knew, was that Oliver's holding would be divided by the new owners into many small parcels, on each of which summer cottages would be built, and the countryside would be swarmed over by intruders. Christopher foresaw these possibilities, but tried not to be obstructive: "Gosh, I can't advise you on it. I'm too damned prejudiced. I've hung onto that place so hard and have put so damned many eggs into that basket that I'm awfully vulnerable now." It was quite possible that, at age fifty, he would have to give up Rhode Island, and he wrote Oliver, "I'm sick of the necessity of making changes—I've about used up my capacity in that regard."

Francis, a cool businessman, emotionally attached to both brothers but with some partiality toward Oliver (he once complained that Christopher could not get along with fewer than three servants, and never arose before noon) was blunt in his advice. "I would disregard all the special pleading regarding his age and the rest. You cannot possibly be run by his special problems. Fit them in if you can but that is all. . . . I would look upon it almost entirely as an investment."

When the sale was made, Christopher never again alluded to it, and he stayed on at the River Farm. For Oliver, what might have been a disappointment, a failure of achievement, the relinquishment of his Rhode Island acreage brought an end to a style of life he could no longer support in fact or in fancy. The social convention which had prompted his purchase originally no longer played a part in his life.

In 1941 Christopher, being the eldest son, took charge of dividing up their father's personal possessions—clothing, guns and fishing tackle, letters, photographs, and some jewelry. The quantity was not great and the items were valuable only as remembrances of their father and the life they had shared together. But to get the job done, since none of the others was at hand to consult, Christopher made four approximately equal piles—one for their sister Margaret and one for each brother—and then cast lots, "for there seemed no other fair way to divide them."

What followed after that was a period of meticulous negotiation, each acting properly, but not yielding anything. Two items in question were a 28- and a 20-gauge shotgun, of which Christopher remarked: "I think it was agreed I was to have the 28."

Oliver replied: "The only thing I question is about the 28. As a matter of fact, the question of the 28 and the 20 seems a little tough to solve. For the last year or so, I've always oiled them and so forth. As long as we have a common center, the 20 is a nice gun to have in reserve for wives or for special uses, but I think that eventually that kind of ownership in common becomes difficult, and I suppose some settlement ought to be made of both guns now. . . . If you feel that you have a special claim to the 28 (did Daddy buy it originally for you?), that's important."

Later, Oliver tempered his statement. "What I said about the 28 was just a consideration. I don't want to be grabby. Franny and I each received a gun, I got the long knockabout 12, which is still in Daddy's room in the leather case, Franny the short one, on the basis that neither of us had a gun. . . . So you have a claim on the 28 or the 20. . . ."

Beneath all the sharing, the tidying up of small debts, the balancing of gifts, the occasional stresses that marked the relationship, ran an undeviating loyalty. Francis, the little brother, about whom both elder brothers worried as they watched him building a career in Wall Street and forsaking intellectual interests, became the anchorpost of the family. To him fell the thankless task of eking out the precariously slender resources of the father and mother—with a father often rebelling against austerity. Only once did he protest.

This was in September 1943—Christopher Grant La Farge was dead, the mother failing, Oliver was with the Air Transport Command, and Christopher was writing war stories in the South

Pacific. Francis had the full burden of providing nursing care and living arrangements for his mother, while carrying a heavy schedule for his investment partnership. He wrote Oliver: "I wonder what would happen if I let out a really loud yell and pulled out. I guess everyone believes too strongly that I never will. Well, I get a little tired once in a while. You can answer this one from China." Oliver was then traveling to the far corners of the embattled world, and civilian Wall Street was a dull affair.

Realizing perhaps that Oliver might not return from one of his flights, Francis wrote: "I believe that the time has come to put your income and capital on a sound basis and on as permanent a one as possible. He had been managing Oliver's investments ever since the publication of *Laughing Boy,* and, as the letter indicates, the investment record reflected the convulsions in the American economy.

> I am going to turn over to you one-fifth of the share of the Bingham that mother gave me as part of her estate.
>
> You will remember that your money came in at the top of the stock boom in 1929 and that I put it in a joint account for you and myself. The crash in 1929 wiped out forty percent of the account. In March 1930, the outlook for the stock market appearing distinctly sour, I took the balance of our funds and invested them in a small company of a friend of mine. . . . At the time it seemed a safer move than leaving the money in the stock market and at the same time getting a good income.

The deepening depression caught up with the company and regular dividend payments were suspended in 1931. After 1935, nothing had been paid. Francis explained:

> Because I had some hope that the company would get back on its feet, I have been paying your income and capital withdrawals out of my own funds. They have totalled $7,600 over the actual income. The 1938 depression and then the war restrictions have made it virtually impossible for the company to come back.
>
> It is impossible, of course, to tell at this time what would have

happened to your funds if I had pursued a different course. The stock market did decline from 393 in the average in the fall of 1929 to 43 in 1932, or 89%. . . . It is now at 137, or 65% below the 1929 level. On these bases and others, and without making any adjustments for the differences in income payments over receipts or capital withdrawals, your funds and income would be no larger today and possibly less than the value and income of the Bingham. . . .

When he received the letter, as he wrote to Consuelo in Santa Fe, Oliver showed both surprise and chagrin at what had taken place without his knowledge. "The sainted man has been kicking in to me out of his own pocket for years, when he certainly did not need to. . . . I have written him that he owes me nothing. The Bingham dividend went to him because he gets no real estate [from the mother's estate]."

All this, this way of acting responsibly whatever the personal cost, had entered into their ordering of their lives. In another realm it accounted for Oliver's anger when he encountered irresponsible men and irresponsible public policy operating in Indian affairs. Now, though surprised by it, he understood and approved of what his brother had done.

At the very time that Oliver was pulling up his Rhode Island roots, he had to face one of his most crushing disappointments. In the spring of 1948 the La Farges were expecting a child. Oliver made only casual mention of the coming event in his family correspondence of the time, but as the days passed the likelihood was an engrossing prospect. La Farge families had always been large families, comprising children, relatives of all degree, household pets in and out of doors—with noise and confusion. He and Consuelo had lived alone until they moved to Santa Fe, where the Baca family had settled after giving up the Rociada home. The La Farge's house in Santa Fe was always open to visitors and they entertained frequently. Still, it was a childless house, tacitly reminding Oliver of the children who had become strangers to him.

All of this was in his mind as he and Consuelo counted off the days. He went to New York in May for the annual meeting of the association, and while he was enroute to the airport for the return trip, and out of communication, Consuelo was taken to the hospital. Oliver reached Santa Fe just before their baby girl was born.

From the moment of birth their jubilation was tempered. The birth was premature, otherwise Oliver would not have been out of the city. The infant failed to overcome a gastric obstruction and lived for only a week.

When he could write about it at all, after some days had passed, Oliver recited the details to Christopher and asked a favor: "I'd appreciate it if you'd circulate the essence of the information above, I can't go writing it over and over."

There had been disappointments, losses, transformations—none as grievous as this.

✤ XIX ✤

An Orderly Withdrawal

LA FARGE possessed an extraordinary capacity for entering into warm and enduring relationships, sharing himself deeply and unreservedly, and being himself renewed by personal attachments. This sharing was not limited to family, where it might be expected, but extended to the relationships he sustained through the years with Vidal Gutierrez of Santa Clara Pueblo, with the leaders of the Jicarilla Apache tribe, and with a number of individuals. With the Association on American Indian Affairs and its predecessors he had, in effect, a long love affair.

Oliver's marriage to Consuelo and his subsequent acceptance in the Baca family were ideal objects for these qualities in Oliver. He had not simply married into a family but became a participating member. In writing to Christopher soon after he and Consuelo moved to Santa Fe in 1941, Oliver explained: "The Bacas are less divided than the La Farges, and I should say, in view of their limited means, more swiftly generous, but nonetheless they are running into problems and personalities. I find myself taking on to some extent the role of elder brother, and everything I have learned in our cooperation is of enormous value."

Within that first year of the move to Santa Fe, Consuelo's mother was seriously ill, with a major operation in prospect. The cost of travel to a medical center plus the medical expense involved a sum of money which neither Mrs. Baca nor any of her children possessed, and when Oliver mentioned his role of elder brother, he had a specific incident in mind. Each of the children wanted to contribute toward the expense, and Oliver persuaded them to pool their funds, instead of each offering a gift, for reasons which he explained to one of the absent daughters:

> One principle we learned within our own [La Farge] dealings with my mother and father. I've urged it on the kids here, and they're all agreed to it. Contributions of money must not be personal. We shall pool our funds here, deposit them to [Mrs. Baca's] credit, and give her a slip in a tactful way. . . . When an individual kicks in, a mother is bound to think in terms of the individual's situation and so forth. There is a danger of creating a sense of obligation, even discomfort, which is the death of generosity. . . . We must keep a schedule, of course, of the contributions among ourselves, so as to know what the total is, and do what we can to keep track of the costs incurred and the sums paid out.
>
> Your mother has no idea of what's going to be given her, and she is worried about finances. If it can be properly handled, having her family pick up the ball should give her real pleasure. And that leaves all of us feeling good, and closer together than ever.

At first it was a startling procedure when suggested to the "swiftly generous" Bacas. Oliver told Christopher, "Consuelo had felt that we, in our planning for Mother and what she heard of our relations with Daddy, as well as our balancing of efforts among each other, were heartless. This upset me, for I had felt that, un-emotionally, we had done pretty damn well. Now she understands, and her whole feeling about it has changed."

As it worked out, Oliver was designated by the Baca children to act as treasurer for the group, receiving and depositing con-tributions, making a record of expenditures, and keeping all mem-bers informed of income and outgo. And he was the one selected to inform Mrs. Baca, which he did by formal letter, saying, "It gives me the greatest pleasure to enclose with this a deposit slip for a small fund raised by [your children] jointly to help you with your expenses in New York, medical and otherwise. . . . I can assure you that no one has made what could be properly called sacrifices: the contributions have been spontaneous tokens of everyone's affection for a grand person, and if the use of the money gives one-tenth as much pleasure to you as producing it has to your family, we shall have attained our goal."

He also informed the La Farges in New York and Rhode Island of Mrs. Baca's impending visit, and she was wined and dined, taken to Macy's and to the Metropolitan Opera. It was a most successful siege of illness.

It was out of this background of family association, which grew always closer as the years passed, that the incidents and characters emerged which went into the writing of the Rociada stories, published in the collection *Behind the Mountains* (1956). Oliver had been listening to the remembrances of childhood told by the Baca children for some time before he realized their story value. Once he started writing, it became a kind of family collaboration, with everyone interested and contributing something out of the buried past. It was an extraordinary performance, a kind of autobiography of a family, told through a friendly interpreter.

The stories have a magical quality, a compound of remembrance and reality, that sets them apart from La Farge's other writing. Using actual names and actual happenings demanded a decent regard for veracity, but people and events are presented principally through the eyes of the Baca children, and this allows for a blurring of character and event, as in "Snow Too Deep," or for mystery and even a suggestion of terror, as in "Visit of Politeness" and "Cap in the Snow." The shock of reality as registered in sensitive adolescence emerges in "The Loss of a Hero."

The first of the stories was submitted to *The New Yorker* in July 1950, at a time when sales had been slow and Oliver was feeling impoverished. He wrote Christopher at the time: "Keep your fingers crossed and burn candles for me. *The New Yorker* has taken the first of what I hope is to be my new series, and I believe they're going to take the second. It looks as if I might really be in business."

By the end of November the magazine was "sitting on four pieces . . . , waiting for me to send in some more before they start running them." In keeping with its policy, the magazine paid for every piece on acceptance, and each story after the fourth, including the first four retroactively, earned a percentage bonus.

Oliver had published occasional pieces in *The New Yorker,* at least since 1938, and in 1950 he signed a "First Reading" agreement with the magazine, which was renewed annually through 1962. The agreement gave the magazine a first option, limited usually to one year, to accept or reject "all fiction, humor, reminiscence and casual essays," to be bought at a rate above the magazine's "going" rate.

In the years after 1950, while La Farge and the Association on American Indian Affairs were battling in Congress and with the executive branch of government to salvage some of the reforms of the earlier years, writing for a living for Oliver was especially difficult. Arguing policies and issues was distracting, to say the least, while planning and launching strategies consumed great blocks of time. His attempt to limit Indian work to two days a week was regularly thwarted, and his trips east to attend meetings of the association drained his energies in later years.

In spite or perhaps because of the difficulties, however, these were the years in which his writing matured. He produced no major work because of the prohibitive investment of time required, but the more carefully wrought of his short stories often have depths of perception and emotion usually found only in a fully conceived novel.

Such a story is "Old Century's River," published in the *Atlantic Monthly* in September 1950, at the beginning of that period. A jungle and river tramp, facing certain death somewhere in Central America after an airplane crash that left him with a gangrenous shattered leg, achieves a kind of triumph within himself and poses a contrast between Indian and white man with startling relevance. In the flow of consciousness which La Farge uses here with great skill, Old Century, as he is known among jungle Indians and in the bars of river towns, muses, "An Indian would have given up by now. An Indian's reason would have told him that it was all over days ago, and very reasonably he would have given up and avoided a lot of discomfort by deliberately dying, the way Indians know how to do. A white man goes beyond reason—and so a lot of times he wins out when he ought not to."

The Northern Cheyenne Indians who battled Dakota blizzards and the U. S. Army and in the end won freedom in Montana—the few who were left—could quarrel with Old Century's theories. Certainly they went beyond reason—and won because they were entitled to win. La Farge was well aware of this distinction— but Old Century had no way of knowing about that and so he saw the white man enduring when there was no hope. It was part of the small triumph he achieved for himself.

La Farge is saying here that white men have been seeing Indians in just such contrasting terms since the first landfall in the Western Hemisphere and asserting a spurious primacy on which they thrive in some small inner world. "Old Century's River" covers a lot of history.

The stories appearing in the posthumously published *The Door in the Wall* (1955), with one exception, were written in those last years, and all have this maturity, the searching revelations, and seemingly effortless structure. The stories draw upon anthropological material, normally not subject matter to fascinate a nonprofessional reader. La Farge makes judicious use of jargon, not for the sake of authenticity, though it contributes to that, but as part of the narrative drive.

"Independent Research," the earliest of these stories (1937), deals with traditional material—the cultured Western man, in this case scientist, who has stayed too long in a lax native world and gone to the bottle—but the narration is freshly detailed, each item a telling stroke which condemns and yet evokes pity. "Journey in Remembering" (1960) traces the web of associations by which a man's complex career is pieced together.

In "The Senior Assistant" (1959) and "The Timely Death of Wallace Caswell" (1965) he fully uses archaeological apparatus, which is not only believable and exciting, but conveys touches of humor. Perhaps the most effective of the stories in this vein is the title story, "The Door in the Wall" (1965), which derives more or less directly from La Farge's efforts to track down and correlate the esoterics of the Mayan belief system. In part, at least, it is a fictional treatment of the data reported in several of his scientific papers, primarily *Santa Eulalia.*

Yet even the success that came along during those years was punctuated with awkward stretches of time when nothing sold. His letters to Christopher have a fairly constant refrain: "If I sent you a hundred bucks at present [to pay his share of a joint obligation], I'd either have to miss the rent or have the light and phone cut off" (1949). . . . "My sales this year have been but lousy" (1952). . . . "Right now my unpaid bills, some going back three months, considerably exceed my bank balance" (1954). . . . "I have been writing and writing and not selling much of anything" (1955). . . . "I haven't sold a damned thing this summer, other than items such as book reviews" (1955).

A dance drama, "The White Shell Cross," which he wrote and helped to stage for the Tucson, Arizona, Festival Society, in the spring of 1951, was a disappointing failure. It was to have been the focal attraction of an annual civic celebration, but it was not repeated after that first performance.

He wrote two children's books, the first, published in 1953, was "Cochise," a fictionalized life of the Apache warrior, and the second, "The Mother Ditch," a collaboration with Karl Larsson, a Santa Fe artist, which appeared in 1954. Neither sold as well as expected.

One financially successful publication was "A Pictorial History of the American Indian," published in 1956, although it was a worrisome book to produce. La Farge had to inspect many hundreds of illustrations the publisher gathered from a variety of sources, following an outline and instructions Oliver had prepared in advance. From these he selected the pictures for his text and prepared captions and the text—all of which involved copious correspondence. A children's edition, "The American Indian," was brought out in 1960, and this contained prints of original paintings as well as many new illustrations. While he referred to these works as "potboilers," the writing is lean and spirited. He meant them to be instructive.

For the La Farges the year 1951 was "a wonderful year, with a lot of interesting work, Consuelo well, lots of fun together"; at the very end of the year, on December 28, their son was born. "It looks like a new baby," Oliver wrote his brothers, "and probably is."

This event was of more than ordinary importance, wholly belied by this casual reference. His estrangement from the children of his first marriage was a continuing anguish, and repeated efforts at reconciliation achieved only frustration. The son, who discarded the name Oliver and became Peter La Farge, and as such was known as a rodeo performer and folk singer, caused special grief. Oliver went to extraordinary lengths to help the developing boy, who possessed a variety of talents but seemed incapable of maturing any of his gifts. He died suddenly, soon after Oliver's death, still in search of himself. Povy, the daughter, remained aloof through her growing-up years, and as a young woman entering her own marriage, refused to invite her father to her wedding. Oliver wrote her a scolding letter, reminding her of the social amenities of such an occasion. He wrote a story, "The Bright Faces" (in the collection *A Pause in the Desert*) exploring the emotional context within which a father must deal with the children of a sundered marriage.

The loss of his and Consuelo's daughter in 1948 after one week of life denied him once again the pleasure of having a child in the house, hence the arrival of their son was of deep importance and joy. They named the boy John Pendaries, linking Consuelo's mother's family name with La Farge, and promptly familiarized that to "Pen," to avoid "the profusion of Johnnies in the La Farge family." Oliver wrote: "Calling the infant 'Pen' is proving profitable, as we have made a house rule that anyone who makes a joke about 'Pen and Ink' sticks a dime in his piggy bank." And then, "It will be a miracle if I can lay up the money to send him to Harvard." Shortly, after a church christening, Pen was taken to

Santa Clara Pueblo, where Uncle Vidal, quite old now, sang over him and named him "Tanyi Hwan."

The readers of Oliver's weekly column in the Santa Fe newspaper, *The New Mexican,* were kept informed through the next years of the joys and hazards of growing up with a child—a child who could take a house apart handily and grow new grass where his father's efforts yielded only bald earth. These were healing experiences. With a child to absorb his hours and a writer's precarious income to earn, the politics of Indian affairs were more than ordinarily obtrusive during those years, or so it seemed. There were compensations, however.

The congressional and executive onslaughts against Indian people that characterized the Eisenhower administration had quickened the Association on American Indian Affairs into a more effective and better known citizen group. Much of this growth after the mid-fifties was attributable to the efforts of the talented and energetic La Verne Madigan. On one occasion she remarked on the transformation of the association from an agency of agitation to one of action, referring to programs then in operation or soon to be initiated. Action can have a limiting, unilateral purpose, which culminates when an objective has been attained. Miss Madigan was speaking rather of the kind of action that arises from a social idea or principle and gives release to many community forces in an ongoing train of consequences.

Such was the demonstration project with the unwieldy name We Shake Hands, which she described as "a method by which conquered American Indian communities may rediscover their power to act on their own behalf, and fulfill their desire for independence by relating themselves as political, economic, and social equals to other communities of the United States."

The program was initiated in 1957 in the Great Plains Area, under an even more unwieldy title: "An action to create neighborly relations between Indians and non-Indians of the Great Plains." As a program in community development, the emphasis was on the internal structure of the community as acted upon, most often negatively, by the external surrounding environment. Of the Great Plains tribal groups, La Farge had observed: "These tribes are lonely and in need of friends in their home states."

Miss Madigan explained in 1961,

> Social mobility can be restored to Indian communities only by restoration of the Indian people's belief that they can have purposes of their own and can act effectively to accomplish them.
>
> The recovery of this belief was preceded by anguished efforts to escape . . . because it involved facing the hated, humiliating image of themselves as conquered people, and facing the true meaning of their dependence upon federal government. . . .
>
> Once looked at squarely, this intolerable self-image had to be replaced by the image of themselves with the unrelinquished political right to reverse their conquest. The means to this end was seen to be the economic and social development of their communities to the point at which they could themselves declare their colonial dependence upon the federal government at an end. . . . The action took the form of the exercise of citizenship, first within the Indian community itself, in relation to tribal government, then increasingly within the county and the state.

It proved to be a social instrument of great effectiveness, as reservation communities cooperated with their white neighbors on problems involving civil rights, race relations, fair employment, and equal treatment in the courts. By first setting their own houses in order, the tribes that worked with the We Shake Hands program went on into economic planning and resource development and invariably found that the outside, non-Indian community was friendly and responsive in contributing technical skills and experience to the solution of reservation problems.

The Northern Cheyenne Tribe of Montana, one of the early participants in the program, found for example, that residents of the neighboring city of Billings readily formed a committee of assistance which recruited skills as needed. Miss Madigan reported: "The members of this committee are persons of greater local influence and deeper sensitivity with respect to Indians than can usually be mustered together in an Indian area, and are working quickly and smoothly with Cheyennes in a number of interracial sub-committees, each assigned the task of developing a specific economic enterprise." It was a leader in this tribe who introduced a tribal development program by declaring: "Take each of us alone, a man apart from the Cheyenne people who remember the same things and wish for the same things. Take each one of us that way, and you have nothing but a man who cannot respect himself because he is a failure in the white man's way. . . . Now take all of us together as Cheyenne people. Then our names are not the names of failures. They are the names of great and generous hunters who fed the people, fighters who died for freedom just as white men's heroes died, holy men who filled us with the power of God. Take us together that way and there is a drink for every man in the cup of self-respect. . . . The more we progress as Cheyennes, the more we will progress as Americans."

The ideas and methods of We Shake Hands quickly spread beyond the northern plains. By 1961 work was initiated with the Lumbees of North Carolina, the Miccosukee Seminoles of Florida, the Mississippi Choctaws, and the tribes of western Washington—all groups neglected, in some cases not even recognized, by the Bureau of Indian Affairs. Miss Madigan traveled to all of these out-of-the-way places. Brooklyn Irish that she was, she made lasting friendships and inspired loyalties wherever she worked in Indian communities.

Her last effort was with the Eskimos of the far north, the Arctic slope, and the problem on which she worked was complex and difficult. It involved nothing less than finding a means by which the natives of Alaska—Indians, Aleuts, Eskimos—might save for themselves the lands which they used and occupied from aboriginal times, now threatened with expropriation by the newly created state of Alaska.

For La Farge, seriously ailing, the work in Alaska meant fresh effort to acquaint himself with a history and a present situation of which he, like most Indianists, had been ignorant. To give guidance and make tenable decisions about the association's Alaska involvement he had to know the issues. He never accepted the judgment of others, however competent, without searching out the facts for himself. He very quickly discovered that the exploitative practices which had ruined the economics of the tribes in the so-called southern forty-eight would certainly determine the fate of the native peoples of the forty-ninth state, unless public concern was forcefully expressed. This was the theme of his 1962 report to the association. He observed:

> As far back as 1884 the Congress formally recognized that the natives had rights in the lands they used, and reserved to itself the task of determining just what territories belonged to the natives. . . . The enabling act of this new state does recognize that the native rights exist. It does so in general terms, raising only an uncertain shield between these people and simple expropriation of the earth on which they have so long abided. . . .
>
> Theoretical recognition of an undefined right is all very fine, but such recognitions are of no avail unless they are backed by firm intent and unquestionable authority.
>
> The Alaska Enabling Act authorizes the state to select 102,-550,000 acres of public domain, not otherwise occupied. We can argue that the state cannot lawfully obtain land that in fact belongs to communities of natives. We can argue, and history can repeat itself, and we can have all over again in Alaska what happened . . . in every part of the older, forty-eight states, wherever the natives of the land stood unaided against the furious land hunger of the white man.

Miss Madigan traveled through the north with local leaders, sitting in on community meetings, and reading extensively, and became remarkably well informed in a brief period. She was concerned to discover a basis on which the Eskimos especially could assert claims to the lands from which they gained their subsistence. Settled communities are few, and those few are widely scattered across vast spaces, and the people themselves are not corporately organized and prepared to act in unison. The style of life is well described in her letter to Oliver of August 19, 1962:

At Point Hope, Barrow, and every other Eskimo village I have visited, the most meaningful of all relationships and the least changed by impact with our culture seems to be the relationship of members of families to each other. A man seems to derive his feeling of security from his family. That is, every member seems to have an inescapable obligation to every other. This applies, apparently, to members of immediate family and in-laws, and also to quite distant relatives in other villages. When Guy [Okakok] and I were traveling last spring, "cousins" of his turned up in every single village we visited. . . . I teased Guy about having so many relatives so far from Barrow. Finally he said that in the old days the people of a village always rushed out to kill any stranger, and the stranger therefore would run as fast as he could to the home of a relation. He explained that a hunter made it a point to beget as many relations as possible in the course of his travels—and kept close track of them. The other Eskimo men I know say the same thing and say that the family tie is the strongest tie of all. . . .

I think the Eskimos will act together when a way has been found to get the families to act together. This should not be difficult . . . since the families have recognized heads, and neither the families nor the villages are too numerous.

There would be no point in our working out a plan for action by the families, the plan would be imposed. However, I think the Eskimos themselves should at their next meeting discuss the question—from what source can they derive the authority and power to act to help themselves—as individual villages and as Eskimo people. They will know whether the families are this source. If it is, they are smart enough to figure out how to tap it. It is not strange, really, that they have to go through this process. After all, they never were a unified people, and are only just now trying to become one.

The Eskimos did come together and they did make a proposal, based on discussions and agreement among themselves.

The Guy Okakok Miss Madigan mentioned presented the proposal following La Farge's address at the 1962 meeting of the Association on American Indian Affairs in New York. It was, he said, the "considerate and unselfish way," since it would not "take anything away from our fellow citizens in Alaska or all over the United States" and "it will save our Inupiat Paitot," which translates as Eskimo tradition or heritage.

He asked that "all the land north of Brooks Range from Barter Island through Ahnaktukvak Pass to Noatak be held in trust for the Eskimos by the United States. . . . Eskimos or Inupiat will gladly share mineral rights and administration with State of Alaska —maybe twenty-five percent of minerals to State and seventy-five percent to be invested in area to develop it economically for the Inupiat residents."

Miss Madigan played a decisive part in bringing home to the Eskimos an awareness of the peril in which they stood with respect to their land and their livelihood. Their response, as she had anticipated, was born of unity and a tradition of sharing. The land they asked for was the barren Arctic slope, where only Eskimos know how to survive, but they would share the buried minerals, which white men coveted.

It was the last service she performed for the native peoples of North America.

Two days after she wrote that letter to La Farge, while vacationing in Vermont, she was thrown from a horse and fatally injured. Oliver was battling his own health problems at the time, and the news staggered him. He wrote a letter to Alden Stevens, secretary of the association, a cry of sheer anguish.

When I try to think about this thing, I keep running into a sort of block because I begin by thinking immediately of consulting La Verne. I've worked very closely with her since she became exec [in 1956], and her not being there is very strange.

More than ever, I wish to God I'd never heard of American Indians. They've been a trap and a ruination for me. However, I had at least the satisfaction of having got a going concern set up and a hope of pulling back little by little, or maybe in a few jumps. Now, I wonder sourly whether all the work and the cost, and the hell it has raised with my work and income, are going to end in a flat tire.

He was tired and ailing. In a memorandum to the Executive Committee, October 5, 1962, he asked that the committee "start giving serious consideration to replacing me." As he explained: "I have been in very poor condition ever since last spring. In the beginning of September I underwent a thorough examination. It turns out that, in addition to a pair of lungs that I would not wish on the tomcat next door, I have a peptic ulcer and a somewhat enlarged heart. I am now on a very severe regimen."

The following spring, as he prepared for his annual trip east and the meeting of the association, his condition was really grave. His doctor tried to dissuade him from going, calling the effort "suicidal," and Oliver gave a lot of thought to ways of avoiding unnecessary meetings with individuals and time-consuming discussions. He wrote his new executive director, William Byler, "It rather makes me ashamed to have to play the invalid and ask for so much consideration, but it is the only way in which I can seriously consider another trip East."

Later in the letter he suggested, "If you think it worthwhile, I can arrange to reach New York on the morning of Friday, May 3, and hold myself at your disposal that day, although it is rather a waste of the Association's money to maintain me then over a weekend." The annual meeting would not take place until Monday.

As it turned out, the eastern trip was almost as disastrous as his doctor had anticipated. On June 11, Oliver wrote his closest friends on the board:

"I returned here to learn that I had water on my lungs, and had to take to my bed. . . . We might as well all make up our minds now that further trips East by me are most unlikely." He had gone to Taos earlier that month, at a cost of two days in bed.

"I am faced with the likelihood of an early, rather slow, and expensive death, which cannot be covered by insurance," he further confided to his board members, and again urged that he be relieved of responsibility as president. He concluded his letter: "It is not easy for me to make this withdrawal. With the exception of the interlude 1941–47, I have carried the burden of this Association since 1933, seldom, of course, without co-workers. If at times the load has been galling, and of recent years increasingly so, the work has also been an integral part of my life. It goes back to my first intimate association with Indians in 1921, and has woven through many personal relationships and rich experiences. However, I have no choice."

As he planned the growth of the association, so now in the last weeks and days, he planned an orderly transition for the workers who would succeed him.

* XX *

The View from the End

JOHN LA FARGE, the painter, marked well the lineaments and the personalities of his descendants. Doubtless the traits and physical features ascend beyond him, but no record exists. Royal Cortissoz, writing in *The Dictionary of American Biography,* describes John La Farge as "six feet tall, deep-chested, with long and slender hands and feet. His dark brown hair . . . crowned a magnificent head. His grey-green eyes were set in deep sockets; his nose was long, straight, and aristocratic; his skin . . . fairly warm."

Of himself, John La Farge wrote to his close friend, Henry Adams: "My temper is frightful and the world is stuffed with sawdust." The letter is quoted by the Reverend John La Farge, S. J., Oliver's favorite uncle, in his autobiographical *The Manner Is Ordinary.* Father John also reports that Grant La Farge, Oliver's father, had an even worse temper than John the painter, by the latter's acknowledgment. This particular trait, at least, had an ancient lineage. Jean-Frédéric de la Farge married Louisa Binsse, and this family, originally emigrants out of Ireland into Britanny, were "inclined to be quarrelsome" and "had a tradition of dissent, talkativeness, and charity which appeared in one generation after another," according to Father John.

Oliver appears through the haze of these antiquities, and even more clearly, perhaps, in a further description of John La Farge, the painter, written by his son, John, the Jesuit.

> He was interested in everything that concerned man and mankind; yet not in the spirit of the mere sentimental humanitarian,

233

in fact, he was curiously unsentimental. His dry, humorous cynicism was in accordance with ancestral traditions. He was concerned in somewhat eighteenth-century fashion with all varieties of human beings, near and far, different races and types of men, their ways, their habits, their songs, their dances, their customs, and their wars, their psychology, the peculiarities of old and young, men and women—particularly the strange things that women do to you when you are trying to get through your work as an artist.

A description to fit an ethnographer—or a novelist—or both. Such inheritance laid the gridwork, on which experience fashioned the overlay. That experience began in the twenties, about which Oliver's Harvard classmate Archibald MacLeish had written: "A generation born in [a] century of stability and order—of reliable events, forseeable consequences. . . . It was not easy for us . . . to accept the fact that that world was no longer there. . . . It was not the Lost Generation which was lost: it was the world out of which that generation came. And it was not a generation of expatriates who found themselves in Paris in those years but a generation whose *patria,* wherever it may once have been, was now no longer waiting for them anywhere."

As an age of protest the twenties seem mild, in retrospect, but an age can be seen properly only against its time. The jazz age—bobbed hair, short skirts, bathtub gin, and country club extravaganzas—seemed disturbingly outrageous even violent, to a society seeking to recapture the pre-war days of "stability and order." Certainly the causes for protest were real, with a complacent Harding administration giving rise to public scandals, with an Attorney General seeking to crush dissent, with strike-breaking goon squads, and with the searing experience of the Sacco-Vanzetti tragedy.

Oliver's sheltered growing-up years had left him with a sense of belonging to a secure world, a world that would continue, and he did not experience the first intimations of illusion until late adolescence. His contacts with reality were still so tentative that his only arena for protest was internal and subjective—and he did not express even that until much later, when he wrote about his Groton years.

Oliver followed his own course of interest, digging out archaeological ruins. That brought him, in time, to the realities of the Indian world, where the absurd and brutal actions of the dominant society, *his* society, stirred him to deep protest. And there he found himself.

The feeling of inadequacy, of certain defeat—if not this time, then the next time—which troubled his early years, was first tempered on the trip across Black Mesa in the summer of 1924. Bart Hayes, who shared that journey of discovery, talked about it in later perspective: "Oliver was not running away, but exploring, expanding his own inner life by coming close to the lives of others."

His involvement with the West and with Indians may have started as escapism, as he insisted, but to let it go at that is to ignore those qualities of the West, largely intangible, sometimes overpowering, which could attract and hold a man with La Farge's capacity to absorb sensuous impressions. The truth is leaner in the West. The whole of creation is exposed to the knowing eye in thousands of canyons and upthrust mesas. Something of this directness of communication affects the relationships between people after long acclimatization. It is a pronounced characteristic of Indian relationships.

The West, when La Farge first came to know it, had a poor image of itself. The sons and daughters of Western families felt that they had to go East, if they wanted to amount to anything. The first settlers of the region were frankly exploitative, or they were "lungers" and asthmatics with no ambition except survival. Many of these latter, upon regaining their health, became builders and contributed to the humanizing of the raw society which the exploiters left behind. As to the latter, they took what they could easily get and then left, and what remained after them were ugly scars in the mountainsides, slovenly little towns that died as fast as they were born. The Indians were part of the wreckage left behind—their economies destroyed, their choices denied, their survival jeopardized. At best, they were curiosities, like the flora and fauna of the region, gazed upon by Easterners traveling through the Indian country.

The West needed a time perspective and a sense of belonging on the same continent as the East. United States' history was eastern seaboard history. American culture was Eastern culture.

The archaeologists of the southwestern digs began to supply the perspective, and in a few years they had completely recast the pre-history of the Western Hemisphere, in which the high plains and arid deserts were seen as the great highway for one of the major migrations in world history.

The West also needed a maturity in dealing with its human and physical resources: Teddy Roosevelt's conservation movement had lost headway and had succumbed to apathy as soil was mined and water polluted. The dust bowls of the thirties foretold disaster to come.

La Farge's training and experience—and inclination—fitted him to act in both areas. He knew from personal involvement about the achievements of southwestern archaeology, and hence he could write about the culture of the American West with insight and objectivity. What doubtless was his most significant contribution was that he brought Indians into the consciousness of Americans as something other than casual savages without tradition or style.

While he was concerned with the preservation of human values, early in his western travels he realized the fearful destruction being wrought upon the land and saw the interdependence of land and people. He reported on these matters to his own associates as well as to administrators, and he directed his Indian Association in support of the conservation movement.

He was determined to be a good Westerner and was outraged during an early visit to Colorado Springs to find the Chamber of Commerce urging vistitors to that city to "be an armchair pioneer on this civilized frontier." He went about in all seriousness to learn about western-type horses, about trail riding and camping, and taking care of himself in open country. His knowledge was first-hand and intimate. And once he moved to the West, to become a permanent resident of Santa Fe, he left behind something of the strain of his early years.

He was in all respects a new man in the West, concerned with cultural relativism, with city planning, with responsibility in public life, with conserving resources for the future, with the free flow of ideas into and out of the West, within a nation of many parts.

These solemnities notwithstanding, the weekly column in the Santa Fe *New Mexican* that La Farge wrote faithfully from 1950 until his death was rarely solemn. And it rarely had to do with Indians. All of Santa Fe was his beat, and by turns he scolded, praised, castigated, admired, ridiculed, defended, and obviously loved what he called by turns "The City Different" and "The City Difficult," whose streets are "very old and hence . . . very tired" and full of ruts. It reflected the infinite variety of a well stocked and ambient mind.

A selection of these columns, compiled by his friend, Winfield Townley Scott, and published under the title *The Man with the Calabash Pipe* (1966), shows La Farge's versatility as a writer and a commentator. Some of this writing indeed ranks with his best—for leanness of phrase, for liveliness, and for a warmth that is often lacking in his formal pieces.

Two characters appeared frequently in these weekly columns—"The Man with the Calabash Pipe" and "Horned Husband Kachina Chief." They bespoke La Farge's wanderings between the world of the urbanite intellectual—remote, austere, at times difficult—and that of the earth-born, earth-centered, laughing Indian—a kind of unconscious self-portrait of his proper self, for which he had been searching since his ordeal at Groton.

The day came when he could write no more. After a two-day meeting he attended at Taos, June 6 and 7, he failed rapidly. He was taken to Albuquerque where surgery was attempted. There his strength failed entirely, and on August 2, 1963, Oliver La Farge died.

❖ Index ❖